REMAINS OF THE SOCIAL

REMAINS OF THE SOCIAL
DESIRING THE POSTAPARTHEID

Edited by Maurits van Bever Donker,
Ross Truscott, Gary Minkley & Premesh Lalu

WITS UNIVERSITY PRESS

Published in South Africa by:

Wits University Press
1 Jan Smuts Avenue
Johannesburg, 2001
www.witspress.co.za

Compilation © Editors 2017
Chapters © Individual contributors 2017
Published edition © Wits University Press 2017
Artworks and Photographs © Copyright holders. See image captions.
Music lyrics © Copyright holders.
First published 2017

978-1-77614-030-5 (print)
978-1-77614-031-2 (PDF)
978-1-77614-032-9 (EPUB North & South America, China)
978-1-77614-033-6 (EPUB Rest of World)

This book is licensed under a Creative Commons CC-BY-NC License. To view a copy of this license, visit http://creativecommons.org/licenses/by-nc/2.0/.

An electronic version of this book is freely available, thanks to the support of libraries working with Knowledge Unlatched. KU is a collaborative initiative designed to make high quality books Open Access for the public good. The Open Access ISBN for this book is **978-1-77614-038-1**. More information about the initiative and links to the Open Access version can be found at www.knowledgeunlatched.org.

All rights reserved. No part of this publication may be reproduced, stored in a retrieval system, or transmitted in any form or by any means, electronic, mechanical, photocopying, recording or otherwise, without the written permission of the publisher, except in accordance with the provisions of the Copyright Act, Act 98 of 1978.

All images and music lyrics remain the property of the copyright holders. The publishers gratefully acknowledge the publishers, institutions and individuals for the use of images and music lyrics. Every effort has been made to locate the original copyright holders of the images and music lyrics reproduced here; please contact Wits University Press in case of any omissions or errors.

Cover artwork: 'Life and Death' by Dathini Mzayiya, artist in residence in the Centre for Humanities Research, Factory of the Arts
Editor: Russell Martin
Proofreader: Alison Lockhart
Indexer: Marlene Burger
Typesetting: Integra

CONTENTS

Acknowledgements
vii

Preface
Gary Minkley
ix

Chapter 1
Traversing the Social
Maurits van Bever Donker, Ross Truscott, Gary Minkley and Premesh Lalu
1

Chapter 2
The Mandela Imaginary:
Reflections on Post-Reconciliation Libidinal Economy
Derek Hook
40

Chapter 3
The Return of Empathy: Postapartheid Fellow Feeling
Ross Truscott
65

Chapter 4
The Ethics of Precarity: Judith Butler's Reluctant Universalism
Mari Ruti
92

Chapter 5
Hannah Arendt's Work of Mourning:
The Politics of Loss, 'the Rise of the Social' and the Ends of Apartheid
Jaco Barnard-Naudé
117

Chapter 6
Souvenir
Annemarie Lawless
146

Chapter 7
Re-Cover: Afrikaans Rock, Apartheid's Children and the Work of the Cover
Aidan Erasmus
172

Chapter 8
The Graves of Dimbaza: Temporal Remains
Gary Minkley and Helena Pohlandt-McCormick
195

Chapter 9
The Principle of Insufficiency: Ethics and Community at the Edge of the Social
Maurits van Bever Donker
225

Chapter 10
The Trojan Horse and the 'Becoming Technical of the Human'
Premesh Lalu
249

About the Contributors
275

List of Figures
279

Index
281

ACKNOWLEDGEMENTS

In early 2011, the South African Research Chair Initiative (SARChI) Chair in Social Change at the University of Fort Hare and the Centre for Humanities Research (CHR) at the University of the Western Cape, now the home of the Department of Science and Technology and the National Research Foundation (DST-NRF) Flagship on Critical Thought in African Humanities, began a long-term collaboration, a research and pedagogical experiment that took the form of a Winter School for doctoral and master's students. The chapters collected here have emerged largely out of this collaboration. Together, they constitute an intervention into the concept of the social as such. There is much more to be said of this collaboration between two universities that were produced by apartheid thought and legislation as precisely not capable of such an intervention. We would, however, simply like to acknowledge these two projects – and there have been other important partners, most notably the Interdisciplinary Center for the Study of Global Change at the University of Minnesota – for providing the space in which this intervention was able to take shape.

This volume would, of course, not have been possible without the investment and collaboration of all our contributors. Each one of the contributors has been, at some point in the past few years, a participant in the projects convened by the CHR and the SARChI Chair, whether as students, postdoctoral fellows, visiting faculty or participants in the various seminars and colloquiums that have taken place over the years. The contributors to the volume have been patient over a very long process, always responsive and positive, and have produced what are quite clearly in their own right outstanding interventions into the social.

The project has benefited from the intellectual friendship and direction offered by many who are associated with the CHR and SARChI Chair. For the care with which this volume has been read, critiqued and encouraged, we would like to thank John Mowitt, Brian Raftopoulus, Adam Sitze, Qadri Ismail, Cesare Casarino, Jane Taylor, Sanil V, Arunima G, Patricia Hayes, as well as our reviewers from the Press. We would also like to extend our sincere thanks to Wits University Press for the care and patience with which they have handled the publication of this book.

We thank the Estate of Stephen Spender for kind permission to reprint his 1964 poem titled 'An Elementary School Classroom in a Slum' from *New Collected Poems* by Stephen Spender © 2004.

Ross Truscott's chapter is derived in part from an article published in *Safundi* on 5 May 2016. Thanks are due to Taylor and Francis for permission to reprint it here. The original article is available online: www.tandfonline.com/ dx.doi.org/10.1080/17533171.2016.1172825. He would also like to thank the Stevenson Gallery and Nandipha Mntambo for permission to reproduce images from *The Encounter*.

The editors thank the Stellenbosch Institute for Advanced Studies and the Andrew W. Mellon Foundation for research grants that supported this project and for intellectual input along the way.

PREFACE
Gary Minkley

Remains of the Social is, as we note in our acknowledgements, a product of a critical engagement between the SARChI Chair in Social Change at the University of Fort Hare, the Centre for Humanities Research at the University of the Western Cape, and their respective research partners. As such, this volume, read as a coherent project in itself, might also be read alongside wider collaborations and developments, and in anticipation of subsequent volumes that broaden, deepen and extend the discussions around the social into areas that might seem absent from this volume.

Most studies on the social as it comes to bear on the postapartheid – and studies of social cohesion could be included here – take the social as an ideal that must either be vigorously defended or triumphantly declared. *Remains of the Social* offers another perspective. Pressuring assumptions of rational progress for society and the subject, we begin by putting the social into question, asking after the ways in which, and the ends to which, it is invoked and given its itineraries, attending to the epistemological grounds of the social. In doing so, the volume inquires into that which is remaindered in the production of the social. In other words, *Remains* treats the social as a problematic, one from which it is difficult to emerge unscarred.

The interventions collected here ask after what is rendered unliveable as a condition of possibility of the social. This unliveability most readily recalls Judith Butler's concept of precarity – the ungrievability of certain lives that engenders their unliveablility, a theme taken up by several contributors here – but it recalls, also, and importantly, the rupture that, for Walter Benjamin, clears the ground for his critique of time and progress in his 'Theses on the Philosophy of History'. Indeed, what is explored here, in various ways, is the notion that the very question of loss, as Zita Nunes has argued, might be read not only as constitutive of, or constituted by, the social – the social produced through loss, the grave as its first commemorative sign, or the social apportioning life and death and designating its grievability – but rather as a masking of that which enables the constitution of the social: the remainder, which we propose against conceptions of mourning and its failures, melancholia and nostalgia, which one finds more frequently in studies on the social.

There is an echo here, as we discuss in the introductory chapter, of Fanon's critique in *Black Skin, White Masks* of the social as it is constituted through the concept of Man, an echo that brings with it not only the urgent task of posing questions of racial formations, but also a need to turn attentively to modes of narration that enable an encounter with these remainders as resistant: to read this resistance back into the social as a demand that orders a future which is, as Fanon puts it in his opening lines, always too soon and too late, out of time. Such a demand is what threads the ethical weight that the chapters in this volume bring to the question of the social.

REFERENCES

Benjamin, Walter. 'Theses on the Philosophy of History.' *Illuminations: Walter Benjamin Essays and Reflections*, edited and translated by Hannah Arendt, Schocken Books, 1969, pp. 253–264.

Fanon, Frantz. *Black Skin, White Masks*. Translated by Richard Philcox, Grove Press, 2008 [1952].

Nunes, Zita. *Cannibal Democracy: Race and Representation in the Literature of the Americas*. U of Minnesota P, 2008.

CHAPTER 1
TRAVERSING THE SOCIAL

Maurits van Bever Donker, Ross Truscott, Gary Minkley and Premesh Lalu

What is South Africa? We have perhaps isolated whatever it is that has been concentrated in that enigma, but the outline of such analyses has neither dissolved nor dissipated it in the least. Precisely because of this concentration of world history, what resists analysis also calls for another mode of thinking. If we could forget about the suffering, the humiliation, the torture and the deaths, we might be tempted to look at this region of the world as a giant tableau or painting, the screen for some geopolitical computer. Europe, in the enigmatic process of its globalization and of its paradoxical disappearance, seems to project onto this screen, point by point, the silhouette of its internal war, the bottom line of its profits and losses, the double-bind logic of its national and multi-national interests (Derrida, 'Racism's Last Word' 297–298).

The blackmail of whiteness

As Jacques Derrida reminds us, it is not possible to 'forget about the suffering, the humiliation, the torture and the deaths', in short, the weight of lived experience that was and is apartheid. At the same time, particularly when we consider apartheid as a question that extends beyond its own borders, it remains both necessary and urgent to distil the question of what he calls 'South Africa', to shape it and focus it as a problem for thought, so as to enable the possibilities of thinking what we in this volume call, without hyphenation, the postapartheid, neither a point in time nor a political dispensation, but rather a condition that names the labour of coming to terms with and working through the desires, principles, critiques and modes of ordering that apartheid both enabled and foreclosed. One of the tasks that we set for ourselves in this introduction is to provide a sense of this terrain on which the postapartheid unfolds.

Let us begin, then, by turning to a recent intervention into the social. Introducing their edited volume, *Re-Imagining the Social in South Africa: Critique, Theory and Post-Apartheid Society*, Peter Vale and Heather Jacklin argue that 'when apartheid ended, critical thinking ended' (1). The conditions of this 'shift from critique to subservience' (2) are to be found, they argue, in 'post-apartheid South Africa's incorporation into the logic and exigencies of global neo-liberal capitalism' (7). With this 'incorporation', the value of humanities scholarship was reduced to its capacity to contribute to economic growth, always subject to tests – often in terms of 'impact', 'efficacy' and 'efficiency' – against the imperatives of the market. It is a counterintuitive claim – South Africa's freedom has coincided with a constraint of thought – by the editors of *Re-Imagining the Social*, with which we are, to an extent, in agreement.

However, there is a jarring line in Vale and Jacklin's introduction that makes this volume necessary. They write: 'Even the most casual reading of these chapters will confirm that this collection, like most writing in critical social theory, is an exercise interested in promoting Enlightenment values' (11). Precisely what values might this mean? As if to respond to the question, they refer, further on, to the 'counter-Enlightenment authoritarian tendencies' (17) which the state assumed in South Africa during apartheid. So, in their construction of it, 'promoting Enlightenment values' is an antidote to apartheid as an 'authoritarian' impediment to the 'Enlightenment', leaving the postapartheid to come as the Enlightenment's fulfilment. To point out the Eurocentrism of this view is hardly necessary.

As for the question of which Enlightenment they are 'promoting', we are left guessing, for the Enlightenment was not a unified project. Given their subtitle, and their leanings, it is likely a call for those forms of critique that take their point of departure from Immanuel Kant.[1] If we take Michel Foucault's reading of Kant's elaboration of the concept of the Enlightenment as a touchstone, the itinerary to which Vale and Jacklin commit the postapartheid must be read as a 'way out' of the 'immaturity' of humanity with respect to the proper use of reason, that is, reason's autonomous use as 'humanity's passage to its adult status' ('What is Enlightenment?' 308–309). This presents what Foucault famously called 'the "blackmail" of the Enlightenment' (312), for the only way to counter the Enlightenment is on the very terrain of reason. That the game is rigged presents, in Foucault's words, a 'philosophical *question* that remains for us to consider' (312–313, emphasis added). Rather than being for or against 'Enlightenment values', it is perhaps more apt to say that we are both constrained and enabled – conditioned – by this double bind, this false choice.

The question of Enlightenment – of the autonomous use of reason – is inseparable from questions of race. Kant's *Anthropology* was, as Foucault argues in *Introduction to Kant's Anthropology*, central to his critiques, the two projects traversing each other. Both the philosophical and the political project produced race as a necessary function rather than as a timely accident, as Gayatri Spivak in *A Critique of Postcolonial Reason* and Tony Brown in *The Primitive, the Aesthetic, and the Savage* have argued. Apartheid here is not an impediment to but is, rather, coextensive with the Enlightenment, for apartheid is not purely an anomaly, a perversion of 'Enlightenment values', but their fulfilment.[2] This is not a small issue, for it informs how we might clear the ground for the arrival of a sense of difference that will not be apartheid's difference.

It is, arguably, in response to a version of this 'blackmail' that Steve Biko in 'Black Souls in White Skins?' offers a diagnosis of the problematic named by apartheid. On the apartheid policy of separate development, Biko states: 'Everyone is quite content to point out that these people – meaning the blacks – will be free when they are ready to run their own affairs, in their own areas' (20). His specific concern, however, is not this indefinitely deferred autonomy, but the tutelage under which liberals place blacks, treating them as children, 'claiming a "monopoly on intelligence and moral judgment"' (22–23). As he continues: 'There is nothing the matter with blacks. The problem is WHITE RACISM and it rests squarely on the laps of white society' (25). Here, Biko takes a position 'against integration' if it means 'an assimilation and acceptance of blacks into an already established set of norms' that will keep in place 'the superior–inferior white–black stratification that makes the white a perpetual teacher and the black a perpetual pupil' (26). While explicitly dealing with the relations between liberals and the black consciousness movement in apartheid South Africa, what Biko is drawing attention to in this formulation is the very question of racial formations as these structure the present in South Africa, both his and ours. If we consider the invisibility of whiteness, apart from accusation, in the framing of the postapartheid, the course opened by Biko's intervention acquires a fresh and purposive urgency. To state this intervention more pointedly, liberals, rather than concerning themselves with 'helping Blacks', must rather 'fight for their own freedom' (27) through confronting 'the real evil in our society' (25). To grasp the force of this injunction we need to briefly invoke, as Biko does, Frantz Fanon's *Black Skin, White Masks*.

Fanon similarly argues that 'there is no black [*noir*] problem' (13). Rather, he suggests that the problematic that structures the social derives from a deeper terrain. That Fanon refuses the definition of the problem as 'black' does not mean that he defines it as 'white', nor does it mean that he is dismissive of, or ignores, what he calls the 'lived experience of the black man' (89–119) – this in fact orders his intervention. For Fanon, however, the problem has to do with the 'metaphysics' of blackness and whiteness as these come to structure society in relation to the concept of Man. As he argues, Man is the concept on which both blackness and whiteness are articulated, as well as the function that 'brings society into being' (xv). It would, however, be too quick to focus only on dismantling Man and producing a new terrain for humanity (the focus of most critiques of Eurocentrism); the question of blackness is not so easily dismissed. For Fanon, Man as a concept does not designate an entity in itself; rather, Man is a becoming that in modern society is produced through the operation, the differential function, of whiteness/blackness. As he phrases it: 'The black man wants to be white. The white man is desperately trying to achieve the rank of man' (xiii). This relationship, where black and white are both 'locked' in place (xiv), where 'whites consider themselves superior to blacks' and 'blacks want to prove' their equality with whites (xv), and where blackness is relegated to a position of 'non-being' (xii), has produced a 'massive psycho-existential complex' (xvi) which Fanon's intervention attempts to destroy. In short, it is the conceptual terrain produced through the mechanism of blackness/whiteness that leads Fanon to declare that 'an individual who loves Blacks is as "sick" as someone who abhors them' and that, conversely, the black man who strives to whiten his race is 'as wretched as the one who preaches hatred of the white man' (xii).

It is because whiteness and blackness constitute a mechanism in the project of Man which produces blackness as non-being and whiteness as the potentiality of man that *any* relation to whiteness or blackness *as such* is a sickness. Biko directs our attention to this structural formation when he invokes the 'real evil' in our society. What he names with the signifier 'evil' is the mode by which the white man is produced as Man through the objectification of the black man. As an injunction that is laid in the laps of whites, this enables a reinscription of Biko's formula that 'the most potent weapon in the hands of the oppressor is the mind of the oppressed' (74). While clearly dealing with the question of a mental attitude, this statement also indicates the process of objectification outlined by Fanon in which whiteness becomes mind and blackness becomes body. Here it is both the mental condition of viewing the self as white or non-white that is a potent weapon, and the existence of those who claim to be white as such.

Itinerary

In this volume we seek to address the problem of the social as it is diagnosed by Fanon and reoriented by Biko. In what follows, and as a way of anticipating the chapters in this volume, we turn to two interventions into the postapartheid social which we have found productive to think with and against, one by Mark Sanders, the other by Achille Mbembe. We select these two texts for the way their juxtaposition brings into view the shifts in the social that are under way and the conceptual turns we seek to make. Despite our clear equivocation over their recourse to psychoanalysis, our initial invitation to contributors to write on the remains of the social was framed largely in psychoanalytic terms, and several of the contributions stage their chapters, at least in part, in or against psychoanalytic language. Thus, critically assessing these two texts is useful in underlining the wager of the volume itself.

We take the work of Sanders and Mbembe as an invitation to begin to elaborate what we call the remains of the social. Rather than advancing Kantian critique – and we cannot be sure that this is what was called for in *Re-Imagining the Social* – we turn, in framing this volume and as a point of departure, to an heir to the Kantian problematic: Sigmund Freud, to whom Fanon also turned.[3] We do so not as a means of imposing a different Enlightenment figure – the best word to describe Freud's relation to the Enlightenment is, perhaps, troublesome – on the social after apartheid, but as a means of making adequate what is immanent in the discourse on the social in South Africa; that is, there is already a form of austere psychoanalysis in the air, a weak psychoanalytic sensibility lodged in, and ordering, the social, largely as an effect of the work of the Truth and Reconciliation Commission (TRC) in the 1990s and, it has been argued, its most immediate precursor, the colonial Commission of Inquiry, which the TRC inherited and had to make function in a new way.[4] Within this frame, we aim to traverse the social in the wake of apartheid.

Traversal, in the psychoanalytic sense, is an act of passing through repetition after repetition – acting out – until the signature of the unconscious has been written in the rhythm of a transferential relation, the production of a repetition without which no new configuration of desire would be possible.[5] To traverse the social in the wake of apartheid, in this sense, is to attend to the repetitions that impede but also make possible another social beyond the horizon of apartheid, beyond apartheid's ordering of extrinsic difference. And if traversal is a means of grasping the social as a series of repetitious acts, it is also an act through which the social is constituted.[6] We are not 'promoting' psychoanalytic 'values', then, nor do we wish to close off the potential of the psychoanalytic as a discourse adequate to the question of the postapartheid social. We take a position neither pro nor contra psychoanalysis, but *versus* it, which suggests, for us, not only to turn against, but also to face, to turn towards, to return to, even (simply) to turn, to turn the soil of and, thus, to till, to renew, and – in its etymological link to the German *werden* – to turn it into what it might become, turning it away from its therapeutic, institutionalised uses so as to activate its critical potential. We abide by psychoanalysis, then, reading it for its productivity despite what we see as its several false turns.

If a crude form of psychoanalysis was set to work in and around the TRC, producing a form of mournful sociality that marked the end of apartheid, we want to turn the conception of mourning towards a wakefulness, not that of reason, but rather as a question of our present, a visceral articulation of a lived experience ordered by the undercurrents of apartheid. These undercurrents – and we discuss some of their symptoms below – persist in this time named by the adjective 'postapartheid' as a form of remainder: as the remains of apartheid, as those remains that apartheid produced and, indeed, continues to produce, as the very conditions through which the social coheres in this time and, as such, as that which produces this social as (perhaps) already out of time, even before it has properly begun. All of this, the contributions to this volume suggest, shape what is grasped as life, shaping life to such an extent that, now as a noun rather than only an adjective, the postapartheid operates as a signifier for a condition. The postapartheid, a condition of life, not only an adjectival signifier: this is one of the moves that this volume makes, a move that asks that we grasp difference as a marker of life that is, precisely – and, to repeat ourselves – not apartheid's difference.

Following the next section, 'The wake of apartheid', we dwell on the concept of 'global apartheid', particularly as it is figured in the work of Michael Hardt and Antonio Negri (*Empire* and *Multitude*), as a means through which to rethink the category of difference as this operates in the social. The concept of global apartheid, we argue, asks that we rethink the social lived in the wake of apartheid, that we rethink apartheid itself and thus rethink what a postapartheid social will be.

The wake of apartheid

The work of Sanders on the TRC serves as a useful starting point in conceptualising social acts and the remains of the social. In 'Remembering Apartheid', Sanders argues that apartheid was and continues to be an 'interdict against the development of a social formation' (61), the essence of apartheid being the 'foreclosure of the other, and thus of any historical possibility of another social formation' (61). The question of a social to come is at the forefront of his concerns. Though the parameters of such a foreclosed social formation against which Sanders writes were never clearly stated by the theoreticians of apartheid, at the heart of apartheid's discourse – Sanders argues – there is 'a proscription on mourning, specifically of the other' (60). For Sanders, 'mourning, as the giving up of a loved object, presupposes desire for that object' (65), and it is for this reason, he argues, that mourning the other was proscribed.[7] The conclusion Sanders draws for a postapartheid social is that 'apartheid would be undone through condolence' (72).

Sanders turns to Freud's 'Group Psychology and the Analysis of the Ego', traditionally read in order to critique the psychology of Fascism and its persistence. For Freud, it is identification with the figure of the leader that produces secondary identifications between individuals who love the same object and are, thus, a part of the same social formation. Sanders makes two key moves. Firstly, he underscores the importance of Freud's earlier 'Totem and Taboo' to 'Group Psychology' and its conception of the social. In 'Totem and Taboo', the revolt against, and the murder of, the primal father is the constitutive act through which the social emerges, an act recalled by the totem meal, re-enacting and forgetting the murder, the meal as a sacrament through which reconciliation with the father is brought about. Secondly, Sanders highlights the point that mourning (the pain of relinquishing the lost object) and melancholia (the pain of that loss lived as a part of oneself through identification with the lost object as a means of refusing the loss), while often opposed to each other, are for Freud inseparable. There is no mourning without a structurally anterior, constitutive melancholia: it is loss that inaugurates the subject, a subject that, paradoxically, does not pre-exist the losses it is to bear. Loss hollows out the subject, as it were, engenders the very psychic interiority within which the lost object is incorporated. In sum, loss conditions not only sociality but subjectivity, a theme elaborated upon by several contributions here.[8]

By discerning the centrality of mourning to Freud's group psychology, and the inseparability of mourning and melancholia, Sanders argues that we have here a means to grapple not only with authoritarianism but also 'the social formation in general and its lines of fissure' (75–76), a social formation, that is, produced through identification with the dead. As Sanders argues, 'The dead one – not necessarily the "father" – can occupy the place of the ego ideal' (76). The object mourned, identified with, could well be a slain activist. What is intriguing here is the constitutive function of remains to this formulation of the social, as well as the constructedness of the social, a social produced through acts of mourning, the social as an assemblage of egos bound together through a common introjection of an object.

Sanders also draws attention to the wager of mourning as a social act, most notably the rivalry that attends mournful sociality, an inevitable rather than exceptional eventuality. To mourn is not only to have loved, to have desired, it also, as an identificatory act, sets in play 'lines of fissure' over the parameters of who may mourn and, thereby, be a part of the social thus constituted.[9] As he suggests, the person refused the right to mourn is effectively barred from the social. Refracted through Sanders's argument if read at the limit of what is for us its productivity, the title of this volume would set out to abide, in some way, with those who have been excluded in the production of the social under apartheid and who, to the extent that the difference that constituted that social is still the grammar of the social that is ostensibly *ours*, remain still excluded: those policed by apartheid's difference, who refuse to inhabit that difference, persist as the remaindered in this social as well as perhaps the markers of its death.

The lens of mourning offers one way to think the remainder. This volume, however, articulates a hesitancy around such an argument's figuration of difference, which we can begin to sound out through a discussion of Mbembe's 'The State of South African Political Life'. Mbembe argues that postapartheid South Africa is facing 'a crucial moment in the redefinition of what counts as "social protagonism" in this country'.[10] While Sanders is, in his own terms, interested in 'the makings of a minor group psychology or general psychoanalytic theory of social formation' (76), Mbembe's widening and deepening of the problem of the social after apartheid suggests that the terms for such a social are, in themselves, in flux.

Mbembe begins by drawing attention to the protests that erupted and reverberated across South African university campuses in 2015–16. The problem to which these events were a reaction is, however, both wider and deeper than the immediate framing assumes. The 'winds blowing from our campuses', Mbembe states, 'can be felt afar, in a different idiom, in those territories of abandonment where the violence of poverty and demoralization hav[e] become the norm'. We have here, then, a somewhat different articulation of social acts, 'lines of fissure' and, as we will see, of remains of the social. The state of which Mbembe writes is being called in different quarters, as he notes, 'decolonisation'. It is, as he puts it, '*a psychic state* more than a political project in the strict sense of the term' (original emphasis), and he marks three shifts that characterise this 'cultural temperament' (each of which entails the elements of time, affect and value or, rather, libidinal economy): a politics of waiting has been supplanted by one of impatience, for people can no longer wait; an identity politics of pain, suffering and anger has replaced the affirmation of blackness, worldliness and cosmopolitanism, which characterised the early 1990s; and the ideal of reconciliation, through which the postapartheid nation was constituted, has been dislodged in favour of the settling of accounts.

Referring to this, as Mbembe does, as an 'age of fantasy and hysteria', suggestive of acting out rather than social acts, might be said to echo Jacques Lacan's observation in *The Seminar of Jacques Lacan* that student protesters in May 1968 risked, in their ostensibly hysterical revolt, reinstalling a new master. Mbembe is clear, though, that this is a new threshold even as it recalls the past. Nor is South Africa on the same brink of revolution that Fanon wrote of in *The Wretched of the Earth*, however much those vaunting 'decolonisation' invoke it.[11] The tensions across the country, of which campus protests are one manifestation, are reactions to a problem at once old and new. They are, as Mbembe puts it, 'structural repetitions of past sufferings in the present', a repetition, a stumbling, produced by an apartheid past not adequately worked through.

It is worth pausing over the difficulty of diagnosing the condition of anticipating a postapartheid social. 'If we cannot find a proper name for what we are actually facing,' Mbembe writes, 'then rather than simply borrowing one from a different time, we should keep searching.' Caught beneath the gaze of authoritarian images from the colonial and apartheid pasts, words ready to hand are grasped for: 'They speak in allegories and analogies – the "colony", the "plantation", the "house Negro", the "field Negro", blurring all boundaries, embracing confusion, mixing times and spaces, at the risk of anachronism.' As we argue in this volume, rather than rushing to name that around which or through which the social might cohere, it is necessary to undertake the slow work of reading, of marking limits, abiding by their motile edges, and constructing concepts that might be adequate to their demand.

Among those names given to the problem within this discourse of 'decolonisation' is whiteness. Mbembe seeks to listen, attentively, to the indictments of white privilege and the structures that uphold it. With the subtlety of an analyst he attends to the more symptomatic iterations of the problem, to the address of bodies tense with revolt and to the language of the wounds of bodies occupying university spaces, to the hieroglyphics, as one might say, of excrement-covered statues. At the same time, however, he issues a caution over whiteness being installed as an 'erotogenic object', keeping the problem firmly in place. To name the problem as one of whiteness, he argues, will not offer an easy exit to the script that has produced a politics of impatience, which is also a politics of pain and anger; at least, it may keep those who rail furiously against whiteness libidinally cathected to it, continuing to orient and shape life in the wake of apartheid. This is certainly one problematic that several contributions in this volume explore.

Rather than disagreeing with whiteness as the problem, Mbembe offers a more rigorous definition. For him, the problem of whiteness has a South African particularity, though it cannot be confined to South Africa. The problem is at once local and global, whiteness understood as 'a necrophiliac power structure and a primary shaper of a global system of unequal redistribution of life chances'. The crux of Mbembe's argument comes when he speculates on whether cathexes of whiteness, pain and suffering are 'typical of the narcissistic investments so privileged by this neoliberal age'. Therein lies the wager, not only of a repetition of the past in the very attempt to move beyond it, of remaining passionately attached to whiteness, even if in hatred, but also the possibility that what is being called 'decolonisation' shares certain traits with whiteness itself, a politics of pain, upon which identitarian claims are increasingly staked, leading to 'self-enclaving', finding its reflection in a form of whiteness that has sought to 'fence itself off, to re-maximize its privileges' – two markedly different and, at the same time, isomorphic symptoms of 'an astonishing age of solipsism and narcissism'.

Mbembe's diagnosis of the present is not without hope. If, as he puts it, 'the capacity to resume a human life in the aftermath of irreparable loss' – a task as urgent as it is difficult and slow – is to be nurtured, it will be necessary to abide by an *'ethics of becoming-with-others'* (original emphasis).[12] He states: 'The self is made at the point of encounter with an Other. There is no self that is limited to itself. The Other is our origin by definition. What makes us human is our capacity to share our condition – including our wounds and injuries – with others.' Mbembe situates a hope for a future social adequate to the postapartheid in the realm of ethics, in the encounter with the other as such, conjuring most immediately the work of Emmanuel Levinas, for whom the encounter with the other always confronts the self with an excess of the idea of the other in the self – the Other is not simply another 'I' like me – a confrontation with what he calls 'infinity' that always puts the consciousness of the self into question.[13] The key point here, given this Levinasian current in Mbembe's diagnosis, is that the other is always similarly affected; there are no whole selves in play.

Mbembe's intervention calls for new kinds of social acts, beginning with a deconstructive reading of the myths of whiteness as well as the snares of its libidinal economy. 'There will be no plausible critique of whiteness, white privilege, white monopoly capitalism,' Mbembe argues – and this is where we circle back to our opening comments about the neoliberal university – 'that does not start from the assumption that whiteness has become this accursed part of ourselves we are deeply attached to, in spite of it threatening our own very future well-being.' Moreover – and this is the crucial point – the repetitions of which Mbembe writes are not produced by repression of desire or a failure of mourning; rather, they have to do with the production of desire, which employs such repression and mourning as its mask.

It is here that we mark a departure, through our reading of Mbembe, from the concept of remains in the work of Sanders, which is also an attempt to clear the ground to affirm the possibility of a social different from the one he was reading over a decade ago. What Sanders calls a proscription on mourning the other, and thus on desiring the other, takes the other as already constituted as such.[14] This field of extrinsic difference – what we have been calling apartheid's difference – determines the terrain in such a way that critique often results in amplification. Addressing apartheid within the terms of its expression, it seems to us, can only return that expression to itself. This, we might say, is what remains apartheid's trap.

Contrary to this, the work of traversing the social is what enables, in the Fanonian language that Gilles Deleuze uses in his reading of Freud in *Difference and Repetition*, a 'primary sense of repetition' (25) that posits a difference altogether more common. The primary repetition invoked here is articulated by Deleuze through the language of masks. It is not that a mask covers over an original or primary substance held in common. Rather, what exists is always a multiplicity of masks whose existence as such is repressed in the selection of particular masks. As Fanon makes clear both in his *Black Skin, White Masks* and *The Wretched of the Earth*, 'the native' is produced through the thingification of colonialism as the damned of the earth, as less than human, and as sliding into the category of 'the animal' due to an apparent 'insensibility to ethics' that the European is said to embody (*The Wretched of the Earth* 32). For Fanon, while violence enables a certain 'taking of place' (47) in the moment of decolonisation, it is not able to deal with the 'Manichean problem' (31) of Man as the conceptual terrain that produces the native as such – it maintains the binary, the mask of whiteness, even if it shifts positions within it. More urgent is what might come after the moment of decolonisation: the project of 'working out new concepts, setting afoot a new man' (255). Such a construction requires the production of a difference that is not apartheid's difference. This difference can be neither ontological nor extrinsic; it amounts to an affirmation of becoming at the limit. Such a difference is not accessible, or rather available, in the field of mourning, where mourning parries a loss. It is produced on the screen of transference as an encounter in which such a selection takes place. At stake in its articulation is the very understanding of difference on which a postapartheid might be constructed, a difference, to use Deleuze's term, resistant to the 'deafness' (217) that characterises repetition as it takes place within the mask of resemblance.[15]

After global apartheid

Central to the task of thinking the social in the postapartheid is, we have suggested, grasping precisely what this social might come after. The concept of global apartheid, first coined by Gernot Köhler, has recently gained critical currency as a way to critique neoliberal politics (see, for instance, Bond; Dalby; Fregoso; Loyd; Žižek), resulting in race being foregrounded where other approaches may leave it in the background.[16] Within most deployments of the concept, global apartheid functions as an analogy that enables the global West and North to hold up a mirror to itself in a gesture towards self-critique.[17] For many, the corollary is hope for a different world, for if apartheid has been dismantled in South Africa, the logic goes, it can be dismantled globally. Not simply the analogue of the world, the story of apartheid functions as an allegory, a tale of an unjust order rehearsed to give to the structure of an unfair, rapidly changing world a face or, at least, a familiar name, as well as the possibility of a resolution.

Along this line of thinking – which, admittedly, we reduce to some of its bare turns – the path that global apartheid leads down, hopeful as it seems, is circular, for the end of apartheid in South Africa coincides precisely with the country's entry into the neoliberal order of global apartheid; the ending, upon which hope hinges, leads back to the very problem it is supposed to lead out of. It is this version of global apartheid we would want most rigorously to resist – yet another symptom, perhaps, of the 'age of solipsism and narcissism', the Eurocentrism of the world staring into the screen of South Africa, projecting, as Derrida puts it, 'the silhouette of its internal war, the bottom line of its profits and losses, the double-bind logic of its national and multi-national interests' ('Racism's Last Word' 298). There is, however, another line, which is discernible from the first elaboration of the concept of global apartheid, but which has in most cases dropped out, wherein the genealogy of apartheid stretches back to the dawn of modernity and to the beginnings of European colonialism. Although it is given almost no sustained attention (cf. Dalby; Köhler, 'The Three Meanings of Global Apartheid'), it is this that we find most productive and attempt to draw out here, the idea that apartheid was always already global or, rather, is lodged within a genealogy of the modern world system.

Among the various renderings of global apartheid, Hardt and Negri's *Multitude* is, for our purposes, the most provocative:

> We are living in a system of global apartheid. We should be clear, however, that apartheid is not simply a system of exclusion, as if subordinated populations were simply cut off, worthless, and disposable. In the global Empire today, *as it was before in South Africa*, apartheid is a productive system of hierarchical inclusion that perpetuates the wealth of the few through the labor and poverty of the many. The global political body is in this way also an economic body defined by the global divisions of labor and power (166–167, emphasis added).

In a shift from the analogous to the emblematic, apartheid here is one name for what Hardt and Negri call Empire, apartheid exemplifying its logic of 'hierarchical inclusion'. This system is different, they insist, from the logic of colonialism, which includes in so far as it can exploit but, failing this, exterminates the 'worthless, and disposable'. For Hardt and Negri, the world we currently inhabit is no longer colonial; it has been superseded, they argue, by a new global order. And they are emphatic on the point: 'Empire is not a weak echo of modern imperialisms but a fundamentally new form of rule' (*Empire* 146).

In *Empire*, Hardt and Negri's previous book, it is interesting to note the different figuring of apartheid as 'one form, perhaps the emblematic form, of the compartmentalization of the colonial world' (125). Apartheid is, on the one hand, the emblem of the modern world, the world where European nations extended their borders through colonisation, and, on the other hand, one name for the current state of a postmodern world, a fundamentally new world of global Empire.

Given their insistence on the paradigmatic difference between Empire and colonialism, on their incommensurability, this is not a small contradiction.[18] Nevertheless, the key point is that apartheid is utilised to name systems of exploitation and inequality. It is, however, not only the structure of apartheid's violent inclusions that repeats in our global present, but also the modes of resistance that it elicits, a point to which Mbembe also draws attention. Resistance operates, for Hardt and Negri, along an axis of tension between centralism and network, between guerrilla war and people's army, a tension that they suggest has continued into the postapartheid present. The terrain for the emergence of a subject that might exceed Empire is found in what they call Multitude. Quite simply, if modernity required the emergence of a subject coterminous with its socioeconomic and political moment, then they suggest this new moment, which is shot through with 'immaterial labour' (109), produces a subject adequate to it, expressed in a class of the 'properly alienated' (as labour is not only productive, but is now also affective, immaterial) – articulated in the South African protest slogan 'we are the poors' (152).

Thus, their formulation – 'Empire today, *as it was before in South Africa*', echoing earlier formulations like 'apartheid, *as formerly practiced in South Africa*' (Dalby 137, emphasis added), '*as is South African apartheid*'

(Köhler, 'Global Apartheid' 266, emphasis added) – uses apartheid in order to 'remember that another world is possible', apartheid standing between 'our desire for a better, more democratic world' (Hardt & Negri, *Multitude* 227) and its arrival. That is, they are interested in the productivity of Multitude, the image of which is flesh: 'This common social being is the powerful matrix that is central in the production and reproduction of contemporary society and has the potential to create a new, alternative society. We should regard this common social being as a new flesh, amorphous flesh that as yet forms no body' (159). Hardt and Negri invoke here modern political philosophy and its body politic – a body with various heads, arms and organs – but also Deleuze and Félix Guattari's body without organs. Thus, Empire not only includes and exploits, but also, recalling Empire as a 'global political body', organises the flesh of the Multitude into a body, 'transforming its singularities into divisions and hierarchies' (212). In short, the flesh of the Multitude is constantly being organised; in turn, it resists, organising itself in ways that allow singularities to encounter one another, enabling networks of communication, new habits to form, new performativities to emerge, which break down hierarchies and call into question sovereignty, all of which might be called 'symptoms of the common dreams, common desires, common ways of life, and common potential that are mobilized in a movement' (213).

Hardt and Negri use flesh in two senses that they claim are derived from Maurice Merleau-Ponty. On the one hand, 'flesh' is understood as 'elemental' and shared; on the other hand, it is taken as 'singular' (193–194). In this way, Multitude allows differences, and does not reduce difference to any single category, whether nation, class or race. As they phrase it, 'the multitude is the subjectivity that emerges from this dynamic of singularity and commonality' (198). It seems to us, however, that the concept of the flesh might be pushed further in their argument, towards the constitution of new senses of difference and desire, which can be outlined through a brief consideration of how Merleau-Ponty comes to flesh.

For Merleau-Ponty, the body is not simply a physical thing (meat and bones) that can be located inside a field of extrinsic difference; rather, it is an 'intertwining of vision and movement' ('Eye and Mind' 353). Stated differently, it is a place of the intertwining of senses so as to leave them with no strict division. As such, the body would be considered as a quilting point with sense. Within this understanding, which goes against the dominant understanding of the subject since, at least, René Descartes, Merleau-Ponty argues that it is in fact perception which is primary, not thought.[19] In positing the 'flesh' as primary, Merleau-Ponty displaces the possibility of a self that can know its existence internally (*cogito ergo sum*); instead, the self exists always already in relation to other existents, different from them owing to a matter of style. The emphasis on style is important as in it is maintained an element of an 'I' that is unique to itself due to its particularity as a peculiar kind of object in perception.

The swerve from the Cartesian subject that Merleau-Ponty enables is crucial. For Hardt and Negri, the genealogy of apartheid can be traced to the early modern world, which for them emerges with a new and radical concern with immanence and its possibilities in terms of desire, democracy and freedom, among other things. The foreclosure of desire, the reinstallation of a transcendental principle and, thus, sovereignty – largely, national sovereignty – is one of the tragedies of the crisis of modernity, the crisis through which modernity has been revealed. What we know of modernity, they argue, is in fact a reaction, a second phase coextensive with the first, a foreclosure of this radical potential that took place first in Europe and then in the colonies.[20] The key philosophical figures in Hardt and Negri's itinerary of modernity are Baruch Spinoza and Descartes, the latter's significance being that he reinstates a transcendental principle against the insurrectionary potential of a field of immanence: God is the guarantor of knowledge, as it is God who laid down the law of nature. To trace apartheid's genealogy, and thus to track what the social was and is under apartheid, it is necessary to read not only widely, across the globe, but back to at least Descartes: the thinking upon which apartheid is grounded finds one of its beginnings there, in the division, the separation, the apartness of mind and body, and the subjection of body to mind he inaugurates.[21]

In contrast with the positing of an understanding of subjectivity open to learning from the other, which, as we saw in our reading of Mbembe, is central to the constitution of a social to come, here in the Cartesian itinerary, through the insistence on an always already individuated subjectivity endowed in itself with the sovereign properties of knowledge and freedom, the subject which holds the social field is endowed with what we might figure as the obligation to instruct the other – to reduce the other to the self. Without even the preliminary uncertainty of the Hegelian subject, whose movement towards Spirit is necessitated by its internal contradiction between the 'for-itself' and the 'in-itself' (Hegel 104), the subject here stands forth, already self-recognising, ordering a field to its own predetermined measure.[22]

It is in the haunting of language, brought about through intercorporeality, that Merleau-Ponty locates the social field as something that comes after and is 'held' by the 'flesh' ('The Intertwining' 411), and it is this sense that is taken up by Hardt and Negri in their concept of Multitude.[23] For Merleau-Ponty, however, language haunts the flesh, language touches and is touched in the intertwining of the flesh, which is primary. In language, the 'I' recognises the other, which is held in the world in the same manner as it is. As such, the other in language is for the 'I', not one of its phenomena; it 'imposes itself not as true for every intellect [ideal], but as real for every subject who shares my situation' (94).[24] This social world is neither 'personal' nor 'ideal'; the subject is lodged in it through its interactions with others only, as Merleau-Ponty phrases it: 'History is others, it is the relationships we establish with them, outside of which the realm of the ideal appears as an alibi' ('The Primacy of Perception' 101). This understanding of flesh would enable a very different reading of both Multitude and the concept of global apartheid that Hardt and Negri develop in relation to it. Here the subject is outside itself, a constellation of singularities resistant to its ordering within subjective certainty. Global apartheid is, then, an ordering of desire and not only its structuring, an ordering from which Multitude might try to escape.

The Multitude is described by Hardt and Negri in two ways, as an ontological and as a historical conception of insurrection. There has always been, through the ages, a Multitude in revolt and yet there is still a Multitude to come, which is latent within contemporary political praxis: 'The multitude, then, when we put these two together, has a strange, double temporality: always-already and not-yet' (222) – resonant with Fanon's formulation in *Black Skin, White Masks*.[25] But contrary to Hardt and Negri's casual dismissal of the necessity of the subaltern in the political constitution of the Multitude, we suggest that it matters from where and in what articulation difference is broached. Anticipating the deconstructionist critique, Hardt and Negri state: 'Every identity, such critics say, even the multitude, must be defined by its remainder, those outside of it, call them the excluded, the abject, or the subaltern' (225). To which they reply: 'Its boundaries are indefinite and open. Furthermore, we should remember that the multitude is a project of political organisation and thus can be achieved only through political practices. No one is necessarily excluded but their inclusion is not guaranteed: the expansion of the common is a practical, political matter' (226). This practical political resolution of the question of the Multitude that finds it palatable to make the 'inclusion' of the 'subaltern' 'non-necessary' (226) misses in our view both how the destruction of the world produced through global apartheid is ordered precisely through the lived experience of that subaltern, and how it is that lived experience which guards against, which orders, the arrival of a future which might produce a difference that is not apartheid's difference. In other words, 'the poors' are not only a local articulation of an abstract category; the poors live. As Deleuze phrases it in his discussion of the Hegelian dialectic, this is the difference between 'the point of view of the slave who draws from the "no" the phantom of an affirmation, and the point of view of the "master" who draws from "yes" a consequence of negation and destruction' (54). The resonance in this statement of a project such as negritude is unmistakeable.[26] This is, however, not an argument for a repetition of extrinsic difference from the perspective of the subaltern. Such an expression would amount to a conservation of 'old values', what we have termed the remains of apartheid. Rather, we need a sense of difference that might enable 'the creation of new values'

(54), a difference that carries, in an echo of Aimé Césaire, a 'freedom for the end of the world' (293).

If the only way that Hardt and Negri can render apartheid as emblematic of paradigmatically different systems of exploitation is through taking apartheid as a concept of world history, it repays the effort to turn to Derrida's 'Racism's Last Word', where apartheid is the name of a worldly racism, 'the unique appellation for the ultimate racism in the world, the last of many' (291).[27] Here, apartheid 'exists within a worldwide network' (292) and is, echoing the terms of Hardt and Negri's *Multitude*, 'a sinister swelling on the body of the world' (294). That is, rather than an analogy, apartheid is a 'concentration of world history' (297), unthinkable without the armature of a Western concept of Man.[28] Yet, as Derrida notes, despite its worldliness, apartheid is an 'untranslatable idiom' – or, rather, an untranslated idiom – 'as if all the languages of the world were defending themselves, shutting their mouths against a sinister incorporation of the thing by means of the word' (292). Thus, if the cardinal feature of apartheid is its obsessional logic, if its primary objective is to differentiate and to keep apart, as Derrida puts it, a 'compulsive terror, which above all forbids contact', then worldwide denunciations of apartheid enact the same logic, the denunciators 'refusing to let themselves be contaminated' (292), keeping such a heinous crime against humanity *over there*, in South Africa, repeating the obsessional logic railed against.[29] In this sense, to speak of global apartheid allows the delocalisation of the problem of apartheid's persistence after the demise of official apartheid, but the concept performs a double move: on the one hand, it recalls the worldliness of apartheid, its place in a long genealogy of modern colonialism, but, on the other, the detachment of apartheid from its South African inscription is effectively crossed out by leaving apartheid untranslated, marking it as South African. Indeed, there is something irreducibly South African about apartheid, which is perhaps why it is left untranslated even as it is used to speculate on the world's future. The knot in the concept of global apartheid is that apartheid both *must* and yet *cannot* be detached from South Africa. It is *necessary* that apartheid be detached from

South Africa and, at the same time, *impossible* to fully detach it, leaving an untranslatable remainder.

Interventions

In arranging the chapters, we have not set up 'reserved domains' for disciplines (Derrida, 'But Beyond, ... ' 170).[30] Nor have we created designated areas for the separate development of themes, those concerned with mourning, precarity, futurity in their allocated neighbourhoods, those explicitly focused on South Africa over *here*, those on pure theory over *there*, in their respective homelands. This was advised, and the temptation to go that route was great, not just to organise the body of the text more rigidly but to follow through this obsessional impulse so thoroughly to its conclusion that its logic is laid bare. This is not the line we have taken. Rather, we have sought to arrange the chapters in a way that sets in play their multiple currents, so that they might encounter and run up against, interrupt and lean on each other.

Opening the volume is Derek Hook's chapter, 'The Mandela Imaginary: Reflections on Post-Reconciliation Libidinal Economy', which engages several themes discussed thus far, most notably mourning and the constitution of the social around a totemic father figure, namely, Nelson Mandela. Hook considers the notable anxiety expressed around Mandela's ailing health in 2013 and the tendency towards hagiographic memorialisation. Not only does such idealisation run contrary to Mandela's own political thought, Hook argues, but it also bears the marks of the mortifying repetitiveness of obsessional neurosis. This is another familiar theme, though Hook gives obsession a specifically Lacanian gloss, considering Mandela as a master signifier that stabilises multiple libidinal investments in the postapartheid social, traversing Mandela as a 'shared social fantasy' (53). Hook concludes his deft analysis with the suggestion that if the primary role delegated to Mandela since the 1990s has been to make possible the bridging of inherited social divisions, if the name 'Mandela' has had the function of sheltering within its associative field various meanings of the social after apartheid, then the task of producing common grounds that do not homogenise the social, that allow the coexistence of multiple singularities, will in his absence have to be assumed, identified with; but, consonant with Mbembe, this is a caution against narcissistic identification.

Ross Truscott's chapter stays within the psychoanalytic in order to think through some of the predicaments of postapartheid psychosocial transformation. While attentive to what Foucault called in *The Order of Things* the 'calm violence' (376) of the psychoanalytic transference, this chapter also poses the question of what a postcolonial psychoanalysis would entail, doing so through a reading of the ambiguous place of empathy within psychoanalytic discourse. The significance of this chapter to the themes of the volume is underlined by the fact that the concept of empathy has been set to work, across a range of fields, to mark a break with the relational patterns of apartheid, frequently in the language of psychoanalysis. Similarly, empathy has been identified historically as that which, within apartheid and colonial rule more generally, exceeded or escaped relations of domination, a relation to be recuperated and enabled.[31] Taking empathy as a concept embedded in colonial thinking, Truscott focuses on the incorporation of empathy in Freud's work, specifically in Dora's case and his analysis of Michelangelo's Moses, which are read alongside the images and installations of contemporary South African artist, Nandipha Mntambo. Three scenes are conjured wherein empathy confronts its own violence. But rather than foreclose on empathy, it is through the disclosure of the irresolvable contradictions of empathy, Truscott suggests, that it might be brought into the realm of the ethical through a practice of reinscription and through the figure of Echo that attends the narcissism and penetrative violence of empathy. It is thus, despite all, a defence of empathy as an impossible social act.

Mari Ruti's chapter, 'The Ethics of Precarity: Judith Butler's Reluctant Universalism', carefully outlines and ultimately – although within certain limits and with a good deal of caution – affirms the potential of Butler's Levinasian ethics of precarity, an ethics that has much in common with many of the contributions to this volume, as well as the position advanced by Mbembe. It is an ethics, as Ruti reads Butler, that, in seeking to respond to the other within a global context of uneven distributions of precarity, forgoes universals in favour of a relational ontology. Such an ethics turns on a shared condition of human vulnerability – shared, however, in different ways; in Butler's terms, not all lives are equally grievable and, thus, liveable. Ruti then locates a difficulty with this as a terrain for ethical action. The care that Levinas takes in structuring the encounter of the face-to-face through the realm of the third, justice, is absent in Butler's ethics of precarity. As Ruti notes, for Levinas 'justice places limits on our ethical accountability', whereas Butler 'for the most part ignores the distinction between ethics and justice, attempting, as it were, to apply Levinasian ethics to questions of global justice' (104). This absence, in turn, is accounted for through an implicit turn to the *a priori* norms of the Enlightenment in Butler's pronouncements on political questions, a scenario that, Ruti argues, might in fact unravel the very force of Butler's own critique of such norms. This is not to suggest that precarity is something to be rejected. Instead, the task is to find a mode through which the critique expressed in precarity can be performed while holding onto the capacity to order the social that might arrive in its wake. What Ruti's chapter does so powerfully for the volume is draw out how this same tension runs through the analogy of global apartheid.

Jaco Barnard-Naudé's chapter, 'Hannah Arendt's Work of Mourning: The Politics of Loss, "the Rise of the Social" and the Ends of Apartheid', can be read as giving Hardt and Negri's notion of Multitude a serious precursor in Arendt's writings. It is a figuring of Multitude – as plurality, freedom and acting in concert – that is quite different from what we find in Hardt and Negri. Arendt, as Barnard-Naudé points out, is frequently read as yearning for a form of politics, in the classical Greek sense of the term, lost with the modern rise of the social question as a concern with poverty. As Barnard-Naudé argues, Arendt conceives the mourning of this loss of politics as a form of political action in and of itself that can and does abide by the other, that can and does concern itself, politically, with poverty. Mourning, as it is understood here, drawing on the Derridean reworking of the distinction between mourning and melancholia, enables Barnard-Naudé to offer an alternative sense of a social act or, rather, political act in the wake of apartheid. While recalling Arendt's ontological distinction between the social as necessity and politics as freedom, Barnard-Naudé suggests a reading of Arendt that inaugurates a 'politics of the social' (117) by force of the very mourning for politics that animates her work. Political acts, he suggests, occur in the remains of a loss of politics (Arendt's social) that stands to be mourned and yet can never fully be mourned, this failure being the condition (and here he follows Derrida) of all political responsibility and action. At stake here for Barnard-Naudé is a relation to the other, fidelity to the otherness of the other that can only be carried out through a form of mourning which, of necessity, as a matter of ethics, must fail. Thus, Barnard-Naudé, following Arendt, traces Multitude back further than Hardt and Negri, to antiquity and, unlike them, perhaps because of this different genealogy, he affirms coming to terms with this loss as, paradoxically, the only grounds upon which to act in accordance with what has been lost. To mourn politics is precisely, and paradoxically, a form of fealty towards its lost possibilities. Barnard-Naudé's notion of mourning as the condition of the postapartheid social is resonant with, but also calls into question, Sanders's mournful sociality. If there is a concept of remains mobilised here, it is as an encounter, through Arendt, with the ancient Greek concept of political action that, in being mourned, that mourning always failing, is also, as Barnard-Naudé argues, narcissistically appropriated. While Sanders designates apartheid as a proscription on mourning the other, Barnard-Naudé offers a somewhat different reading of apartheid (140): 'What is it if not a homogenising logic that attempted to deny at all cost the plurality of the human condition?' It is precisely this plurality as politics that we might mourn, that we will always fail to mourn, and that we might abide by.

Annemarie Lawless's chapter can be placed in relation to a mode of the postapartheid social outlined by Truscott's chapter, a social that has congealed around calls for empathy between those apartheid divided – empathy as the supposed threshold of a postapartheid social – a figuring that, like the mourning discussed above, entails desire for the other. It is precisely such a capacity for empathy that is at stake in Lawless's chapter, 'Souvenir', which begins from a consideration of the uncomfortable performance of an encounter with the other located in the work of Alphonso Lingis, asking what that discomfort might express and how it might be read as a haunting placed under the name of 'love'. Lawless, however, offers a call for an encounter of empathy that is starkly different from those made around the TRC, and that is also quite unlike those forms of anthropological empathy that critics take as predatory, penetrative and grounded on a colonial temporality and spatiality. In particular, Lawless asks 'what it is for one thinking, feeling, breathing body to encounter another thinking, feeling, breathing body – not a subject-to-subject encounter, still less a human-to-human one, but rather a creaturely one, epidermis to epidermis' (147). And through her lucid reading of the touches between the texts of Walter Benjamin, Roland Barthes, Spinoza and Deleuze, Lawless conjures what apartheid, from the seventeenth century, foreclosed. (Recall that the philosophical figures in Hardt and Negri's itinerary of modernity are Spinoza and Descartes.)[32]

Aidan Erasmus, in his chapter, 'Re-Cover: Afrikaans Rock, Apartheid's Children and the Work of the Cover', considers the articulation of whiteness in the postapartheid as a question of inheritance through reading it as a script that is worked through the 'angst of a community' (182). In Erasmus's reading, whiteness – in the epistemic project of apartheid as this came to be expressed in popular culture, particularly music – was always already a question of repetition, of what comes after. This futurity is what he suggests the rock group Van Coke Kartel (VCK) trouble in their repetitions of traditional Afrikaner singer Carike Keuzenkamp's utopic misrepresentations of the 1980s in South Africa. Through the lack of a sense of futurity, this repetition marks VCK as the passive inheritors of an anxiety that the apartheid regime struggled to repress. The epistemic structure of apartheid is maintained in this repetition: there is no new sense of the social affirmed in VCK's music. And, by implication, this anxiety might still order the present named by the postapartheid.

If the concept of global apartheid has turned on the notion that global geopolitics find their analogue in the relation between the South African state and its homelands, then the reading offered in Gary Minkley and Helena Pohlandt-McCormick's chapter, 'The Graves of Dimbaza: Temporal Remains', has direct bearing on how we think global apartheid. They attempt, as they put it, to 'refigure the South African bantustan as constitutive of a South African "empire"' (196), elaborating a concept of what they call an 'empire of liberation'. It is anything but a recapitulation of Hardt and Negri's 'Empire'. Minkley and Pohlandt-McCormick attend to the ways in which race is embedded, archaeologically as it were, in the overdetermined discourse of liberation, a global discourse to which the postapartheid has adhered. In short, that race haunts the postapartheid is not, in their montaged reading of the archive of Dimbaza, a failure to have delivered on liberation. Rather, the spectre of race has been internal to the promises and premises of liberation as such, an 'empire of liberation'. Minkley and Pohlandt-McCormick find one opening onto this predicament through Foucault's 1975–1976 lectures at the Collège de France, *Society Must Be Defended*. The genealogy Foucault sketches begins with 'race war', an insurrection at the end of the Middle Ages when the concept of history became not simply the praise of kings or the re-establishment of mythical ties with Rome, but a form of counter-history from the perspective of those subject to the violence of the sovereign's rule, a history that was for the first time prospective, offering 'prophecies of emancipation' (80). Foucault distinguishes, but discerns a filiation between, the discourse of 'race war' and its transmutation into modern racism, 'born at that point when the theme of racial purity replaces that of race struggle' (81) – totalitarian politics and the bureaucracy of Fascism bearing a distant echo of a liberatory discourse. With this genealogy, recast as an 'empire of liberation', Minkley and Pohlandt-McCormick abide by the figure of the 'native' subject, reading for what they term (via Arendt) social acts, 'the act' as that which articulates the subject and the social as co-constitutive expressions. Acts, as formulated by Minkley and Pohlandt-McCormick, are neither about arriving at nor about fleeing a scene but rather about engaging in its creation. In an echo of Louis Althusser's aleatory materialism, social acts have a virtual existence that may be actualised under certain conditions and, in that actualisation, produce a potential rupture along which a newly constituted expression of the subject might become possible.

It is precisely the potential for such an opening, produced in the fragility of the touch of writing, that is constructed in Maurits van Bever Donker's chapter, 'The Principle of Insufficiency: Ethics and Community at the Edge of the Social'. Beginning from a consideration of Maurice Blanchot's troubling of the concept of community in *The Unavowable Community*, Van Bever Donker suggests that being adequate to the postapartheid requires the ethical task of thinking the social in a more conceptual and yet rigorously lived sense. A key element in this is what he calls 'the principle of insufficiency' as a condition with which to abide, rather than from which to depart, in the becoming expressive of community. As such, he suggests that the task is not to recover, to redeem or to rediscover community, but to abide by the edge of its concept so as to open the possibility of the new. Community, in the formulation against which his chapter works, is an integral element in what we have termed 'global apartheid', both in respect of the subject that it encloses and the social that it envisages. The ethical weight of unsettling this terrain of community through abiding by the principle of insufficiency is brought into focus through a brief consideration of the character of Antigone in the Oedipus myth. In Van Bever Donker's reading, the character of Antigone works to maintain the disjuncture between autochthony and copulation, between the fixing of the human through either the land or the state, so as to open the potential of a sense of the subject, and hence of the social, that might be resistant to such a closure. It is in Phaswane Mpe's reworking of the principle of insufficiency in relation to the weight of lived experience in postapartheid South Africa that the ordering potential of this opening is perhaps most clearly worked out. Reading Mpe's novel, *Welcome to Our Hillbrow*, as an intervention into the social, Van Bever Donker argues that the tensions of autochthony, copulation, community, nation and race are all dislocated and reworked in the ethical potential of a community of the touch constructed through the 'unworking labour' of writing. This, he suggests, constitutes an opening that presses beyond the figuring of the principle of insufficiency in Blanchot, or the mediating role of Antigone, precisely to the extent that it is ordered by the weight of lived experience, the ethical burden of 'not owning life'.

If Van Bever Donker situates this opening as a possible site through which to rethink the postapartheid, Premesh Lalu, in his chapter, 'The Trojan Horse and the "Becoming Technical of the Human"', similarly begins to ask what duration is necessary for the thinking of life *now*. Proceeding on the philosophical terrain opened up by Bernard Stiegler and Gilbert Simondon, Lalu intervenes in the relation between technicity and a condition of life that he designates as a 'memory of the future' (250). Lalu asks after the work of naming as this has been brought to bear both on the student movement of the 1980s and on the acts of violence against these movements and their subsequent memorialisation. Dwelling on the 'movement' at work in 'student movements', Lalu asks after a rhythmic potential he locates in 'the cinematic notion of interval', not merely a break between two films but 'the interval as an opportunity to change directions' (263). While the ways in which the 'student movement' sought to change the course of schooling cannot be reduced to the filmic apparatus that provided the basis for an aesthetic education in Athlone, Cape Town, Lalu's intervention suggests that 'student movement' marshalled the force of the interval and its capacity to effect the movement of a swerve, a potential that was foreclosed in the 1985 Trojan Horse massacre. It is the double articulation of 'schooling' and 'bioscope' that lends a grammar to the work of remaining with the 'memory of the future' that, Lalu suggests, the 'movement' sought to make possible. This is a grammar of the interval, of a Bergsonian dilation of time that might enable an alternate trajectory, one resistant to the closure of the interval by the naming of this movement as 'violence' and as 'anti-school'. As a desire for a return to the interval, Lalu brings his argument to bear on the 'condition of the human as undulating sadness' in which the human has already folded into the 'industrialisation of memory' (269). For a social to come, Lalu argues, it is this folding – a fold against the fold of duration – that must be resisted.

NOTES

1. We assume that this amounts to an affirmation, following Martha Nussbaum, that 'Kant more than any other Enlightenment thinker, defended a politics based upon reason rather than patriotism or group sentiment, a politics that was truly universal rather than communitarian, a politics that was active, reformist and optimistic, rather than given to contemplating the horrors, or waiting for the call of Being' (3). Of course, we may fall into a trap here of making Kant's 'What Is Enlightenment?' stand in for an entire heterogeneous field of thought.

2. If, however, by 'promoting Enlightenment values' Vale and Jacklin mean taking it to its deconstructive limits, we are in sympathy. In different terms, there is a tendency to auto-destruction in the Enlightenment that Max Horkheimer and Theodor Adorno discern in *Dialectic of Enlightenment*: 'The curse of irresistible progress is irresistible regression' (28). While freedom, for Horkheimer and Adorno, *is* dependent on Enlightenment thinking, all the cautions against totalitarianism sounded out in their opening chapter are directed not at 'counter-Enlightenment' forces but at those forces within the Enlightenment itself.

3. Put in the barest possible terms – Freud's own – Kant's categorical imperative finds its cognate in the Oedipus complex. Here, the superego, as the agent and enforcer of morality, provides a portion of the very enjoyment it forbids; the superego begins to sweat with the forbidden wishes it supposedly keeps in check, Enlightenment accruing, on Freud's reading, a sadistic element.

4. On the talking cure elements of the TRC, see Ross Truscott's chapter in this volume. On the relation between the TRC and the colonial Commission of Inquiry, and their mutual reliance on a psychotherapeutic discourse, see Adam Sitze.

5. On the psychoanalytic conception of traversal, see also Derek Hook's chapter in this volume.

6. To traverse also retains an archaic meaning of opposition. Thus, the traversal of the social is an act that forms the social by questioning it, interrogating it; a social act, then, of abiding by and inhabiting repetition whose wager is precisely antisociality, a wager shared by movements that, more recently, have gathered under the banner of 'decolonisation' – though

this is not what we are calling for, even if it is a call we hear and to which
   we respond.
7. It is possible to read in Sanders's formulation an unstated resonance with
   Fanon's formulation of racism in *Black Skin, White Masks* as a defence against
   desire for the other.
8. That is to say, psychoanalysis works against any notion of a unified,
   preconstituted subject. However, it presents the same 'blackmail' to the
   subject: one is never at home, always split, doubled, alienated; indeed
   knowledge of the world, of others and self-knowledge is torn from certitude,
   but that impossibility of certitude remains within the psychoanalytic frame,
   about which there is limited doubt. Anticipating this, Freud produces the
   concept of epistemophilic pleasure, within which he counts psychoanalysis.
9. Sanders implicitly operates in a Derridean mode of reading Freud as a proto-
   deconstructionist, as a dismantler of accepted binaries: if there is sociality on
   the one hand and antisocial violence on the other, Freud shows, for example
   in 'Totem and Taboo', that violence, murder, is inherent, indeed constitutive
   of, the social; similarly, if narcissism, as an immature stage of development,
   is opposed to the maturity of social bonds, Freud refuses this opposition, in
   this particular instance as melancholia, as a form of narcissism, is inseparable
   from, even making possible, the mourning of the social bond.
10. Mbembe's article was published online in the forum *Africa Is a Country*. It
    is, nevertheless, an exceptionally concise, accessible and clear statement on
    the social in South Africa today. The forum does not define the weight of its
    intervention.
11. Mbembe himself uses the Fanonian language of bodily tension that anticipates
    the explosion of anticolonial revolution.
12. This understanding of 'becoming-with-others' is explored in Chapter 9 in
    this volume.
13. For Levinas, who sets his philosophy against that of René Descartes, Georg
    Wilhelm Friedrich Hegel and Martin Heidegger, the central problem is
    resisting 'the transformation of the other into the same' ('The Trace of the
    Other' 348). As he continues: 'The I loses its sovereign coincidence with itself,
    its identification, in which consciousness returned triumphantly to itself and
    rested on itself. Before the exigency of the other, the I is expelled from this

rest' (353). This loss of identity in the self situates the self as an 'I' that is not its own adequate cause. While the self is still 'riveted to itself' (*On Escape* 66), is still absolutely responsible, it is no longer at rest in this responsibility as though it emanates from its own goodwill (*Otherwise than Being* 114).

14. There is additionally a nagging sense that Sanders's formulation may confuse an effect, a proscription on mourning, for a cause, apartheid; that is, it sets to work on the very terrain that, in our reading, apartheid sought to produce in the first place.

15. As Deleuze phrases it: 'The mask, the costume, the covered is everywhere the truth of the uncovered. The mask is the true subject of repetition. Because repetition differs in kind from representation, the repeated cannot be represented: rather, it must always be signified, masked by what signifies it, itself masking what it signifies ... I do not repeat because I repress. I repress because I repeat, I forget because I repeat' (18). This truth of repetition is what Deleuze locates in his reading of Freud's positing of the death instinct. On the proximity of this understanding of the construction of the subject to Fanon's discussion of the mask as a fixing in place, as a covering over of repetition so as to locate the subject within the realm of representation constituted through the figure of Man, see *Black Skin, White Masks*, particularly the Introduction as well as the fifth chapter, 'The Lived Experience of the Black Man'.

16. The term that recurs through Köhler's initial formulation, and several after it, including his own subsequent essay, is structure, the idea being that 'the structure of the world is very similar to the structure of South Africa' ('Global Apartheid' 266). This is, as we saw above, similarly Mbembe's reading of the postapartheid as the manifestation of a structural repetition.

17. Köhler argues that, from a statistical point of view, 'the income inequality of the world is even worse than that of South Africa' ('Global Apartheid' 268).

18. Invoking the language of Thomas Kuhn, Hardt and Negri call the shift from imperialism to Empire a 'paradigm shift'; the emergence of modernity, itself a revolutionary discovery of the plane of immanence, was a 'paradigmatic and irreversible change' (*Empire* 14, 74).

19. An integral element in the development of this idea of the body is the concept of the gaze. For Merleau-Ponty perception, or what he later terms the gaze,

envelops and palpates things: 'It is not simply a thing *seen* in fact (I do not see my back), it is visible in principle, it falls under a vision that is both ineluctable and deferred' ('The Intertwining' 398). In order to understand the gaze in this way, it is necessary to 'emigrate' into the outside, into what he terms 'flesh'. In other words, being is moved outside of the self or, rather, the self is located on the other side of the body. The gaze emanates from the intertwining of the flesh which leaves no self-sufficient ego; rather, there is only an 'I' due to touching, to the palpation of the gaze. It is in this formulation of the 'flesh' that Merleau-Ponty situates his concept of a pre-individual field, a field of singularity that might be available to the repetition of difference as such. This 'I', which exists due to being entwined with other 'I's' in 'flesh', leads to a notion of 'inter-corporeal being, a presumptive domain of the visible and the tangible which extends further than the things I touch and see at present' (403).

20. Hardt and Negri are of course alert to the violence of colonialism, though they are at pains to recall 'the utopian tendencies that have always accompanied the progression toward globalization' (*Empire* 115), a utopian tendency shared by Vale and Jacklin, an idea that will surely be met with resistance from those whose thought is routinely bracketed as 'postcolonial'.

21. See, for example, *Meditations on First Philosophy* in which Descartes enables a relation to the world and the other taken as fact on the subject's own terms and in relation to a subject that is always already there – there is no world apart from his thinking. This basic assertion of subjective certainty structures the terrain on which the modern concept of the subject, and the social that follows, are lodged, even if the particularities of its expression differ in meaningful ways across this itinerary. This is evident in Hobbes's *Leviathan*, written a decade after the publication of Descartes's *Meditations* and critical to Kant's understanding of the movement of reason across the world as set out in his *Perpetual Peace*. For Hobbes, as for Descartes, the subject is taken as primary; in fact, it is through an understanding of 'man' that you come to the necessity of the 'common-wealth'. Understanding, 'being nothing else but conception caused by speech' (25), is derived from sensory encounters which are then held in thought and placed into a form of causal relation (deduction, science) – the subject applies itself to the sensory.

It is this aptitude to apply itself so as to deduce the cause of things which characterises the subject, in Hobbes's formulation, as human and which produces the subject as a capable agent with an independently active will that it applies to the world so as to make sense of it. See also John Locke's *Second Treatise on Government* and John Stuart Mill's *On Liberty* for two iterations of this itinerary that take the separation between mind and body, and the subordination of the latter to the former, as constitutive assumptions in the construction of their respective socials.

22. Of course, as Hobbes declares toward the end of his section on the commonwealth, causing this ordering to take hold is the problem – that is, unlike Vale and Jacklin, he anticipates the failure of what he sees as the Enlightenment's productivity.

23. The potential of this concept, however, can be located in Lacan's reading of Merleau-Ponty in relation to the Real and desire. He suggests that his concept of the Real should be thought in relation to the concept of the 'flesh' (*The Four Fundamental Concepts of Psychoanalysis* 68). More particularly, it is in his discussion of the gaze, as a non-total ontology, that Lacan draws on Merleau-Ponty's concept of the 'flesh' as the locus both of perception and language. For Lacan, we are 'beings who are looked at'; in other words, we are located as patients within perception, we are 'in the spectacle of the world' (75). This necessitates that Lacan formulate a distinction between the Sartrean gaze and the gaze in psychoanalysis. Principally, the Sartrean gaze emanates in the realm of Others, from Others as subjects. It is thus always locatable, even if it carries an ethical imperative that is not easily answered. On the other hand, the gaze for Lacan is more primordial, 'presented to us only in the form of a strange contingency, symbolic of what we find on the horizon, as the thrust of our experience, namely, the lack that constitutes castration anxiety' (72–73). In other words, the psychoanalytic gaze is that of the Real from which 'I' am extracted as 'eye' (84); this extraction, this emergence of a subject, situates it within the realm of resemblance and representation, as a field for a certain rendition of desire. The gaze in which the subject occurs, which is located in the Real (flesh), is the 'underside of consciousness' (83) in which Lacan locates the lack by which the subject emerges as fixed to itself. As he later asserts, 'the *objet a* in the field of the visible is the gaze' (105).

24. Merleau-Ponty's concept of the 'flesh' is near to Levinas's encounter with the other, though, of course, not reducible to it. Although Levinas in *Otherwise than Being* very quickly shifts this relation to the other into the realm of language, and particularly that of discourse (spoken language for Levinas), it is important to note that it is first a relation that occurs in sense – on the surface of the body, being in one's 'own skin' (110). In his discussion of this being at the edge of oneself, in one's 'skin', Levinas suggests that his understanding of 'skin' is akin to that of the 'oneself' which he posits in discourse (195, n. 11). His shift to language from sense seems to indicate that, for Levinas, sense is always already foreclosed in language.
25. 'The explosion will not happen today,' Fanon states, 'it is too soon, or too late' (*Black Skin, White Masks* 7).
26. For a reading of negritude that resonates with the reading of the postapartheid social that we develop here, see Souleymane Bachir Diagne, *African Art as Philosophy*.
27. 'Racism's Last Word' was first published in the catalogue to *Art contre/against Apartheid*, assembled by the Association of Artists of the World Against Apartheid.
28. Derrida goes as far as to suggest, 'The survival of Western Europe depends on it' ('Racism's Last Word' 295).
29. It is not that Derrida's essay is without hope; not only is apartheid 'the most racist of racisms', but it is also the name for what, in the future perfect, 'will have been abolished' ('Racism's Last Word' 291). The problem Derrida allows us to isolate in formulations of global apartheid, however, is that South African apartheid is known in advance, whereas, with Derrida, we might ask, 'But hasn't apartheid always been the archival record of the unnameable?' (291). This point in particular was objected to by Anne McClintock and Rob Nixon, to which Derrida responded in an open letter ('But Beyond, ... ' 155–179).
30. Derrida accuses his interlocutors, McClintock and Nixon, of a form of apartheid logic, in what he reads as their adherence to strict academic disciplines, chiding them that they are arguing for 'reserved domains, the separate development of each community in the zone assigned to it'; in short, that 'apartheid remain or become the law of the land in the academy' (170).

31. One frequently reads of *new* empathic relations since the end of apartheid or of the presence of empathy *despite* apartheid rule.
32. Lawless's chapter offers one response to the question an anonymous reader asked about the significance of Deleuze to the volume. Deleuze is the best of Spinoza's readers. And grasping Spinoza's thought is central to thinking the postapartheid.

REFERENCES

Biko, Steve. 'Black Souls in White Skins?' *I Write What I Like*, Picador, 2005 [1978], pp. 20–28.

Blanchot, Maurice. *The Unavowable Community*. Translated by Pierre Joris, Station Hill Press, 1988.

Bond, Patrick. 'South Africa Tackles Global Apartheid: Is the Reform Strategy Working?' *South Atlantic Quarterly*, vol. 103, no. 4, 2003, pp. 817–839.

Brown, Tony. *The Primitive, the Aesthetic, and the Savage: An Enlightenment Problematic*. U of Minnesota P, 2012.

Dalby, Simon. 'Globalisation or Global Apartheid? Boundaries and Knowledge in Postmodern Times.' *Geopolitics*, vol. 3, no. 1, 1998, pp. 132–150.

Deleuze, Gilles. *Difference and Repetition*. Translated by Paul Patton, Columbia UP, 1994.

Derrida, Jacques. 'Racism's Last Word.' Translated by Peggy Kamuf. *Critical Inquiry*, vol. 12, no. 1, Autumn 1985, pp. 290–299.

———. 'But Beyond, ...' Translated by Peggy Kamuf. *Critical Inquiry*, vol. 13, no. 1, Autumn 1986, pp. 155–170.

Descartes, René. *Meditations on First Philosophy*, 3rd edition. Translated by Donald A. Cress, Hacket Publishing Company, 1993.

Diagne, Souleymane Bachir. *African Art as Philosophy: Senghor, Bergson and the Idea of Negritude*. Translated by Chike Jeffers, U of Chicago P, 2011.

Fanon, Frantz. *The Wretched of the Earth*. Translated by Constance Farrington, Penguin Books, 1990 [1961].

———. *Black Skin, White Masks*. Translated by Richard Philcox, Grove Press, 2008 [1952].

Foucault, Michel. *The Order of Things: An Archaeology of the Human Sciences*. Vintage Random House, 1994 [1970].

———. 'What Is Enlightenment?' *The Essential Works of Michel Foucault: Volume 1, Ethics: Subjectivity and Truth*, edited by Paul Rabinow, translated by Robert Hurley, Allen Lane, 1997, pp. 303–320.

———. *Society Must Be Defended: Lectures at the Collège de France 1975–1976*. Translated by David Macey, Penguin, 2003.

———. *Introduction to Kant's Anthropology*. Edited by Roberto Nigro, translated by Roberto Nigro and Kate Briggs, Semiotext(e), 2008.

Fregoso, Rosa-Linda. 'Voices Without Echo: The Global Gendered Apartheid.' *Emergences*, vol. 10, no. 1, 2000, pp. 137–155.

Freud, Sigmund. 'Group Psychology and the Analysis of the Ego.' *Standard Edition of the Complete Psychological Works of Sigmund Freud, vol. XXVIII*, translated and edited by James Strachey, Hogarth Press, 1953 [1921], pp. 69–143.

———. 'Totem and Taboo: Resemblances between the Psychic Lives of Savages and Neurotics.' *The Standard Edition of the Complete Psychological Works of Sigmund Freud, vol. 13*, edited and translated by James Strachey, Hogarth Press, 1955d [1913], pp. 1–161.

Hardt, Michael and Antonio Negri. *Empire*. Harvard UP, 2000.

———. *Multitude: War and Democracy in the Age of Empire*. Penguin Press, 2004.

Hegel, Georg Wilhelm Friedrich. *Hegel's Phenomenology of Spirit*. Translated by Arnold V. Miller, Oxford UP, 1977.

Hobbes, Thomas. *Leviathan*. Edited by Richard E. Flathman and David Johnston, W.W. Norton, 1997 [1651].

Horkheimer, Max and Theodor Adorno. *Dialectic of Enlightenment: Philosophical Fragments*. Edited by Gunzelin Schmid Noerr, translated by Edmund Jephcott, Stanford UP, 2002 [1944].

Köhler, Gernot. 'Global Apartheid.' *Alternatives: Global, Local, Political*, vol. 4, no. 2, 1978, pp. 263–275.

———. 'The Three Meanings of Global Apartheid: Empirical, Normative, Existential.' *Alternatives: Global, Local, Political*, vol. 20, no. 3, 1995, pp. 403–413.

Lacan, Jacques. *The Four Fundamental Concepts of Psychoanalysis*. Edited by Jacques-Alain Miller, translated by Alan Sheridan, W.W. Norton, 1998.

———. *The Seminar of Jacques Lacan: The Other Side of Psychoanalysis (Le Séminaire #17)*. Edited by Jacques-Alain Miller, translated by Russell Grigg, W.W. Norton, 2006.

Levinas, Emmanuel. *On Escape*. Translated by Bettina Bergo, Stanford UP, 1982.

———. 'The Trace of the Other.' *Deconstruction in Context: Literature and Philosophy*, edited by Mark C. Taylor, U of Chicago P, 1986, pp. 345–359.

———. *Otherwise than Being, or Beyond Essence*. Translated by Alphonso Lingus, Duquesne UP, 2009.

Locke, John. *The Second Treatise of Government and a Letter Concerning Toleration*. Dover Publications, 2002 [1689].

Loyd, Jenna M. 'Carceral Citizenship in an Age of Global Apartheid.' *Occasion: Race, Space, Scale*, vol. 8, 2015, pp. 1–15.

Mbembe, Achille. 'The State of South African Political Life.' *Africa Is a Country*, 19 September 2015, africasacountry.com/2015/09/achille-mbembe-on-the-state-of-south-african-politics/. Accessed 7 August 2016.

McClintock, Anne and Rob Nixon. 'No Names Apart: The Separation of Word and History in Derrida's "Le Dernier Mot du Racisme".' *Critical Inquiry*, vol. 13, no. 1, Autumn 1986, pp. 140–155.

Merleau-Ponty, Maurice. 'Eye and Mind.' *The Merleau-Ponty Reader*, edited by Ted Toadvine and Leonard Lawlor, Northwestern UP, 2007a [1961], pp. 351–379.

———. 'The Intertwining – The Chiasm.' *The Merleau-Ponty Reader*, edited by Ted Toadvine and Leonard Lawlor, Northwestern UP, 2007b [1961], pp. 393–414.

———. 'The Primacy of Perception and Its Philosophical Consequences.' *The Merleau-Ponty Reader*, edited by Ted Toadvine and Leonard Lawlor, Northwestern UP, 2007c [1947], pp. 89–119.

Mill, John Stuart. *On Liberty and the Subjection of Women*. Edited by Alan Ryan, Penguin Books, 2009.

Mpe, Phaswane. *Welcome to Our Hillbrow*. U of KwaZulu-Natal P, 2001.

Nussbaum, Martha. 'Kant and Stoic Cosmoploitanism.' *The Journal of Political Philosophy*, vol. 1, no. 5, 1997, pp. 1–25.

Sanders, Mark. 'Remembering Apartheid.' *Diacritics*, vol. 32, no. 3, 2002, pp. 60–80.

Sitze, Adam. *The Impossible Machine: A Genealogy of South Africa's Truth and Reconciliation Commission*. U of Michigan P, 2013.

Spivak, Gayatri Chakravorty. *A Critique of Postcolonial Reason: Toward a History of the Vanishing Present*. Harvard UP, 1999.

Vale, Peter and Heather Jacklin. 'Framing and Revisiting: Debates Old and New.' *Re-Imagining the Social in South Africa: Critique, Theory and Post-Apartheid Society*, edited by Peter Vale and Heather Jacklin, U of KwaZulu-Natal P, 2009, pp. 1–28.

Žižek, Slavoj. *Demanding the Impossible*. Edited by Yong-june Park, Polity Press, 2013.

CHAPTER 2
THE MANDELA IMAGINARY: REFLECTIONS ON POST-RECONCILIATION LIBIDINAL ECONOMY

Derek Hook

Throughout June, July and August 2013, much of South Africa's news media was preoccupied with the question of Nelson Mandela's ailing health. Leaving aside for the time being the question of South Africa's tendency to exhibit a type of media fixation on a single iconic person – the cases of Oscar Pistorius and Julius Malema are clear examples – my objective here will be to offer some speculative comments on the social and psychical significance of this period of uncertainty leading to Mandela's death in late 2013. Considering the meaning of Mandela in this period – as opposed to the period immediately after his death – represents a very different line of inquiry from any ostensibly objective assessment of Mandela's political or symbolic legacy. The reason for this is that I broach the topic of Mandela's role in the what, following Jean-François Lyotard, can be called the libidinal economy of the South African nation, that is, in terms of the various clusters of affect and unconscious ideation that his role represented at the time and beyond.

Societal hagiography

I begin by asking: how might one approach the obsessive media speculation concerning Mandela's declining health prior to his eventual death? Popular media commentaries on Mandela during the middle of 2013 as a rule wavered between requests that the public honour appropriate cultural customs – to respect the privacy of Mandela and his family – and an unrelenting thirst for ever more details pertaining to the former South African president and his feuding family. The obvious point to note here is that each such impulse effectively undoes the other, in a to-and-fro, self-perpetuating fashion.

A related tension was also at play. A variety of political personalities and media pundits made the call – presumably preparing us all for the inevitable – that the public needed to 'let Mandela go'. Verne Harris of the Nelson Mandela Foundation made such a request as early as 2011: 'He is already gone – as an active voice who offers us a last resort. He is no longer with us. He has been frustrated by our dependence on him. He wants to see us walking without him. We must allow him to go' (Nuttall & Mbembe 283). Given Mandela's advanced age in the months before his death, and the various ordeals he had lived through, this call to relinquish our hold on Mandela seemed wholly reasonable. The problem was that, once voiced, such sentiments were almost immediately paired with the contrary demand, to the effect that we – as it was then stated – 'can't let him go' (see Dawes).

The commemoration industry that has been built up around Mandela gives one reason to wonder if the country has become vaguely fearful of its many other struggle heroes. None of these men and women even vaguely approaches the quasi-mythical status attained by the name of Mandela. It is an odd quirk of human psychology and, indeed, of human sociality more generally that societies so often feel it necessary to predicate an entire social or political order on the image or the legacy of a single person (Adorno; Freud, *Mass Psychology*). In view of the history of fascist, totalitarian and dictatorial regimes of the past century, regimes which unfailingly relied on elevating the figure of a single totemic leader to the place of the sublime Thing of the nation, it is understandable that there are many who feel discomfort at the impulse to thus embody the nation in the figure of a single leader. This gives rise to our first question: Despite Mandela being a hero, a champion not only of the Left but of the struggle against global forms of apartheid, is it not worrying that he has been elevated so far above the many other political actors, past and present, who have posed forms of resistance to inequality and injustice? Differently put: What are the shortcomings of seeing Mandela as the encapsulation of all that is good in South Africa's history, as the sublime embodiment of the nation? Are we not in danger of a form of societal hagiography?

What might a psychoanalyst make of a patient who spends time on the couch directing adoring praise towards a single heroic figure? In such a situation, one would be forced to question the function of such praise, and to locate it in reference to a broader array of affects. That is to say, when one views idealisation of this magnitude one can only suspect that it is proportionately related to – and maybe even works to conceal – a considerable quantity of negative emotion, guilt perhaps or a sense of inadequacy. If one adopts such a psychoanalytic view, then the amount of celebration and love directed at Mandela seems less than innocent. We can take the argument further: such levels of idealisation could be seen as an indication of shame, certainly so inasmuch as they possibly function as the necessary counterbalance to a history that cannot – even now, after South Africa's Truth and Reconciliation Commission – be fully admitted.

Mandela against Mandela

I would not be the first person to make the argument that a politics of lionisation stands diametrically opposed to Mandela's own emancipatory struggle. Truly progressive political revolutions arguably share this as their aim: not so much to celebrate the icons of the struggle, but to serve the people. Mandela's struggle as outlined in his autobiography *Long Walk to Freedom* was, to risk a simplification, that of attaining a non-racist and democratic state in which the equality and rights of millions of ordinary men and women were protected. It was not – at least in my view – to set up a moneyed political elite or to enshrine the image of a single faultless revolutionary hero. Nic Dawes has essentially the same point in mind when he notes that Mandela's leadership style was instructive in sending the message that South Africa must be a nation of laws and of institutions, not of single lauded men and women, and certainly not of one man. In his biography of Mandela, Tom Lodge makes much the same point: 'Neither before nor during his presidency, Mandela neither demanded nor received an entirely unconditional devotion; in power he expected his compatriots to behave as assertive citizens not as genuflecting disciples' (225).

Lodge goes on in fact to credit this as Mandela's single overriding achievement: to prioritise the workings of democratic political processes and institutions – essentially, types of participatory democracy – over the authority of any one totemic leader. With this in mind, we may go so far as to say that to idolise Mandela is also, in a very significant sense, to undermine him. If a radical and emancipatory politics is about calling attention to those forms of oppression that have been ignored and unchallenged, then the glare of celebratory Mandela fanfare cannot but be seen as diverting attention from forms of human subjugation that are far less edifying to contemplate. This provides us with a case of Mandela against Mandela, of celebratory image trumping emancipatory values. The role of political hagiography in undermining the political agency of the people is nowhere better made than by the radical historian Howard Zinn, who decries

> the mountain of history books under which we stand ... so tremblingly respectful of states and statesmen ... All those histories ... centred on founding fathers and presidents weigh oppressively on the capacity of ordinary citizens to act. They suggest that in times of crisis we must look to someone to save us ... They teach us that the supreme act of citizenship is to choose between saviours by going into a voting booth ... The idea of saviours has been built into the entire culture ... We learn to look to stars, leaders ... thus surrendering our own strength, demeaning our own ability (143–414).

We can extend this argument by referring to Jacob Dlamini, who, more bluntly yet, enables us to understand how the Mandela imaginary functions in a disempowering way:

Mandela is the hero whose presence allows us not to be heroes in our own lives ... He is the big man in whose shadow we can walk, convinced that we cannot emulate his example ... [A]ll this evasion does is to ... dehistoricise him and make him larger than life while absolving us of the moral responsibility to become better people.

Perhaps more cuttingly yet, Malaika wa Azania argues that the danger of the deification of Mandela

> is that it distorts history. When Mandela is posited as the liberator, something atrocious happens: the people of South Africa are reduced to mere decorations in our liberation history ... While Mandela was languishing in prison, ordinary citizens intensified the Struggle ... The reality is that ordinary South Africans liberated Mandela in more ways than Mandela liberated them ... [Mandela] became a symbol of our struggle – by deliberate design. But he is not a liberator of black people. It is both ahistoric and apolitical to appropriate the liberation of millions of people to a single individual, especially one who spent most of his activist years incarcerated as ordinary people were continuing the Struggle and resisting their own oppression.

Overlapping the arguments of Zinn, Dlamini and wa Azania helps us make a broader point about the role of Mandela internationally and about global forms of apartheid. Wherever Mandela is venerated as a political celebratory there is the chance that the discourse of the saviour comes to eclipse an effective belief in the agency and role of single political subjects. One can even imagine, disconcertingly, that as apartheid was being dismantled in South Africa, the historical glamour of this event – piloted by no one other than Mandela – distracted attentions from a global array of various 'new apartheids'.

Neurotic vacillation

Let us return, though, to the contrary impulses displayed in public discussions of Mandela's ailing health in mid-2013. How are we to understand this double-step oscillation whereby an instance of action or assertion is immediately paired with its negation (letting Mandela go/refusing to do so, respecting and then undermining his privacy)? Psychoanalytically, one cannot deny the obsessional quality to this self-cancelling set of actions, which clearly represents an impacted ambivalence, a clear 'stuckness', an unwillingness to proceed. This is not, for the most part, an encouraging sign, because it so strongly resembles, as in the case of the classical psychoanalytic model of obsessional neurosis (Freud, 'From the History of an Infantile Neurosis'), a form of paralysis.[1] When it is extrapolated to the social sphere, we have a mode of societal stasis in which ambivalence becomes entrenched, where opposing movements perennially counterbalance one another. We have something akin to the dynamic of a perpetual motion machine, continually moving, but never progressing beyond the site to which it is affixed. It is in this way that the obsessional subject avoids the new, forestalls the possibility of making significant choices, and thus, in effect, annuls life. Hence the Lacanian idea of the obsessional as constantly marking time, effecting a kind of deadness-in-life (Fink, *The Lacanian Subject*; Melman).

Such a deadening of life is typically characterised by ritualisation, by structured patterns of living or compulsive behavioural tics (radicalised in the case of obsessive compulsive acts) that ensure that nothing new can ever emerge. It is perhaps unnecessary to add that, classically, such a psychic structure or disposition to life often takes the form of the son or daughter chronically overshadowed by a larger-than-life father figure. Such a symbolic figure – not necessarily, of course, one's actual father, a man or even biologically a father at all – is one whose influence cannot be metabolised and who thus remains a model of ambivalent affective responses, typically disguised by processes of idealisation. Here another motif of Lacanian psychoanalysis comes to the fore: that of the obsessional patient who, despite protestations to the contrary, is essentially waiting for the father to die so that he or she can start to live. What this obsessional (and typically unconscious) aspiration overlooks is the fact that the influence of such a father will only grow and attain an ever greater status after his demise – when, by virtue of ascending to a wholly symbolic existence, he becomes in effect immortal.

45

Many questions arise here, not the least of which is whether a society or the 'affective economy' of a nation's investment in a given figure could exemplify a type of obsessional neurosis. Speculation of the sort I have offered can of course be accused of a type of overextension, of generalising the observations of the clinic to the political sphere (Fink, *Against Understanding*; Hook). One should also point out that there is nothing extraordinary about a temporary period of suspension directly preceding or following the death of a national leader. Indecision and prevarication regarding the future would be unremarkable under such circumstances. Nonetheless, this much can confidently be said: the broader pattern of obsessional neurosis, if we are to accept for the moment such an extrapolation from psyche to society, would be ill suited to a nation for which ongoing transformation remains such an urgent injunction. For a country still battling to attain the social equilibrium of a genuinely *post*apartheid era, the prevarications, hidden resentments and repressed ambivalences of the obsessional would prove an immobilising force. The stultifying mode of life lived-as-death is not one that the postapartheid nation can afford. Indeed, if Mandela's symbolic and psychical legacy becomes to the nation akin to that of the overbearing father to the obsessional neurotic, then it would be difficult to see how the nation might move 'beyond Mandela' rather than obsessively repeating gestures of his commemoration.

Mandela, metonymy and enchantment

Importantly, it would be wrong to dismiss the quasi-hysterical nature of the South African public's concerns over Mandela's failing health in 2013 as an excessive or over-the-top response. To the contrary, this wave of anxiety was deeply significant, although perhaps not in the way it may have appeared. It was a token of a more far-reaching and less easily communicable form of social unease than could have been explained simply by reference to the advancing death of a former president. This behaviour can, in other words, be read *symptomatically*, as a crisis of concern that condenses within itself a series of fundamental anxieties underlying the postapartheid condition as such. Before elaborating upon this idea any further, we need to consider the unique status that Mandela's name and legacy have come to acquire in the psyche of South African and global culture alike. Deborah Posel's astute sociological analysis of 'Madiba magic' proves an invaluable resource in this respect. Mandela's stepping out of prison after 27 years to negotiate with his oppressors, says Posel,

> became a metonym of the wider national 'miracle' of a peaceful transition to democracy ... He rapidly came to personify the 'new' South Africa in ways that made the project not merely plausible, but persuasive. He also made it appear proximate, even intimate. Affectionately embraced as Madiba, his clan name, connoting simultaneously his elevated station and popular accessibility, he was the avuncular elder whose appeal breached the sedimented South African divisions of race, class, gender and ethnicity (71).

The politics of enchantment engendered by Mandela's image entailed not only an astonishing symbolic reversal – the refiguring of white South Africa's 'iconic terrorist, public enemy number one, as ... exemplary human being' (75) – but, moreover, his metonymic power to stand in for and enact this 'new' inclusive idea of South Africa. South Africans after 1994 were, as Posel puts it, 'a people in his image' (87).

Posel's engagement with the Mandela imaginary anticipates a series of affective features that I will soon stress from a psychoanalytic perspective. The effects of enchantment, she says, include

> a feeling of being in the midst of truth, but one that is revelatory rather than discursive, blindingly evident rather than produced on the strength of rationally assembled evidence ... we are enchanted, in part, by the absence of any need for further explication, as if the occurrence that produces our feelings of conviction is self-explanatory, tautologically obvious through the sheer fact of what occurs, even if it is impossible to fathom fully how and why it occurred (84).

'Mandela' as transcendent signifier

Let us now take up a more overtly psychoanalytic perspective. A name starts to function as a 'master signifier' when, despite the predominance of a general 'preferred meaning', it comes to signify a great many different things to a great many different people. Moreover, despite the diversity of such personal investments, all related parties – the public as a whole, we might say – remain identified with the name in question. They have, in other words, taken it on as a crucial element of who they are or who they would like to be. The emotive signifier in question – it is always an emotive signifier – be it 'England', 'the new South Africa', 'God', *'die volk'* or, indeed, 'Mandela', makes a type of subjectivity possible and anchors an array of beliefs. This constitutive function of the master signifier is often remarked upon in Lacanian discourse theory: in the absence of such a master signifier, there is no committed or believing subject, no subject of the group – indeed, no viable group or constituency at all (see Bracher; Stavrakakis; Verhaeghe).

What this means is that the name 'Mandela' represents a point of hegemonic convergence at which a variety of incompatible values and identifications overlap. George Frederickson's comment that Mandela succeeded in fulfilling a symbolic role as the 'embodiment of the nation that transcends ideology, party, or group' (28) has by now become a political commonplace. Lodge similarly suggests that the moral prestige embodied by Mandela enabled him 'to bring coherence to previously disparate social forces, and in doing so extend [an] exemplary influence across a range of political constituencies' (224). For some, Mandela is the benign, forgiving father of the nation, the embodiment of hope and reconciliation; for others, Mandela is the radical protagonist of the armed struggle, the African National Congress (ANC) icon who played his part in establishing the Youth League and Umkhonto we Sizwe alike; for yet others, he is an emblem of integrity, a touchstone of moral capital, a figure of global renown who transcended the particularity of his political cause to stand for the goals of a universal emancipatory politics.

The ability of 'Mandela' to function as an encapsulating signifier that brings together a series of ostensibly incompatible values has its own history. Historically, 'Mandela' stood for: proponent of African nationalism, representative of African culture and advocate for the sovereignty of African peoples; democrat and student of the values of Western parliamentary democracy; terrorist, communist, anticapitalist and treasonous enemy of the South African state; ANC leader and representative of the universal ends of justice, non-racialism, equality and freedom. This cross-section of themes is perhaps nowhere better embodied that in Mandela's speech from the dock in the 1964 Rivonia Trial. The event of the trial no doubt proved crucial in transforming Mandela the man into 'Mandela' as master signifier, and it is worth examining again sections of his speech in this light:

> I am one of the persons who helped to form *Umkhonto we Sizwe* ... I have done whatever I did, both as an individual and as a leader of my people, because of my experience in South Africa, and my own proudly felt African background ... In my youth ... I listened to the elders of my tribe telling stories of the old days. Amongst the tales they related to me were those of wars fought by our ancestors in defence of the fatherland (Mandela 349–350).

Mandela likewise proved adept at placing himself in relation to – yet not beholden to – communist allies, from whose ideology he carefully distanced himself. Furthermore, even while espousing fidelity to the African people, he described himself as a man respectful of Western political institutions:

> The ANC['s] ... chief goal was, and is, for the African people to win unity and full political rights. The Communist Party's main aim ... was to remove capitalists and replace them with a working-class government. The Communist Party sought to emphasize class distinctions whilst the ANC seeks to harmonize them. It is true that there has often been close cooperation between the ANC and the Communist Party. But cooperation is merely proof of a common goal – in this case the removal of white supremacy – and is not proof of a complete community of

> interests ... From my reading of Marxist literature ... I have gained the impression that communists regard the parliamentary system of the West as undemocratic and reactionary. But, on the contrary, I am an admirer of such a system ... I have great respect for British political institutions, and for the country's system of justice. I regard the British Parliament as the most democratic institution in the world, and the independence and impartiality of its judiciary never fail to arouse my admiration (352–353).

The 'magic' of the master signifier – which the rhetorical performance above goes some way to embodying – is that it is able to knit together different constituencies, appealing equally, albeit in very different ways, to a variety of classes who are otherwise opposed in their political agendas. Although in different ways, the signifier 'Mandela' was able to perform something of this task, both in 1964 and – in a more encompassing fashion – in the postapartheid years. A master signifier, we can thus say, makes a version of society, a crucial type of social bond, possible. Manqoba Nxumalo's commentary on the different legacies Mandela embodies for whites and blacks seems at first to dispute this idea:

> Mandela of the black community is and will be different to the Mandela of white society. To the black majority, he is a fighter and a radical militant who refused to be broken down even by jail. To them he is a reminder that in order to get justice you must fight because there is honour in struggle. To the white liberal community, he represents reconciliation, forgiveness and peaceful coexistence ... There is a fundamental departure between blacks and whites on what takes precedence in all the things that make up this icon called Mandela.

What these words suggest is that Mandela is a mediator between racial and class groups whose political ideals are not only very different but are at times diametrically opposed. In this respect, the master signifier achieves what seems impossible: it engenders a type of hegemonic appeal whereby various social antagonisms may (however temporarily) be overcome. A further implication can be read out of Nxumalo's observations: part of what was anxiety-provoking about Mandela's declining health was that South Africa would soon lack a crucial 'class mediator', that is, a political figure who not only spoke powerfully to black and white groupings but who also enabled them to speak and engage with one another.

Political theorists such as Ernesto Laclau, also in collaboration with Chantal Mouffe, tend to prefer the notion of an empty as opposed to a master signifier, even though the concept in question is much the same. The benefit of referring to the master signifier as 'empty' is that it draws attention to the fact that it maintains no intrinsic or essential meaning, and also that it permits an endless succession of varying applications and uses. A master signifier, that is to say, can never be totalised; it remains always empty, able to accommodate fresh articulations. This is so obviously the case in respect of Mandela's name – various applications of which are, today in South Africa, seemingly never-ending – that it barely warrants mentioning. Whether in the material form of commemorative architecture or place names; institutions, charities, endowments; commemorative commodities; and even rival political party interests,[2] 'Mandela' is a signifier that can be appended to an endless stream of postapartheid objects and aspirations.

Although I have cited mainly commemorative and commodity objects above, the true measure of a master signifier's strength has more to do with the social bonds and subjective investments that it underpins, that is, with its role in consolidating a social mass. Having said that, one should not neglect the symbolic paraphernalia noted above: the symbolic density connoted by such activities and representations is a clear signal that a society is fortifying a mode of belief, concretising a cherished set of ideals and subjective or societal investments. In short, we don't erect monuments simply to celebrate and affirm what we already know; we build and sustain monuments so that we will continue to know and believe what may otherwise be erased through time, various forms of uncertainty or doubt. So, contrary to assuming that the endless proliferation of Mandela signifiers speaks simply to the historical objectivity, to the security, of the Mandela legacy, we might ask whether this activity is fuelled rather by a need to believe. Moreover, we might ask whether it is propelled by the imminent failure of, or disbelief in, the vision of an integrated South African nation that Mandela championed and, furthermore, whether this multitude of symbolic gestures attempts – desperately perhaps – to affirm such a unified social reality, despite the mounting evidence of growing social and political divisions.

To extend this point, it is worth briefly remarking upon a change that has occurred in South Africa's relationship to Mandela. Writing in 2006, Lodge commented: 'Surprisingly ... there is little evidence of a cult of personality. The only public statue of Mandela is located in Sandton ... His image does not appear on banknotes, or postage stamps, and the museum at his birthplace is low key' (223). All of this, it is safe to say, has changed, and radically so. Mandela's image now adorns South African banknotes; there are a number of museums dedicated to Mandela (at Umtata, Mvezo and Qunu); statues of Mandela in Sandton, Bloemfontein (Naval Hill) and Paarl (Groot Drakenstein) – not neglecting, of course, the Mandela monument in Howick – have now been outstripped by the nine-metre statue at the Union Buildings in Pretoria. Why is it then, we might ask, that we need to celebrate and memorialise Mandela now in the immediate aftermath of his death more than ever before? Might it be because now, as we advance into a *post*-postapartheid era, we are in a time when the exuberance and enthusiasm of the Mandela-led government of 1994–99 already seem to be dated historical phenomena?[3] To reiterate the point made above, we could say that this surge of commemorative practices and signifiers occurs because we need to believe the Mandela myth now more than ever. Such signifiers indicate less the absolute truth of the political changes Mandela helped bring about than the fact that without the constant activity of Mandela signification, we might fail to believe in such changes – promised or otherwise – and begin to fear that many of the country's divisions of old could resurface in novel postapartheid forms.

Lionel Bailly adds an important qualification to the notion of the master signifier which seems crucial here: 'master signifiers usually mask their opposites ... they exist in a polarised form' (63). The openly expressed aspect of the master signifier props up an ego – that is, the imagined identity of a subject or community – while the unenunciated aspect remains 'buried in the unconscious ... constantly pushing up its opposite number' (63). The function of the master signifier is thus to redirect potentially painful or anxiety-provoking signifiers, and to do so in such a way 'that a signifying chain with the opposite, bearable, or even comforting meaning emerges' (63). Following the argument already developed, there could barely be a more apt description of how the signifier 'Mandela' is utilised in the postapartheid context.

The bonds of fantasy

Evident in the elevation of Mandela to the realm of 'pure symbol' is the role of a type of mythologisation. A master signifier is never merely objective in its meaning and value but is animated rather by subjective belief, by the imagination of those who have invested in it. This is to say that the signifier 'Mandela' is today always in part a projection of those who have taken pride in, and identified with, the man and his legacy. There is thus some truth, despite the apparent cynicism, in political evaluations that suggest that Mandela's greatness 'is mainly a creation of the collective imagination' (see Beresford). In speaking of Mandela, we have in mind not just the man or Mandela as historical event, but Mandela as focal point of multiple subjective investments and identifications – Mandela, that is, as shared social fantasy. To make such an observation is by no means to depart from pressing 'real world' political concerns. 'Mandela' has served as a stabilising signifier, a signifier more able than any other to lend moral purpose and meaning to the social contradictions of the contemporary South African era. Indeed, 'Mandela' enables us to knit together the otherwise discontinuous elements of postapartheid experience into a narrative of progress.

A crucial qualification should be made here: in psychoanalytic terms, 'fantasy' is not akin to an imaginary flight of fancy, an idle illusion, something that should be rejected in favour of careful consideration of the objective facts of reality. Fantasy is rather what underlies and mediates what we experience as reality; it is what makes reality as such possible. Fantasy is thus indispensable; it provides the lens through which the chaotic and fragmentary nature of subjective and societal reality is afforded a rudimentary narrative coherence. Although not working from a psychoanalytic perspective, Sarah Nuttall and Achille Mbembe's comments on Mandela's death point to precisely such a fantasmatic function:

> Mandela's death might reveal a void at the heart of a country that has always struggled to mask such an emptiness at its centre: a country that has struggled to define itself as a nation and to draw together its many fragments into a sustained sense of commonality in the wake of a long racist past. More than anybody else, Mandela embodied this sense of commonality, and his passing is likely to reignite the metaphysical anxiety that South Africa is neither a concept nor an idea – just a place, a geographical accident (268).

It was in this respect that the demise of Mandela seemed so anxiety-provoking for the country. It heralded the prospect of a crisis of redefinition and, more than that, of the divergent strands of postapartheid society simply failing to cohere. Or, more dramatically yet – extrapolating a somewhat bleak vision from Nuttall and Mbembe's comments – Mandela's decline may be thought to represent the end of the fantasy, the point at which the concept of South Africa ceases to work in any other way than as a geographical designation. Perhaps it is the case – easy enough to imagine if Mandela's legacy was erased from history – that 'South Africa' is no more than the name for a set of historical events to which no special status, no historical essence, no grand march of progress can rightly be said to apply.[4]

As sombre as such an eventuality might seem, it is nonetheless one worth contemplating; it may have 'therapeutic' benefits. How, for instance, might South Africans see themselves differently; what social, civic and political responsibilities come to the fore once complacent stories of 'democracy achieved' are interrupted? What possibilities for self-interrogation emerge once we suspend the narratives of an extraordinary history and nation that our proximity to the greatness of

Mandela has for so long allowed us to maintain? Despite fantasy making a non-psychotic reality possible, it is also necessary, so psychoanalysis tells us, to work through those fantasies upon which we have become overly reliant. This gives us a different relation to those fantasies which have come to function as a protective shell; those fantasies which routinely obscure disturbing or traumatic conditions that we would prefer to remain concealed.[5]

The ways of love

The question of how – or why – we love Mandela is also crucial. We may distinguish between several different modalities of love. There is a type of love that is largely narcissistic in nature and that operates most fundamentally to facilitate self-love. We love those who enable us to maintain an idealised image of ourselves, to bolster and extend the positive qualities of our own self-image. The loved person here is essentially a prop for our own self-regard, a mirror reflecting what (we believe) is best about ourselves and screening out less admirable qualities. Given the function of this type of love, one appreciates both the importance that the figure of Mandela plays in the libidinal economy of the nation and, once again, why his prospective demise occasioned so much anxiety. The death of Mandela means – at least in part – the loss of what South Africans feel makes them an exceptional nation, remarkable in the eyes of the world.

There is also the more abstract love of shared social and historical ideals. This type of love concerns those beliefs – what we might call 'to live and die for' values – that not only ground a society, but also link it to its history and set out the ideals that it will continue to strive for. Such a constellation of social and symbolic ideals necessarily exceeds the role of any one person. These comments put us in a position to respond to the question – painful for many – of how, and in what capacity, to let Mandela go. Now that Mandela has died, this may seem a merely academic question; yet his image of course remains, and we should not be too quick to assume that we have in fact relinquished our hold upon him. If it is then the first of the two types of love that underscores our reticence to give Mandela up, if we love Mandela chiefly as a means of loving ourselves, then, surely, it must by now be time to cut the cord, to bid him a final farewell. We can extend this argument. If we love the image of Mandela in ways that enable us to conceal the injustices and inequalities of the postapartheid condition and thus idealise the current social conditions of the country, then it would seem necessary that we leave him behind. More succinctly put: we need to forgo the comforting illusions that the *imaginary* figure of Mandela allows us to maintain.

However, inasmuch as Mandela encapsulated a vision of social bonds traversing apartheid's structural divisions, a vision which made the (imperfect) transition from apartheid possible, then it is appropriate that we cherish the unfinished legacy he has left. For, after all, this set of ideals is bigger than any one figure, even if Mandela did more than most to bring these values to life and lend them a recognisable human face. Dawes makes much the same point, reflecting hopefully on the course that such a permeation of values might take:

> Mandela's long goodbye takes on the form of a return, not as a statue, or as a caricature, but as living potential. That potential is around us in democratic institutions and traditions that, if young, or threatened, are also resilient and powerful … It is visible in the agonisingly slow, but vital change in the shape of our cities, and the refusal of South Africans to be content with half-a-life, or with the outer forms of freedom, absent its content.

Then, again, anxiety may emerge here also, even in respect of Mandela's symbolic legacy. If Mandela made possible 'the postapartheid', as both political era and mode of subjectivity, then his death cannot but imply the question: What comes after the postapartheid era, an era which has been synonymous precisely with the figure of Mandela? Furthermore, if we are to credit the notion that Mandela made a version of South African subjectivity possible, then what types of South African subjectivity will be possible in a future where he no longer exists?

Having intimated that love and idealisation are rarely innocent, we may now turn to a facet of the public obsession with Mandela that few have remarked upon. The universal outpouring of love and idealisation for Mandela in the immediate aftermath of his death has been accompanied by a period of intense vilification directed at his successor as leader of both the ANC and the country, namely Jacob Zuma. Lize van Robbroeck's analysis of 'the visual Mandela' is particularly helpful in this respect, drawing attention, as it does, to the strikingly different portrayals of Mandela and Zuma in contemporary South African popular culture. Zuma, she remarks, has been subject to scathing iconoclasm (the cartoonist Zapiro's showerhead caricature being a case in point), while the figure of Mandela remains the embodiment of good citizenship:

> Zuma ... has managed to rekindle white anxieties and shatter much of the strategic harmony Mandela managed to effect between Africanist symbolic power and the demands of global neoliberal realpolitik. The media's open hostility toward Zuma ... has opened up deep ... fault lines in the South African political and cultural sphere ... Mandela's painstaking stitching together of African traditional values, Western democratic liberal structures, global capitalism, and pan-African communitarianism is in the process of being unravelled. The harmonious multivocality of Mandela ... has now deteriorated into a cacophony of incoherent voices: the tenuous centre established by Mandela is not holding and things are beginning to fall apart (263).

We might add to this commentary by stressing how these respective modes of depiction – idealisation and vilification – are connected. Psychoanalytically, we would be remiss if we did not note how they are linked; indeed, are part of one and the same dynamic. The more Mandela is progressively idealised, the more Zuma's (not inconsiderable) faults are magnified. Mandela is lionised; Zuma is lampooned, reduced to caricature and stereotype, lambasted as the embodiment of everything wrong with South Africa.

This dynamic reflects something of the country's self-ruminations. More to the point yet, it represents the country's inability to bring together what is best and worst, what is most inspiring and most shameful, in its history. One is reminded of the resentful words that the director Oliver Stone puts into Richard Nixon's mouth in a fictitious scene from his 1995 film *Nixon*. Staring with bitterness at a portrait of John F. Kennedy and wondering why the American people loved the younger man so much, he laments: 'When they look at him, they see themselves as they want to be; when they look at me, they see themselves as they are.' It perhaps goes without saying that this perfectly illustrates the libidinal dynamism that Jacques Lacan outlines in his notion of the mirror stage. We have thus on a national level the continual interplay between the loved, narcissistically affirming image on the one hand (Mandela)[6] and the associated rival and much reviled image (Zuma) – both of course reflecting the same subject (the South African nation) – that threatens this idealising self-representation. Resistant as many may be to this conclusion, we should insist: both images stem from the same self-conflicted, narcissistic and yet also self-hating source, namely, the image South Africans have of themselves.

Suffering idealisation

We are all familiar with the figure of the tragic hero, the gallant character who is willing to sacrifice himself or herself for the good of a cause. Importantly, however, the sacrifice in question may not always be the hero's life; it may be of a symbolic sort. That is to say, as in Lacan's notion of being 'between the two deaths', one can die symbolically before one is in fact physically dead. Let us consider a figure – rare at the best of times – that is willing to take on the hate of a community or nation, to assume the role of the villain if this is ultimately what serves the greater public good. One is reminded of the role the psychoanalyst is forced to endure during the travails of negative transference, in which the patient comes – quite unjustifiably – to see in the analyst everything that she or he, the patient, most detests and resents. Or, to provide a more dramatic example from within the domain of popular culture, we might follow the argument Slavoj Žižek makes in *The Pervert's Guide to Ideology* in respect of the character of Batman in *The Dark Knight Returns*. In order to allow the public to continue to believe in the figure of Harvey Dent, a public prosecutor who is seen as pursuing the ends of justice even in the face of insurmountable odds, Batman assumes the role of the criminal 'public enemy number one' which in fact really belongs to Dent. The heroic here has to do not only with the fact of self-sacrifice, but with the fact that this heroism, this very fact of self-sacrifice, may never be acknowledged as such.

It is not hard to find historical examples of leaders who have had to endure such a treatment, who have been vilified beyond what seems reasonable. Both of Mandela's successors as president – Thabo Mbeki and Jacob Zuma – might be considered cases in point. There is a sense of ethical grandeur that, retrospectively, attaches to such a position, even if it is perhaps not, in the final analysis, fully justified. Hated as one might be in present circumstances, there is always the possibility that what one has done, what one has sacrificed one's self for, will one day by recognised by a future generation.

Lonely as it may be to find one's self in such a position, there is another situation which is potentially even more debilitating. Consider the case of the hero who, rather than being sacrificed for or by the people, is lauded, granted every conceivable honour for qualities and actions that are (at least in part) projections, misrepresentations of who they are. A different type of falsity is involved here – not the falsity of the negative transference (when one is not as bad as has been imagined) but the falsity of the positive transference (when one is not as good as has been imagined). Here too, as in the case of the tragic hero, a type of sacrifice is involved, not the sacrifice of one's life, but a sacrifice of what one might privately be, or believe in, for the sake of what people need to see in you. This is part of what Mandela had to undergo: he needed to put himself in the service of the image that others had of him.

Being sublimated in such a way, elevated into the position of 'the most admired person on earth ... a secular saint, an embodiment of greatness and an icon of peace and wisdom' (Stengel), is a necessarily violent process. Such a process would entail the exclusion of many of one's own political values, some of which would have to be silenced so as not to undermine the mythical image one has come to embody. Not all of what one ideally represents, believes or strives for can be shown under such circumstances, particularly in respect of more radical views. This, for a man like Mandela, who was so famously prepared to die for what he believed in, was perhaps more difficult than we at first imagine. Moreover, it was not as if Mandela did not hold controversial views. One only needs to consult one of the many muckraking websites established after his death to see such controversial facts listed: Mandela stood alongside ANC comrades singing 'death to the whites'; Mandela was for many years secretly a member of the South African Communist Party; Mandela was unapologetic about his longstanding friendship with Muammar Gaddafi; Mandela condemned the Iraq War and was an ardent opponent of America's aggressive foreign policy, and so on and so on (see also Malan).

Of course, it can be said that it is better to be loved rather than hated for what one is *not* (that is, for what others have projected upon you). This, surely, is a far more rewarding – even ennobling – form of sacrifice. The rapturous attention of so many might be thought to offset the alienating effects of adopting a persona never quite commensurate with one's own beliefs. Then again, the experience of needing to suffer idealisation, to stifle the radical political instincts that had been his lifeblood, cannot have been easy for Mandela.

The death of the father

The death of an important father figure – particularly one of the stature of Mandela – can represent a great many things symbolically. It can, of course, result in an ugly series of skirmishes in which various family members and stakeholders struggle for their share of the man's legacy and wealth. This often seems, and has sadly proved, unavoidable. This is not the only outcome that may be predicted of such an event. The death of an esteemed father may represent just as much an auspicious beginning as an inauspicious end. This is in fact a well-known literary trope: a grand family story – or historical epic – only in effect really begins following the death of a great patriarch. As US soap operas like *Six Feet Under*, *Dallas* and *Brothers and Sisters* demonstrate, little else provides as much by way of interesting new plot developments as does the demise of a powerful and revered father figure.[7]

What most certainly is signalled by such an event is that the father's descendants need to assume responsibility for what had hitherto been his perceived duty. One of Mandela's tasks – perhaps his overriding achievement – was to pull together a radically divided and diverse society, to enable a postapartheid imaginary that the entire nation could, in very different ways, believe in and identify with. The signifier 'Mandela' provided the basis – historically unimaginable until that point – for a type of social consensus that made the postapartheid public sphere viable. It is this perceived ability to transcend apartheid's lingering culture of hate and separatism, to foster ties of allegiance that cross the boundaries of race, ethnicity and political allegiance, that characterises Mandela's lasting greatness. What the demise of the 'father of the nation' throws into perspective is the fact that we, as individual citizens, will no longer be able to delegate this task to him. This responsibility, the labour of developing a viable postapartheid consensus and, indeed, of supporting a shared public sphere will now fall to those on whom Mandela placed his trust: the people of the country of South Africa.

NOTES

1. The canonical example of obsessional neurosis in the history of psychoanalysis being, of course, Freud's case study of Ernst Lanzer, the 'Rat man', in 'Notes upon a Case of Obsessional Neurosis'.
2. As in the 2013 attempt of South Africa's Democratic Alliance to appropriate Mandela's image in its own campaigning materials.
3. See Dennis Walder for an argument that 2009 represented a turning point in South Africa's recent history. That year saw Jacob Zuma become the country's third democratically elected president; the country was plunged into recession; the HIV and Aids pandemic soared to new levels; new crises of unemployment, crime and corruption came to the fore; and xenophobic attacks and service delivery protests swept through the country.

4. We can elaborate upon this idea of Mandela as fantasy that makes the notion of the South African nation viable by referring to Posel, who in turn cites Ivor Chipkin's analysis of the post-1994 South African people who, Chipkin claims, lacked any distinguishing national marks, had no common culture or race, and had only really an idea of what they were *not*, namely South Africans of old. Posel adds to this (a nice case in point of the anticipatory mode of temporality often stressed in Lacanian psychoanalysis): 'Mandela's metonymic power – to stand in for and enact this "new" people as if it had already come into being – provided a resolution to the paradox: South Africans were now a people in his image and what it stood for, made anew' (87).
5. The notion of 'traversing the fantasy' sometimes taken as a precondition for a successful psychoanalytic treatment entails such a trajectory, namely, a crossing through the multiple layers of a given fantasy which shields the subject from disconcerting 'reals', revealing thus the radical contingency of both their given circumstances and their own status as subject. Importantly, to 'traverse the fantasy' does not imply that the fantasy be completely dissipated or destroyed, but rather that it be 'passed through', resituated.
6. Van Robbroeck makes this point wonderfully. The many photographs of Mandela 'sporting his approving, avuncular smile ... serve to affirm the nation's grandiose narcissism by feeding our sense of specialness' (252).
7. In these TV shows, the 'founding father', that is, the man who has made the wealth and established the name of the family – akin in some ways to the Freudian primal father – dies abruptly within the first few episodes.

REFERENCES

Adorno, Theodor. *The Culture Industry: Selected Essays on Mass Culture*. Routledge, 1991.

Bailly, Lionel. *Lacan*. Oneworld, 2009.

Beresford, David. 'South Africa: Mandela's Greatness Is from Being Here.' *Mail & Guardian*, 7 November 1997, allafrica.com/stories/199711070101.html. Accessed 7 August 2016.

Bracher, Mark. 'On the Psychological and Social Functions of Language: Lacan's Theory of the Four Discourses.' *Lacanian Theory of Discourse: Subject, Structure, and Society*, edited by Mark Bracher, Marshall W. Alcorn, Ronald J. Corthell and François Massardier-Kenney, New York UP, 1994.

Chipkin, Ivor. *Do South Africans Exist? Nationalism, Democracy and the Identity of 'the People'*. Wits UP, 2007.

Dawes, Nic. 'Mandela: The Long Goodbye.' *Mail & Guardian*, 28 June 2013.

Dlamini, Jacob. 'Embittered Histories: The Other Sharpeville and the Making of South African Pasts.' *Open Democracy*, 14 March 2011, www.opendemocracy.net/jacob-dlamini/embittered-histories-other-sharpeville-and-making-of-south-african-pasts-0. Accessed 7 August 2016.

Fink, Bruce. *The Lacanian Subject: Between Language and Jouissance*. Princeton UP, 1995.

———. *Against Understanding: Cases and Commentary in a Lacanian Key, vol. 1*. Routledge, 2014.

Frederickson, George. 'The Making of Mandela'. *New York Review of Books*, 27 September 1990.

Freud, Sigmund. 'Notes upon a Case of Obsessional Neurosis.' *The Standard Edition of the Complete Psychological Works of Sigmund Freud, vol. X*, edited by James Strachey, Hogarth Press, 1909, pp. 153–249.

———. 'From the History of an Infantile Neurosis.' *The Standard Edition of the Complete Psychological Works of Sigmund Freud, vol. XVII*, edited by James Strachey, Hogarth Press, 1918.

———. *Mass Psychology and Other Writings*. Penguin, 2004.

Hook, Derek. *(Post)apartheid Conditions: Psychoanalysis and Social Formation*. Palgrave Macmillan, 2013.

Lacan, Jacques. *Écrits*. Translated by Bruce Fink, W.W. Norton, 2006.

Laclau, Ernesto. *Emancipation(s)*. Verso, 2007.

Laclau, Ernesto and Chantal Mouffe. *Hegemony and Socialist Strategy*. Verso, 1985.

Lodge, Tom. *Mandela: A Critical Life*. Oxford UP, 2006.

Malan, Rian. 'What a Lost Prison Manuscript Reveals about the Real Nelson Mandela.' *The Spectator*, 18 January 2014.

Mandela, Nelson. *Long Walk to Freedom: The Autobiography of Nelson Mandela*. Macdonald Purnell, 1994.

Melman, Charles. 'On Obsessional Neurosis.' *Returning to Freud: Clinical Psychoanalysis in the School of Lacan*, edited and translated by Stuart Schneiderman, Yale UP, 1980, pp. 139–159.

Nixon. Directed by Oliver Stone, Cinergi Pictures, 1995.

Nuttall, Sarah and Achille Mbembe 'Mandela's Mortality.' *The Cambridge Companion to Nelson Mandela*, edited by Rita Barnard, Cambridge UP, 2014, pp. 267–290.

Nxumalo, Manqoba. 'Mandela for Blacks Is Different to Mandela for Whites.' *Thought Leader*, 3 July 2013, www.thoughtleader.co.za/manqobanxumalo/2013/07/03/mandela-for-blacks-is-different-to-mandela-for-whites/. Accessed 7 August 2016.

The Pervert's Guide to Ideology. Directed by Sophie Fiennes, Zeitgeist Films, 2012.

Posel, Deborah. '"Madiba Magic": Politics as Enchantment.' *The Cambridge Companion to Nelson Mandela*, edited by Rita Barnard, Cambridge UP, 2014, pp. 70–91.

Stavrakakis, Yannis. 'Green Ideology: A Discursive Reading.' *Journal of Political Ideologies*, vol. 2, no. 3, 1997, pp. 259–279.

Stengel, Richard. 'Nelson Mandela: Remembering an Icon of Freedom.' *Time Magazine*, 5 December 2013.

Van Robbroeck, Lize. 'The Visual Mandela: A Pedagogy of Citizenship.' *The Cambridge Companion to Nelson Mandela*, edited by Rita Barnard, Cambridge UP, 2014, pp. 244–266.

Verhaeghe, Paul. *Beyond Gender: From Subject to Drive*. Other Press, 2001.

wa Azania, Malaika. 'I Was Not Liberated by Mandela.' *Sunday Independent*, 19 July 2015, www.iol.co.za/sundayindependent/i-was-not-liberated-by-mandela-1887330. Accessed 7 August 2016.

Walder, Dennis. 'Hysterical Nostalgia in the Postcolony: From "Coming Home" to "District 9".' *Consumption, Markets and Culture*, vol. 17, no. 2, 2013, pp. 143–157.

Zinn, Howard. *The Twentieth Century: A People's History*. Harper, 2003 [1980].

CHAPTER 3
THE RETURN OF EMPATHY:
POSTAPARTHEID FELLOW FEELING
Ross Truscott

Empathy between those whom apartheid inscribed as different is widely and confidently posited as a threshold of postapartheid transformation; it is said to mark, if not the arrival of a postapartheid psychosocial condition, then at least the assurance that things are on the right track. At a moment when student movements are coalescing around 'black pain' and 'black anger', it seems worthwhile pausing to consider what has become an assumed good, an ethical response affirmed without question. The assertion of empathy as a postapartheid condition, however, is not new. Around the Truth and Reconciliation Commission (TRC) of South Africa it was argued, largely in the language of psychoanalysis, that empathy stands as a break with patterns of colonial and apartheid domination, the most well-known case being *A Human Being Died That Night*. In it Pumla Gobodo-Madikizela gives an account of her interviews with Eugene de Kock, commanding officer of apartheid's counterinsurgency police unit based at the notorious Vlakplaas farm, with whom she came to identify and empathise, their encounter awakening his 'human' capacity for empathy. It is this particular kind of argument that I want to pressure here.

The aim of this chapter is not to foreclose on empathy as a postapartheid condition but, rather, to offer a critique that might make the concept of empathy adequate to the present historical moment in which South African psychosocial transformation has shuddered and stalled. In staging my concerns, I take the work of South African artist

Nandipha Mntambo, specifically her collection of installations and images in *The Encounter*, as a provocation that asks us to think again about empathy. I regard Mntambo here as a philosophical accomplice rather than an analysand. In short, I want to think with Mntambo's *The Encounter* rather than about her artwork.

It has been suggested that Mntambo's work, like that of photographer Zanele Muholi, elicits empathy from the viewer that their work calls for empathy.[1] It is worth briefly following the contours of this claim. Regarding Muholi's work, Tamar Garb, for instance, argues that 'photographic history provides a resource, not only of critique but of play. Deadly serious about the visual clichés of an oppressive iconographic tradition, she, like the people she portrays, feels free to use them as she likes, exposing their ethnic essentialism while queering their modes of address' (17). Underscoring the stakes of such an appropriative approach, Garb states:

> Photography provided an efficient means through which the unfamiliar inhabitants of the colonized world could be organized into apparently coherent entities and groups for scrutiny, study and delectation by outsiders. In fact it often provided the ground of their intelligibility, and the generic took precedence over the particular. But sometimes the photographs captured distinctive and unique physiognomies and features, and it is possible that empathy was also in place, despite the display of difference and the play of power that exposure to the camera entailed (21).

In so many readings of Muholi's images, empathy appears, as it does for Garb, as a possibility that exceeds the colonial visual codes that Muholi reworks. Like Muholi, Mntambo works within and against a tradition of imaging, but what Mntambo queers is precisely the empathic gaze. This, at least, is the argument towards which I am heading. If empathy has been identified, historically, as that which, within apartheid and colonial rule more generally, exceeded or escaped relations of domination, this chapter approaches the discourse of empathy from a different angle, taking empathy as a concept embedded in colonial thinking, which requires the work of reinscription.

Figure 3.1. 'Emabutfo' © Nandipha Mntambo, courtesy STEVENSON Cape Town and Johannesburg

A part of *The Encounter* consists of installations made of cowhides, moulded on the female body, both the artist's body and her mother's (Figure 3.1). If empathy, as Clifford Geertz puts it in his article 'From the Native's Point of View', discussing the scandal of Bronisław Malinowski's *A Diary in the Strict Sense of the Term*, is 'a task at least as delicate, if a bit less magical, as putting oneself into someone else's skin' (29), then Mntambo 'invites the viewer to take her place, to step into the outline of her body, the moulded cowhide' (May 2010). While these installations provide a comment on empathy, it is in her image 'The Rape of Europa' (Figure 3.2) that, I think, empathy's latent libidinal economy is best grasped and it is to this image that I return below.

In what follows I offer a reading of empathy as it appears in Sigmund Freud's writings, the reason being that if so many calls for empathy have drawn on psychoanalysis, a close reading of Freud will allow us to think through the undisclosed itineraries of subjectivity to which the concept of empathy commits postapartheid transformation.[2] I focus here on two texts: 'Fragment of an Analysis of a Case of Hysteria', or Dora's case,

Figure 3.2. 'The Rape of Europa' © Nandipha Mntambo, courtesy STEVENSON Cape Town and Johannesburg

which opens onto the long and complex tangle between hysteria, art and empathy, and 'The Moses of Michelangelo'.

The impression in the anglophone world that Freud was simply against empathy is, as George Pigman suggests, largely an effect of the *Standard Edition* translation of Freud; it was not Freud but James and Alix Strachey, the editors and translators, who were against the term. As Pigman argues, *Einfühlung*, the German term of which 'empathy' is an early twentieth-century translation, is 'an essential component of Freud's technique, a prerequisite for interpretation' (246). It is not, however, only a matter of translation – the Stracheys searching for English words with which to conceal a term they abhorred. For Freud, 'the process which psychology calls "empathy" [*Einfühlung*] ... plays the largest part in our understanding of what is inherently foreign to our ego in other people [*das Ichfremde anderer Personen*]' ('Group Psychology' 108). Crucial though it is to psychoanalysis, *Einfühlung* is not, strictly speaking, a psychoanalytic concept; it predates the emergence of psychoanalysis and was taken into psychoanalysis from elsewhere. Thus, just as psychoanalysis posits a subject that has, at its core, a foreign object, an other, we find this doubled at the level of psychoanalytic discourse: 'empathy' – for Freud, a concept transposed from psychology, his quotation marks telling of this transposition – is essential to psychoanalytic practice and is, at the same time, a concept foreign to the discourse of psychoanalysis.[3]

Let me now turn to Dora's case and, following that, to Freud's reading of Michelangelo's Moses, from which point I will return more closely to *The Encounter*. My aim in juxtaposing Mntambo and Freud is to conjure three scenes in which empathy confronts its own undoing: its enjoyment, its violence and its narcissism, each of which is commonly taken to be antithetical to the cultivated feeling and refined imagination of empathy.

Dora's predator

Dora presented with various symptoms, among them coughing, aphasia, dyspnoea, stomach pains and catarrh. She was brought to Freud by her father, Phillip Bauer, after he and Dora's mother discovered a suicide letter. She had accused her father of having an affair with Frau K, a family friend. Two years before, she had also accused Herr K of making sexual advances towards her, indeed of pursuing her since she was 14. Though worried about Dora, her father took these accusations as the fancies of a young girl and asked Freud to bring her to her senses. For her part, Dora was furious. She suspected that she had been handed over to Herr K as the price her father was paying for his ongoing affair. And now she had been handed over, once more, to Freud.

While taking Dora's accusations seriously, Freud interprets them. On the one hand, Dora behaved 'like a jealous wife' protesting against a husband's infidelity, 'clearly putting herself in her mother's place' ('Fragment of an

Analysis' 56). The woman her father loved was, however, not her mother and she must also, Freud hypothesises, 'have been putting herself in Frau K's place' (56). Dora was thus, as Freud states, 'identifying herself both with the woman her father had once loved and with the woman he loved now' (56). Extending these lines of Dora's identifications, Freud suggests that her symptoms concealed a secret love for Herr K, behind which was an Oedipal wish. Thus, she was not simply afraid of Herr K: she was afraid of her desire for him, her symptoms providing a means of refusing his advances, of getting him off her path, as it were, but also a means of disguising her desire. Freud's formulation is then given a further twist, which he elaborates for the most part in his footnotes. Dora was not only jealous of Frau K (and her mother), in love with Herr K (and her father); she was also, Freud suggests, in love with Frau K. Indeed, Freud writes of 'Dora's deep-rooted homosexual love for Frau K' (105, n2), a love that was at the heart of her hysteria and that he failed to discern in time.

Freud is frequently charged with a 'lack of empathy with Dora' (Decker 107), 'a lack of empathy with a suffering adolescent girl being victimized by egoistic adults' (Gay 173). Registering the possibility of such a charge, Freud states in his preface that 'the exacting demands which hysteria makes upon a physician and investigator can be met only by the most sympathetic spirit of inquiry [*liebevollste Vertiefung*] and not by an attitude of superiority and contempt' ('Fragment of an Analysis' 15–16). Taking Freud at his word, some commentators have also persuasively argued that he did in fact put himself into Dora's psychic world, that he did empathise with her, and that it is this, rather than his lack of empathy, that is so disquieting about the case. Clare Kahane suggests that, 'as brilliant as Freud was in constructing a narrative of Dora's desire, he essentially represented his own' (20). Stephen Marcus, too, asserts, 'The case history belongs progressively less to her than it does to him' (85). Suzanne Gearhart writes of Freud's 'identification with Dora' (122), a part of his countertransference. And Neil Hertz inquires into Freud's 'unrecognized – or refused – identification' with Dora; indeed, the ways in which 'he "was" Dora' (67).

Freud's letters certainly suggest that he had something like the pitfalls of empathy in mind – 'that the "reader of thoughts" perceives nothing in the "other", but merely projects his own thoughts' (*The Complete Letters* 450) – while writing up the case. We might say that Freud does empathise with Dora but that, in doing so, he situates himself, as Jacques Lacan argues, in the position of Herr K. He assumes or, rather, is cast, through the transference that ensues, in the role of Dora's sexual predator. The transference – as the impression an unremembered experience will have left in the interaction between doctor and patient, organising their relationship – puts Freud in Dora's tracks, as it were.

In Freud's case study of Dora, there are two figures of empathy. The first is Freud; the second is Dora herself. Dora's symptoms allow her to put herself into the place of others. Dora's cough, a copy of Frau K's cough, allowed her to be like the lover of her father, assuming also the place of Herr K's wife. Her cough, which caused her to lose her voice at times, was, however, overdetermined, carrying several wishes. It was also, Freud states, 'an imitation of her father', which enabled Dora to occupy his place and simultaneously express 'sympathy [*Mitleid*] and concern for him' ('Fragment of an Analysis' 82), for his ill health, on account of which he would leave home to carry out his affair, an affair she lived, if only through her affliction, through her suffering. Her suicidal ideation, too, the very reason she was brought to Freud, declared her identification with her father, as on being discovered with Frau K he had conjured a story of wanting to take his life, from which Frau K had saved him. Dora's suicide note is a love letter symptomatically addressed to Frau K, but, like her cough, it was overdetermined. It was also, Freud argues, the double of a letter written by a 'maidservant' with whom Herr K had conducted a brief affair. Indeed, it is in the role of the 'maidservant' that the transference between doctor and patient is acted out, for Dora finally broke with the treatment with Freud by giving him a 'fortnight's warning, just like a governess', and in this way she assumed the fate of the 'maidservant' whom Herr K had taken and then cast aside (107).[4]

Whereas the first figure of empathy in Dora's case – Freud himself – is predatory in kind, the second – Dora – is in flight. Within more orthodox psychoanalytic theory, this pursuit would be taken as the acting out, between analyst and analysand, of her traumatic experience, a repetition of her experience of pursuit in the transference, the transference being both the obstacle to and the condition of possibility for her cure. In this reading, it is a transference that merely *happens* to entail a pursuit. In its rhythms are the traces of her trauma, the key to her haunting memories, which can then be recalled, worked through: Dora's experience of being prey to Herr K, compounded by her parents' complicity. But is this pursuit not, perhaps, an effect of empathy, empathy as an act that is of necessity predatory, an acting out not of her repressed memories but of the roles that empathy offers up? Reconciling these two hypotheses, we might say that it is both: the predation she experienced – which was repressed but echoed through her symptoms, organising the transference – already entailed empathy. That is, if Freud is cast into the role of Herr K, Herr K was not without empathy. At least, my reading of Mntambo's 'The Rape of Europa', when placed alongside Dora's case, leads towards this formulation.

In Ovid's *Metamorphoses*, which is usually taken as the literary source of the visual depictions of Europa's rape, Europa is the Phoenician princess whom Jupiter falls in love with. He changes himself into a white bull and descends to earth. On the seashore where Europa and her friends are playing, Jupiter seduces her, offers himself gently, coaxing her playfully. After placing flowers around his horns, Europa mounts him, at which point Jupiter suddenly bolts, heads into the sea and swims with her on his back to Crete. While the *Metamorphoses* and the many paintings and sketches that depict Europa's rape only gesture towards the rape to come, Mntambo actually depicts the scene of rape, interpreting Europa's rape through Pablo Picasso's etching 'Minotaur Caressing the Hand of a Sleeping Girl with His Face'. Indeed, Mntambo's image is, in terms of its composition, a quotation of Picasso.

If Mntambo's images offer a comment on postapartheid empathy, it is perhaps because empathy is already written into the Ovidian narrative she interprets, at least into its secondary literature. It has been suggested that the frequency with which Ovid wrote about rape – the *Metamorphoses* contains more than fifty tales of rape – and the intense fear in the women raped are evidence of a kind of empathy on Ovid's part. Leo Curran argues that 'flight was for Ovid the consummate means for the expression of the terror of the rape victim, the predatory appetite of the rapist, and the dehumanizing reduction of a woman to the level of a hunted animal' (280). From this, Curran concludes that the hunt is 'an excellent poetic method for putting the reader into the position of the victim, since we have all experienced similar dread in our nightmares and there is a distinctly nightmarish quality in the flight scenes of the *Metamorphoses*'. In short, Ovid asks his reader to empathise (see also Richlin). Although care should be taken wherever rape comes to stand in metaphorically for something else,[5] this is precisely what is at stake in empathy as an ethical act whose form is by definition analogical.

It is the associative drift between empathy and sexual predation that Mntambo conjures through 'The Rape of Europa'. Though Picasso's 'Minotaur' provides the compositional reference point, what is conjured up in the image, through the title, is the island of Crete, where Jupiter took Europa, some interior part, an enclosure in the trees. This enclosure finds a miniaturised double in the enclosures of the installations, made of cowhides, moulded on the artist's body: a hollow in the trees, on the one hand, and the cavities of the hides, on the other. If the viewer is invited to imaginatively inhabit the moulded hides, the skin of an other, the image asks the viewer to identify with the Minotaur straddling Europa, put oneself into the enclosure, into the place of this figure in the act of rape. The viewer's gaze is made complicit through empathy from the start; your eyes are drawn to the Minotaur's eyes, where the light strikes Europa directly, as if from your eyes; the passage of light moves from the place of your gaze to the Minotaur's eyes, and from there to Europa, rebounding back to her hand, where – as if to give your gaze back to you, the viewer, return your empathic look – the circuit ends and begins again. 'The Rape of Europa', alongside Mntambo's cowhide installations, does not merely invite empathy; it solicits it, and then holds up a mirror to it: see yourself in this scene, it says, imaginatively project yourself into the scene, and this will have been an image of your predatory look, erotic and violent. The circuit of light, repeated for as long as one stares at the image, becomes the thrusting of an empathic gaze.

Certainly one can no longer read Dora's case the same way after Mntambo's 'The Rape of Europa'. One cannot but see Freud putting himself into Dora's psychic world, making 'multiple analytic thrusts into her unconscious' (Rieff xvii).[6] If Freud is thrown off by Dora, if his empathy is troubled, it is because he encounters in her an almost absolute, unstable empathy, confronting him with the difficulty of inhabiting the place of an other who intensely enjoys putting herself in the place of others. Just as Mntambo places the empathic gaze within her frame and makes it glare back, in the hysteric (the second figure of empathy) the first figure (the 'physician and investigator') encounters a disturbing reflection of his own enjoyment. Rather than a mere object to be cured or understood, Freud confronts in Dora a figure who has taken to its breaking point the injunction – of which Percy Bysshe Shelley's 'A Defence of Poetry' is merely the nineteenth-century emblem – to 'imagine intensely', to make 'the pains and pleasure' of 'many others' one's own ('Fragment of an Analysis' 6).

A fingerprint of fury

Einfühlung was a concept formed initially in the field of aesthetics and only later posited as an intersubjective condition. It is thus worth turning to a text in which Freud is explicitly concerned with a work of art, 'The Moses of Michelangelo', which will lead us further into the predatory elements of empathy.

Michelangelo's Moses, Freud tells his reader, had been interpreted as a 'calm before the storm'. As this interpretation goes, 'in the next instant Moses will spring to his feet – his left foot is already raised from the ground – dash the Tables to the earth, and let loose his rage upon his faithless people' ('The Moses of Michelangelo' 216). Projecting himself into the movement of the statue, specifically the movement of Moses' index finger caught in his beard, Freud produces a different hypothesis:

> In imagination we complete the scene of which this movement, established by the evidence of the beard, is a part; and we are brought back quite naturally to the hypothesis according to which the resting Moses is startled by the clamour of the people and the spectacle of the

> Golden Calf. He was sitting there calmly, we will suppose, his head with its flowing beard facing forward, and his hand in all probability not near it at all. Suddenly the clamour strikes his ear; he turns his head and eyes in the direction from which the disturbance comes, sees the scene and takes it in. Now wrath and indignation lay hold of him; and he would leap up and punish the wrongdoers, annihilate them. His rage, distant as yet from its object, is meanwhile directed in a gesture against his own body (224).

Freud sees in this 'despotic finger' not the leader's rage to come, but 'the remains of a movement that has already taken place' (223), a sculpture of 'frozen wrath' (229), a hypothesis to which he is brought by imaginatively recreating the history of a gesture, putting himself into the scene of Michelangelo's Moses along three lines. Firstly, he identifies with Michelangelo, an identification recruited by the artist, who, as Freud suggests, 'aims ... to awaken in us the same emotional attitude, the same mental constellation as that which in him produced the impetus to create' (212). Secondly, he identifies with 'the angry scorn of the hero's glance' (213). An editorial footnote draws attention to Ernest Jones's speculation that Freud's interpretation of the sculpture as a departure from scripture – the scriptural Moses destroyed the Tables of the Law while Michelangelo's Moses, in Freud's analysis, preserves them, relinquishes the grasp of his beard, which was the displacement of fury at his rebellious followers – may have been influenced by his own fury at Carl Jung and Alfred Adler.[7] That is to say, Freud was moved by Moses, he identified with him as leader with a group in revolt, 'struggling successfully against an inward passion for the sake of a cause to which he has devoted himself' (233). And thirdly, telling of his many trips to see the statue of Moses, Freud states, 'sometimes I have crept cautiously out of the half-gloom of the interior as though I myself belonged to the mob upon whom his eye is turned' (213). That is, Freud locates himself in the scene as the object of this leader's fury, as part of a rebellious group.

In his interpretation, Freud draws on a technique of connoisseurship proposed by Giovanni Morelli, an Italian physician and art critic. Morelli's method, concerned with distinguishing copies from originals, considers, as Freud puts it, 'the significance of minor details' as a kind of fingerprint of the artist left in 'unconsidered trifles which the copyist neglects to imitate' (222). Morelli's approach is a 'method of inquiry', as Freud states, 'closely related to the technique of psychoanalysis' (222). Indeed, Freud notes the similarity between this method, his own and detective work. Following this 'minor detail', Carlo Ginzburg argues that what unites Morelli, Freud and Sherlock Holmes is a common relation to medicine, more specifically 'the model of *medical semiotics*, or symptomatology' (12). Ginzburg suggests that lurking behind these three forms of 'conjectural knowledge' is a common originary figure, 'the hunter crouched in the mud, examining a quarry's tracks' (14). The hunter, as Ginzburg states, is 'the hypothetical origin of the conjectural model' (22).

Morelli wrote under a Russian pseudonym, Ivan Lermolieff, and Freud first published 'The Moses of Michelangelo' anonymously. If this common concealment of identity recalls two hunters silently tracking their prey, there is nothing necessarily sinister about this for Ginzburg. Indeed, hunting, Ginzburg speculates, may have given rise to writing, the hunter perhaps 'the first "to tell a story" because only hunters knew how to read a coherent sequence of events from the silent (though not imperceptible) signs left by their prey' (13). Ginzburg does, however, note that this mode of knowledge would come into play in colonial governmentality in the nineteenth century through an appropriation of the 'conjectural knowledge' of colonised people, which was then used against them: 'The problem of identifying previous offenders, which developed in these years, was the bridgehead of a more or less conscious project of keeping a complete and general check on the whole of society' (25). Thus, the distance between the footprint of the prey in the mud, the fingerprint at the scene of the crime, and the photographic print in the identity document begins to narrow; all are traces that come to index knowledge of a subject that can be tracked, its history known, its predilections anticipated and controlled.

Buried in 'The Moses of Michelangelo', I want to suggest, is a dialectic of rebellion (the disobedience of the people), retribution (the wrath of their leader) and the sublimation of aggression (the leader's restraint, which allows the Law to be preserved). Associatively read, it is the rebellion of Freud's followers, who would be crushed for their disobedience were it not for the restraint of their magnanimous leader who brings himself under control. Latent, also, is Freud's own rebellion against the scientific community. There is, however, another and, for my purposes, more important associative track to this trace that Freud reads – literally, a fingerprint of fury, a 'violent gust of passion visible in the signs left behind it in the ensuing calm' ('The Moses of Michelangelo' 236) – and to this group in revolt, a people formerly enslaved: the revolt of colonised people and the question of vengeance, retribution and the preservation of the law that arises there.

Given that 'primitive peoples' and children are notoriously rendered by Freud as mutually narcissistic, commonly afflicted by megalomania, perversion and a predilection for Oedipal defiance, the quelling of insurrections against the colonial state is latent in an essay Freud wrote during the same period as his essay on Michelangelo's Moses, published in the same volume of the *Standard Edition*. 'Only someone who can feel his way into the minds of children', Freud states, 'can be capable of educating them; and we grown-up people cannot understand children because we no longer understand our own childhood' ('The Claims of Psycho-Analysis' 189). One cannot but ask whom else this statement might refer to, if not those 'savages or half-savages' who, Freud writes in the opening page of 'Totem and Taboo', represent a 'well-preserved picture of an early stage of our own development' (1). That is, 'we no longer understand' the children of man.[8]

Freud, like the colonial state, is concerned with revolt – with the followers of Moses rebelling against their leader, with rebellious or, at least, badly behaved children and, associatively, with insurrectionary 'savages or half-savages' – and the question of how to respond to it. There is, of course, a crucial difference between Freud and the discourse of the colonial state, as Freud insists that 'forcibly suppressing such impulses' is futile, that its results are no better than 'giving free play to children's naughtiness' ('The Claims of Psycho-Analysis' 189–190). His response, as his analysis of Michelangelo's Moses suggests, is education or, rather, leading by example: Moses quells his own fury, in the sculpture, 'downwards from above' ('The Moses of Michelangelo' 230) – his face already brought under control, his leg not yet subdued, still cutting a path towards the people he would crush, as he crushed his beard, a displacement of fury that, turning on itself, is dissipated.

Freud's analysis of Michelangelo's Moses has direct bearing on a history of psychoanalysis in South Africa, which it has been argued only re-emerged with, and in the wake of, the TRC.[9] The most immediate precursor of the TRC, Adam Sitze argues in *The Impossible Machine*, was the colonial Commission of Inquiry, specifically the 'Tumult Commission', a special category of inquiry whose primary function was to indemnify the colonial state's violent suppression of revolt. Tumult Commission reports, Sitze notes, read like 'a *history and taxonomy of hatred*'; they were 'almost therapeutic in their intense interest in the gradations and thresholds internal to hatred' (166). The Tumult Commission was concerned, no less than Freud, with fingerprints of fury, which it apprehended through an identificatory imagination that could know and thus domesticate it. Sitze's key point is that the TRC is not a new deployment of psychoanalytic ideas, but that it 'reactualizes the therapeutic discourse already at work in the apparatus of the Tumult Commission'; that before 'any integration of psychoanalysis within the administrative apparatus of the TRC', the Tumult Commission operated as a kind of wild psychoanalysis that 'interpreted the etiology of political conflict within a manifestly therapeutic horizon, searching for the psychological antidotes that colonial administrators could apply to dissipate the "fevers" of hatred that always were at risk of swelling into open rebellion' (206).

This is to suggest neither that Freud, with whom I am in sympathy, as it were, is an inadvertent theorist of colonial rule, nor that he can be held accountable for his bad readers. Rather, my interest here is, on the one hand, in the way Freud's texts stage struggles that they cannot fully contain and, on the other, in that which is undisclosed in the apparatus used to mark a break with the apartheid past. A foreign concept at the heart of psychoanalysis, empathy was taken not simply from psychology, but also from ethnology and anthropology, with which Freud was well acquainted. In approaching this incorporation, I take my critical bearing from Qadri Ismail's reading of the concept of culture in the Anglo–US episteme, a concept produced mutually by the disciplines of literature and anthropology.

In Western understanding, the imagination, Ismail suggests, has functioned not as the magical difference of reason, but as reason's supplement, as that which, together with reason, has come to mark the fully human subject. As Ismail reads it, Edward Tylor's *Anthropology* (1881) – and I focus on Tylor because he is one of the anthropologists that Freud read – emplots the 'lower races of men' as helplessly violent towards others, 'much as children are cruel to animals through not being able to imagine' (408). Though seemingly in opposition to a 'primitive' incapacity to imagine the pain and pleasure of others, 'auto-displacement' – Ismail's term for imagining the pain of others – though it appears at first 'an exemplary ethical position', turns out to be violent, for it allows one to '"partake of" – share, participate in – and "enter" – pierce, penetrate, possess – another desire' (100). Bringing 'auto-displacement' into disturbing proximity with rape, Ismail also, in his reading of Malinowski, the empathic anthropologist par excellence, renders the production of anthropological knowledge, in which anthropologists assume the native's point of view, as a kind of hunting. Hence, if psychoanalysis has at its core a concept that is foreign to it, it is a concept doubly foreign to postcolonial psychoanalysis, one whose libidinal economy is both penetrative and predatory.

This is ground we have already covered with Dora and Mntambo, but it repays the effort to go over it again, this time with Grégoire Chamayou's *Manhunts: A Philosophical History*. Chamayou traces the practice of hunting for men back to antiquity, but, rather than an archaic practice, he reads the manhunt as 'the primal scene of conquest' (9).[10] Tracking down and exclusion, Chamayou argues, operate as distinct but complementary operations within the manhunt: technologies of predation on the one hand, but also, crucially, knowledge of the hunted, on the other, which 'explains why, by virtue of what difference, of what distinction, some men can be hunted and others not' (2). Chamayou places empathy within the realm of this 'cynegetic power', as 'hunting presupposes', he argues, 'a form of empathy with the prey: to track prey effectively, one has to put oneself in its place' (65).

Empathy, then, for Chamayou, is a technology of hunting, a necessary procedure, but one that confronts a contradiction at the heart of the manhunt. Empathy with the prey gives the hunt its 'supreme excitement', its pleasure: one is hunting not merely an animal, but an animalised human who is like the hunter. But this leads to 'the denial of the absolute social distance between masters and their slaves that the hunting relationship sought precisely to reinstate' (65). Empathy thus libidinalises and, at the same time, undoes the manhunt, erases the difference that allows the animalised human to be an object of hunting in the first place. 'If the human prey is animalized, so is the hunter, insofar as he has very animal-like feelings. Those who take pleasure in the cruel joys of manhunting are transformed and become savage' (69). Staging the developmental maturity of the modern subject, as we might say with Ismail and Chamayou brought together, empathic predation unravels and fails at the very moment of its accomplishment, a predicament shared by the hunter-anthropologist, whose empathy is precisely what renders him as 'primitive' as the natives whose point of view he inhabits.

The predicament for the prey is different, at first anyway. The prey psychically inhabiting the perspective of the hunter is not empathy, Chamayou states, but the 'mastery of cynegetic logic'. As he writes,

> In order to anticipate the reactions of his pursuers, the hunted man has to learn to interpret his own actions from the point of view of his predator. This internalization of the perspective of the other makes him develop an extreme prudence that at first takes the form of a paralyzing anxiety of a paranoid type: seeing himself in the third person, considering with respect to each of his acts how they might be used against him (70–71).

This produces a form of thought, Chamayou argues, through which the runaway slave can not only evade his predator but also reverse the relation between prey and predator: 'In doing so, the prey escapes the simple state of objectification that constituted his point of departure. By including in his plan of action the logic of his predator, he envelops and internalizes it. Thus he acquires, at the end of this first dialectic of tracking, the mental abilities of a hunter, whereas he is still only a prey' (70–71). The prey can empathise, but not as prey; this remains a form of learning that must pass through anxiety and paranoia to mastery. This is not a true escape but 'the tragic irony of the prey who escapes only by becoming what it sought to escape from' (152). It is only as hunter, the roles reversed, that the prey can empathise. Thus, the prey's predicament becomes, after all and through mastery, that of the predator. Indeed, in Mntambo's 'The Rape of Europa', the artist assumes both roles, that of Europa and Jupiter, who is no longer a snow-white bull but has changed into a dark Minotaur. The Minotaur here is the predator, but the Minotaur, in the mythology and iconography that Mntambo draws on, is also the hunted, the bullfighting images in *The Encounter* recalling the labyrinth in which the Minotaur is killed by Theseus. Here again we have two figures of empathy, two figures that are really one, for the hunted is only empathic inasmuch as she can reverse the relation and become the hunter.

When it is declared that an apartheid-era police operative like Eugene de Kock needed to regain his capacity for empathy after apartheid, it is equally plausible that he already had empathy for his victims, in whose place he put himself, when tracking them down. It could be argued, too, that Gobodo-Madikizela's empathy with De Kock entailed a kind of reversal of roles, the key point being that to stage postapartheid transformation in terms of the mere occurrence of empathy is severely limited, a point that *A Human Being Died that Night* confronts and that is the strength of Gobodo-Madikizela's intervention (see Truscott 2014). But should instrumentalised forms of empathy – counterinsurgency operations, those staged in and around the TRC, the Tumult Commission, those in consulting rooms or in anthropological knowledge production – not be differentiated from more intimate scenes of care and concern, from more ordinary feelings of empathy?

There are strong arguments that empathy can be used for good or bad. However, what all forms of empathy share – from Johann Gottfried

Herder's eighteenth-century formulations onwards – is a concept of History, of progressional time: no conception of empathy, in the modern sense of the word, is possible without History. Which is to say, at the risk of being schematic, the 'target' of empathy is always rendered 'primitive', the gradient of empathy runs downwards and backwards to states apprehended as less mature, less civilised; twisted, the empathic subject is always looking backwards at those before them. It is into this temporality of empathy that Mntambo's 'The Rape of Europa' intervenes, particularly when read in relation to the image it appears alongside, 'Narcissus' (Figure 3.3), which is also an imaging of an Ovidian narrative. If we have already passed through two scenes where empathy encounters its undoing, this is the third scene.

An echo of empathy

For Freud, narcissism is a halfway phase between 'primitive' autoeroticism and the maturity of object cathexes; it is a rehearsal of object love – Moses grasping and then relinquishing his own body, his beard – and also that developmental point to which one regresses from object love. Often taken to be the absence of empathy, the very opposite of empathy, narcissism confronts empathy with a paradox. In empathising with narcissism, one must project oneself into the psychic space of a subject who cannot do so, who has withdrawn all cathexes from the world; one must imagine the impossibility of imagining another's experience. The place where empathy encounters narcissism is where it is cornered, trapped, as it were, in its own discourse. Yet, rather than simply the limit of knowledge of the other, narcissism turns out to be empathy's difference and, at the same time, its disavowed animating kernel. The secret of empathy is that it is itself narcissistic. Empathising with narcissism, the empathic subject is face to face with its own narcissism: I can inhabit your narcissism, the empathic subject thinks, because I see in it the 'primitivity' from which my mature empathic position has developed; I see reflected in the mirror of your 'primitive' narcissism my own lived history (ontogenetic empathy) or that of my species (phylogenetic empathy). The racial undertones of this frame hardly require emphasis.

Figure 3.3. 'Narcissus' © Nandipha Mntambo, courtesy STEVENSON Cape Town and Johannesburg

We are afforded a different, less teleological rendering of Narcissus by both Gayatri Chakravorty Spivak in 'Echo' and Mntambo in *The Encounter*. In 'Narcissus and Echo', in Book III of the *Metamorphoses*, Echo had distracted Juno while Jupiter was with the nymphs. For this, Juno takes away Echo's ability to speak for herself; she can only respond in the words of another she has just heard. Echo catches sight of Narcissus while he is out hunting deer, and falls in love with him. She cannot initiate a conversation and a strange exchange unfolds. Echo – burning with passion for Narcissus, her love unrequited – withers until only her voice remains. Narcissus, too, will disappear. His mother, Liriope, had asked the seer, Tiresias, if Narcissus would live to an old age and she is told that he will, provided he never knows himself. In love with his own reflection – this love, like Echo's, unrequited – Narcissus longs for the death of this other he sees over there, and he too disappears, only a flower remaining.

There is a temptation to read Echo as a figure of empathy, imitative and resonant. For Spivak, however, Echo *undoes* Narcissus; she is not his mature counterpart, not narcissism surmounted, transcended; rather, she abides, critically, by Narcissus. 'We must catch the undoing moment of Echo as she attends, at a distance, every act of cultural narcissism,' Spivak states (27), to which we should add empathy as a form of narcissism. In their encounter in the *Metamorphoses*, Echo responds by repeating Narcissus' words. Spivak's argument hinges on the difference between Narcissus' call to Echo and her response, covered over in Ovid. Narcissus asks Echo why she flies from him, and Ovid, instead of giving her words, reports that Narcissus hears his words given back to him. This holds the possibility, Spivak suggests, of his question becoming her order, 'fly from me'. Rather than a telos – from narcissism to echoic empathy – Narcissus and Echo are a pair through which Spivak might be said to suggest: where narcissism is, there Echo will be as 'the possibility of deconstruction' or, simply, of an '"imperfect" repetition' (37).

In Mntambo's 'Narcissus', the artist is staring at herself in a pool. This narcissistic relation is mirrored in 'The Rape of Europa', where the artist plays both roles, and so, between 'The Rape of Europa' and 'Narcissus', there is a third doubling, the two images asymmetrical doubles of each other. The effect generated is of a reflection of the narcissism of the empathetic gaze itself, 'The Rape of Europa' as a mirror in which empathy's penetrating gaze is offered its reflection, the narcissism of empathy its echo, the empathic gaze staring back at viewers who would put themselves into the enclosure of the trees, into the skin of an other. And it is this gaze that is returned to the viewer, given back, as Echo might, with a difference.

If there is something echoic to be read out of Mntambo's work, it is because she inserts it into an already echoic chain, where the horizon recedes towards an always already echoic beginning: from Albrecht Durer's (1494–1495) drawing 'Rape of Europa'; to Titian's (1559–1562) 'Abduction of Europa' painted for the king of Spain, Philip II; Peter Paul Rubens's (1628–1629) copy of Titian's painting; Rembrandt's (1632) 'The Abduction of Europa'; Claude Lorrain's (1634) etching, and then a later painting, 'Coast Scene with the Rape of Europa'; and Guido Reni's (1637–1639) more simply composed 'The Rape of Europa'. Indeed, the *Metamorphoses* was from the start an echoic text: Ovid rewriting the rape of Europa into Book VI in the tapestries of Arachne, an archive of divine rape, which represents the event after it has been recounted at the end of Book III – an image within the story, a story repeated from the very first, in a text that is itself an unfaithful echo of Virgil.

Spivak notes that a part of the framing of the Narcissus myth often excluded is that Narcissus is born of rape. In *The Encounter*, then, we have, on the one hand, a scene of rape in 'The Rape of Europa' and, on the other, 'Narcissus', the child of rape. In an interview, Spivak explains her interest in writing about children of rape and the postcolonial: 'Rape is something about which nothing good can be said. It's an act of violence. On the other hand, if there is a child, that child cannot be ostracized because it's the child of rape. To an extent, *the postcolonial is that*' ('Bonding in Difference' 19, emphasis added). The rape of Europa is often depicted as Europe's primal scene, its mythical origin, repetitively conjured: Europe born of a mythical rape, European colonialism as an act of rape, the postcolonial as the child of that repetitious scene acted out. Narcissus might be taken, then, as a figure of the postcolonial, at least inasmuch as he is accompanied by Echo.

Mntambo's 'The Rape of Europa' condenses this genealogy within a single frame. The son of this union between Jupiter and Europa, Minos, will marry Pasiphae. Minos will receive a bull from Poseidon, which he will refuse to sacrifice, and Pasiphae and the bull will produce the Minotaur. The Minotaur in this scene of Mntambo's image marks the vertical line of two generations of children to come (Minos and the Minotaur), produced from the horizontal lines of two unions (Europa and Jupiter, Pasiphae and Poseidon's bull), forming what we can refer to as the straight axis of reproductive futurity that orients the viewer to this image.[11] It is this grandchild, the Minotaur – the future, already here – acting out that primal scene. The image is, however, supported by this genealogical axis only for it to confront the viewer with its impossibility: Jupiter is a woman, and so too is the Minotaur, from which we might conclude that, if Mntambo queers empathy, it is through a queer reproductivity, offering reproductions of classical images, placing herself, her own body, into an artistic genealogy to give birth to an impossible line of descent.

If empathy has been proclaimed as a threshold of psychosocial transformation, empathic identifications as the mark of colonial and apartheid relations having been transcended, the claim of this chapter is that, on the contrary, empathy is integral to the order we have still to work through, that such working through – if we are to abide by this psychoanalytic term – will consist in the reworking of the concept of empathy itself. It is this that Mntambo's work makes available: a notion of reproduction through which we may not have to give up on empathy. It is, however, precisely in the disclosure of empathy's dilemmas that the possibility of a postapartheid ethics of empathy might emerge: empathy as a repetition without guarantee, a discursive reinscription rather than a clean break with the past or a threshold to be triumphantly declared.

As is by now clear, my title invokes several senses of empathy's return. In a first cluster of returns, empathy produces a return on libidinal investment, a yield of pleasure that Dora makes it impossible to deny, and a predatory, penetrating, narcissistic empathic gaze that Mntambo returns, gives back, but not without interest. In a second cluster, empathy is lodged in the colonial and apartheid relations that the postapartheid has sought to move beyond or work through. It is not a condition that emerged after apartheid; it returns, but what returns entails the potential of being turned around, not only victim and perpetrator becoming prey and predator or even an inversion of these roles, but an echo that reinscribes and reworks this colonial concept, which returns like a symptom that has lain latent for a time.

Acknowledgement
This chapter is derived in part from an article published in *Safundi* on 5 May 2016, available online: www.tandfonline.com/dx.doi.org/10.1080/17533171.2016.1172825.

NOTES

1. The literature on Mntambo's and Muholi's work, often discussed together, is mountainous and uneven. For reasons of space I do not cite all of it here. For an explicit invocation of empathy in relation to Mntambo, see Sanger. Ruth Lipschitz has written an excellent essay on Mntambo's work and also suggests something like empathy. For a reading attentive to the reinscription of colonial visual codes as well as the wager of Muholi's affective politics, see Van der Vlies.
2. Due to space constraints, I have not catalogued all psychoanalytic interventions that proffer empathy in South Africa.
3. Jacques Lacan comments in his reading of Dora's case that what is constitutive of 'psychoanalytic experience is that it proceeds entirely in a relationship of subject to subject' (93). Considered alongside Freud's assertion that empathy is 'the mechanism by means of which we are enabled to take up any attitude at all towards another mental life' ('Group Psychology' 110), one could say that 'psychoanalytic experience' comes to hinge on empathy, even though, and perhaps precisely because, it is an impossible relation.
4. Indeed, Dora, the pseudonym Freud gave Ida Bauer, is the name of his sister's governess while he was a child, as Jacqueline Rose notes. Read through a postcolonial frame, the figure of the domestic worker gives the case a set of racial associations that are not there or only latent in Freud's written text (see McClintock).
5. Amy Richlin is certainly more cautious here – indeed, her piece can be taken as a critique of this move – than Curran, whose claim is more than a little dubious.
6. Philip Rieff's reading does discern something like empathy at work in Freud's approach, which turns on him seeing in her anger a conflict that he has already worked through in his self-analysis.

7. Jung and Adler were initially a part of Freud's inner psychoanalytic circle and later rebelled against the 'master', particularly concerning sexuality as the source of neurosis.
8. As Gayatri Chakravorty Spivak notes in 'Echo', this isomorphic relation between children and 'primitive peoples' unravels with the figure of the 'primitive' child. If such 'primitive peoples' have children, how can they be the children of man?
9. Re-emerge, that is, after its short-lived institutionalisation in the 1930s and 1940s under the leadership of Lithuanian-born analyst Wulf Sachs, who, incidentally, was also interested in black anger.
10. Chamayou is concerned with three historically specific forms of manhunt that haunt the modern state: 'The slave-master's acquisition hunts, tyrannical sovereignty's capture hunts, pastoral power's exclusion hunts: thus, at the dawn of modernity there were three well-defined forms of cynegetic power' (27).
11. I draw this notion of an axis of straight reproduction from Sarah Ahmed's *Queer Phenomenology*.

REFERENCES

Ahmed, Sarah. *Queer Phenomenology: Orientations, Objects, Others*. Duke UP, 2006.

Chamayou, Grégoire. *Manhunts: A Philosophical History*. Translated by Steven Rendall, Princeton UP, 2012.

Curran, Leo. 'Rape and Rape Victims in the *Metamorphoses*.' *Women in the Ancient World: The Arethusa Papers*, edited by John Peradotto and John Patrick Sullivan, State U of New York P, 1984, 263–286.

Decker, Hannah. *Freud, Dora and Vienna 1900*. The Free Press, 1991.

Freud, Sigmund. 'Group Psychology and the Analysis of the Ego.' *The Standard Edition of the Complete Psychological Works of Sigmund Freud, vol. 28*, edited and translated by James Strachey, Hogarth Press, 1921, pp. 69–143.

———. 'The Claims of Psycho-Analysis to Scientific Interest.' *The Standard Edition of the Complete Psychological Works of Sigmund Freud, vol. 13*, edited and translated by James Strachey, Hogarth Press, 1955a [1913], pp. 163–190.

———. 'Fragment of an Analysis of a Case of Hysteria.' *The Standard Edition of the Complete Psychological Works of Sigmund Freud, vol. 7*, edited and translated by James Strachey, Hogarth Press, 1955b [1905], pp. 3–123.

———. 'The Moses of Michelangelo.' *The Standard Edition of the Complete Psychological Works of Sigmund Freud, vol. 13*, edited and translated by James Strachey, Hogarth Press, 1955c [1914], pp. 210–238.

———. 'Totem and Taboo: Resemblances between the Psychic Lives of Savages and Neurotics.' *The Standard Edition of the Complete Psychological Works of Sigmund Freud, vol. 13*, edited and translated by James Strachey, Hogarth Press, 1955d [1913], pp. 1–161.

———. *The Complete Letters from Sigmund Freud to Wilhelm Fliess: 1887–1904*. Edited and translated by Jeffrey Moussaieff Masson, The Belknap Press of Harvard UP, 1985.

Garb, Tamar. 'Figures and Fictions: South African Photography in the Perfect Tense.' *Figures and Fictions: Contemporary South African Photography*, edited by Tamar Garb, Steidl/V&A Publishing, 2011, pp. 1–85.

Gay, Peter. 'Editor's Introduction: Fragment of an Analysis of a Case of Hysteria ("Dora").' *The Freud Reader*, edited by Peter Gay, W.W. Norton & Company, 1989, pp. 172–173.

Gearhart, Suzanne. 'The Scene of Psychoanalysis: The Unanswered Question of Dora.' *In Dora's Case: Freud–Hysteria–Feminism*, edited by Charles Bernheimer and Clare Kahane, Columbia UP, 1990, pp. 105–127.

Geertz, Clifford. '"From the Native's Point of View": On the Nature of Anthropological Understanding.' *Bulletin of the American Academy of Arts and Sciences*, vol. 28, no. 1, 2009, pp. 26–45.

Ginzburg, Carlo. *Clues, Myths, and the Historical Method*. Translated by John Tedeschi and Anne C. Tedeschi, Johns Hopkins UP, 1986.

Gobodo-Madikizela, Pumla. *A Human Being Died That Night: A South African Woman Confronts the Legacy of Apartheid*. First Mariner Books, 2003.

Herder, Johann Gottfried. *Herder: Philosophical Writings*, edited and translated by Michael N. Forster, Cambridge UP, 2008 [1774], pp. 272–360.

Hertz, Neil. 'Dora's Secrets, Freud's Techniques.' *Diacritics*, vol. 13, no. 1, 1983, pp. 61–80.

Ismail, Qadri. *Culture and Eurocentrism*. Rowman and Littlefield, 2016.

Jones, Ernest. *The Life and Work of Sigmund Freud, vol. 2*. Basic Books, 1953.

Kahane, C. 'Introduction: Part 2.' *In Dora's Case: Freud–Hysteria–Feminism*, edited by Charles Bernheimer and Clare Kahane, Columbia UP, 1990, pp. 19–32.

Lacan, Jacques. 'Intervention on Transference.' *In Dora's Case: Freud–Hysteria–Feminism*, edited by Charles Bernheimer and Clare Kahane, Columbia UP, 1990, pp. 92–104.

Lipschitz, Ruth. 'Skin/Ned Politics: Species Discourse and the Limits of "the Human" in Nandipha Mntambo's Art.' *Hypatia*, vol. 27, no. 3, 2012, pp. 546–566.

Malinowski, Bronisław. *A Diary in the Strict Sense of the Term*. Routledge, 1967.

Marcus, Stephen. 'Freud and Dora: Story, History, Case History.' *In Dora's Case: Freud–Hysteria–Feminism*, edited by Charles Bernheimer and Clare Kahane, Columbia UP, 1990, pp. 56–90.

May, Jackie. 'The Horns of a Dilemma.' *Times Live Online*, 25 March 2010, www.timeslive.co.za/opinion/2010/03/25/the-horns-of-a-dilemma. Accessed 7 August 2016.

McClintock, Anne. *Imperial Leather: Race, Gender and Sexuality in the Colonial Contest*. Routledge, 1995.

Mntambo, Nandipha. *The Encounter*. Michael Stevenson, Catalogue 41, 2009.

Pigman, George W. 'Freud and the History of Empathy.' *International Journal of Psycho-Analysis*, vol. 76, no. 2, 1995, pp. 237–256.

Richlin, Amy. 'Reading Ovid's Rapes.' *Pornography and Representation in Greece and Rome*, edited by Amy Richlin, Oxford UP, 1992, pp. 158–179.

Rieff, Philip. 'Introduction.' *Dora: An Analysis of a Case of Hysteria*, Sigmund Freud, edited by Philip Rieff, Touchstone, 1963, pp. vii–xxviii.

Rose, Jacqueline. 'Dora: Fragment of an Analysis.' *In Dora's Case: Freud–Hysteria–Feminism*, edited by Charles Bernheimer and Clare Kahane, Columbia UP, 1990, pp. 128–148.

Sachs, Wulf. *Black Anger*, Little, Brown and Company, 1947.

Sanger, Nadia, 'Imagining Possibilities: Feminist Cultural Production, Non-Violent Identities, and Embracing the Other in Post-Colonial South Africa.' *African Identities*, vol. 11, no. 1, 2013, pp. 61–78.

Shelley, Percy Bysshe. 'A Defence of Poetry.' *Essays, Letters from Abroad, Translations and Fragments*, edited by Mary Shelley, Edward Moxon, 1839, pp. 25–62.

Sitze, Adam. *The Impossible Machine: A Genealogy of South Africa's Truth and Reconciliation Commission*. U of Michigan P, 2013.

Spivak, Gayatri Chakravorty. 'Echo.' *New Literary History*, vol. 24, no. 1, 1993, pp. 17–43.

———. 'Bonding in Difference: Interview with Alfred Arteaga.' *The Spivak Reader*, edited by Donna Landry and Gerald Maclean, Routledge, 1996, pp. 15–28.

Truscott, Ross. 'A South African Story of Disavowal: Towards a Genealogy of Post-Apartheid Empathy.' *The Ethics of Remembering and the Consequences of Forgetting: Essays on Trauma, History and Memory*, edited by M. O'Loughlin, Rowman & Littlefield, 2014.

Tylor, Edward Burnett. *Anthropology: An Introduction to the Study of Man and Civilization*. Macmillan, 1881.

Van der Vlies, Andrew. 'Queer Knowledge and the Politics of the Gaze in Contemporary South African Photography: Zanele Muholi and Others.' *Journal of African Cultural Studies*, vol. 24, no. 2, 2012, pp. 140–156.

CHAPTER 4
THE ETHICS OF PRECARITY:
JUDITH BUTLER'S RELUCTANT UNIVERSALISM
Mari Ruti

I want to argue that if we are to make broader social and political claims about rights of protection and entitlement to persistence and flourishing, we will have to be supported by a new bodily ontology, one that implies the rethinking of precariousness, vulnerability, injurability, interdependency, exposure, bodily belonging, desire, work and the claims of language and social belonging (Butler, *Frames of War* 2).

I

In her theorising from the last decade, Judith Butler combines Levinasian insights about the primacy of the other with psychoanalytic insights about the intersubjective formation of human beings to devise a post-Enlightenment, postmetaphysical ethics that – as she explains in the epigraph above – is supported by 'a new bodily ontology' based on a rethinking of precariousness, vulnerability, injurability, interdependency and exposure. If Emmanuel Levinas sought, as he put it, to break 'the obstinacy of being' (202) by showing that we owe our very existence to the other, and that we are therefore irrevocably responsible for the other as 'face', psychoanalysis reveals the ways in which our primary infantile relationships linger into adulthood, repeatedly derailing any sense of coherence we might attain. In other words, psychoanalysis reminds us that the other dwells within the self – through the unconscious, through the repetition compulsion and even through our bodily drives – in ways that render us constitutionally incomplete, disoriented, out of joint and riven by alterity. Most importantly for Butler's purposes, our early exposure to the other – what she describes, following Jean Laplanche, as our primordial impingement by the other – is involuntary and always potentially traumatising. Even when we are not treated badly, we are treated unilaterally, which means that we are completely at the mercy of others. And when we *are* treated badly, our masochism is inevitable in the sense that we are forced to cathect to those who harm us; our very survival depends on such wounded attachments, with the result that being injured – and injurable – becomes the status quo of our lives.

Butler thus replaces the metaphysical model of subjectivity as sovereign and self-sufficient with a Levinasian-psychoanalytic model of relational ontology. To 'be' a subject, for Butler, is to be 'interrupted' by otherness, by relationality, which is why her model asks (autonomous) 'being' to yield to (intrinsically non-autonomous) relationality. As she explains:

> If I am confounded by you, then you are already of me, and I am nowhere without you. I cannot muster the 'we' except by finding the way in which I am tied to 'you,' by trying to translate but finding that my own language must break up and yield if I am to know you. You are what I gain through this disorientation and loss. This is how the human comes into being, again and again, as that which we have yet to know (*Precarious Life* 49).

The 'human' here is the name for the disorientation and loss that result from being 'broken' by the other; I am, from the start, mired in otherness for the simple reason that my relation with the other is what 'I' am. Furthermore, I am interpellated into collective systems of normative meaning that form the outlines of my existence, even my bodily existence, in ways impossible to reverse. And because I can only persist, let alone flourish, in such contexts of social crafting, my attempts to claim a degree of sovereignty are always fantasmatic, unable to conjure away my constitutive passivity in relation to the surrounding world.

Butler's conceptualisation of our relational ontology is somewhat extreme in implying that there is nothing about our being that can be separated from the other, so that our experience of ourselves as quasi-bounded entities is purely fictitious or, worse, arrogant and violent. Butler's vision is also somewhat one-sided in assuming that we are invariably overwhelmed rather than, say, enabled by others. I will return to these objections below, but what is important at this juncture is to understand that our unwilled relationality becomes the underpinning of Butler's ethics of precarity, an ethics that takes 'the very unbearability of exposure as the sign, the reminder, of a common vulnerability, a common physicality and risk' (*Giving an Account* 100). Butler thus asks us to recognise that our exposure to otherness – an exposure that can easily be exploited – is something we share with others, and that this shared vulnerability renders us ethically responsible for these others. That is, Butler accepts Levinas's conclusion that our ontological condition of being bound to the other, and particularly our condition of being 'interrupted' by someone else's longing and suffering, gives rise to the kind of accountability that cannot, under any circumstances, be conjured away.

One of the strengths of Butler's ethics of precarity is its capacity to negotiate the relationship between the universal and the singular in ways that do justice to both. Simply put, precariousness is a universal condition of human life, yet we experience it in highly singular ways. Regarding the universal reach of her ethics, Butler states: 'Precariousness has to be grasped not simply as a feature of *this* or *that* life, but as a generalized condition whose very generality can be denied only by denying precariousness itself … The injunction to think precariousness in terms of equality … emerges precisely from the irrefutable generalizability of this condition' (*Frames of War* 22). It is thus the generalisability of precariousness that makes it a suitable foundation for a universal ethics of equality.

At the same time, Butler takes pains to stress that she does not mean to 'deny that vulnerability is differentiated, that it is allocated differentially across the globe' (*Precarious Life* 31), which means that it may be difficult to draw an analogy between one experience of suffering and another. This is due not only to the difficulty of translating from one context to another but also – and centrally – to the ways in which biopolitical and necropolitical forces distribute precariousness unevenly so that some individuals and populations are much more precarious than others. Such differentiation can take place within one society, so that it would, for instance, be difficult – even dangerous – to try to compare the precariousness of a white South African venture capitalist and that of the black woman who cleans his house. Butler's focus, however, has been primarily on global inequalities – some racist, some capitalist, some nationalist – that have historically maximised the precariousness of some populations and minimised that of others. It is this unequal allocation of precarity that, for Butler, forms the point of departure 'for progressive or left politics in ways that continue to exceed and traverse the categories of identity' (*Frames of War* 3).

In the analysis that follows, I consider the strengths and weaknesses of Butler's approach, eventually arriving at the concept of global apartheid that the editors of this volume have used to frame the constituent essays. We will discover that the tension between the universal and the singular that is so central to Butler's work is equally central to recent discussions of global apartheid, which often revolve around the key question of whether globalising apartheid might rob it of its South African specificity or whether there might be real theoretical and political gains to be reaped from insisting that apartheid is not a uniquely South African phenomenon. I will lean towards the latter attitude without thereby wanting to discount the importance of the former. First, however, I want to offer an overview of Butler's ethics of precarity, illustrating that while her early work on ethics stresses the generalisability of human vulnerability in ways that accord with my perspective, her recent work, particularly *Parting Ways*, insists on the particularity of experience to such a degree that it runs the risk of paralysing our ability to build analogies across different sites of oppression. I argue that this is an unfortunate development in so far as it implies that the concept of global apartheid has little theoretical or political purchase. Though I agree that caution is called for when leaping from one historical and sociopolitical location to another, I believe that even more damage is done by insisting on segregation (which, not incidentally, was one of the main tropes of apartheid ideology).

II

In her early formulation of the ethics of precarity in *Precarious Life*, Butler goes a long way towards the universalisation of ethics. Because Butler's social ontology asks us to take stock of our dependence on others, as well as of the interdependence of human beings on a global level, it urges us to object to violence aimed at others even when these others are far away from us or do not seem to share any of our values. Precariousness, as it were, offers a basis for identification, and identification, in turn, offers a basis for ethical indignation: I oppose injustice done to the other because, on a very basic level, I can place myself in the other's position – because I see that, under different conditions, the injustice aimed at the other, or at least something akin to this injustice, could be aimed at me. As Butler asks, 'From where might a principle emerge by which we vow to protect others from the kinds of violence we have suffered, if not from an apprehension of a common human vulnerability?' (*Precarious Life* 30) Speaking of the Vietnam War specifically, Butler notes that it was the apprehension of the precariousness of the lives that the United States army was destroying – particularly graphic pictures of children 'burning and dying from napalm' – 'that brought the US public to a sense of shock, outrage, remorse, and grief' (150), and that led to the widespread protests against the war. There is a great deal one could say here about the special status that the image of the innocent but suffering child holds in the American psyche (see Edelman), but Butler's point is that the pictures – which the American public was not supposed to see yet came to see – reminded Americans of what geopolitical structures of power try to make them forget, namely that the other is just as woundable as they are; it reminded this public of the core of sameness that unites human beings despite their vast cultural, ethnic and religious differences.

One of the obvious risks in raising precariousness to a universal human condition – a risk Butler is clearly aware of – is that it could function as a way for relatively privileged Western intellectuals to imply that we are all equally vulnerable, oppressed, deprived and harassed. Butler counters this risk with a sustained attention not only to the unequal distribution of precariousness but also to the global structures of power that make it difficult for us to acknowledge, let alone empathise with, the precariousness of those who do not inhabit our immediate, intimate lifeworld. The American public may have been outraged at the images from Vietnam in the same way that many were outraged at the images from Abu Ghraib, but this ethical response depended on a momentary failure of power: people saw pictures they were not meant to see. As Butler deftly demonstrates, one of the ruses of power is to delimit the domain of grievability so that – under normal circumstances – we are prevented from mourning the suffering (or death) of those deemed different from, or inferior to, ourselves. According to Butler, it would be easy to enumerate 'a hierarchy of grief' (*Precarious Life* 32) that determines which lives count as mournable and which do not, and even – and perhaps most fundamentally – which lives are recognisable as human and which are not. This is why Butler's ethics of precarity pivots on our ability to recognise the other as human, why, as she explains, it is 'not a matter of a simple entry of the excluded into an established ontology, but an insurrection at the level of ontology, a critical opening up of the question, What is real? Whose lives are real?' (33)

The derealisation (through dehumanisation) of the enemy is one of the basic strategies of warfare. It is easier to kill those we do not consider fully human or human in the same way as we are, and it is also easier to deny that the loss of such people is a real loss and therefore something that should be mourned. Violence against such people, Butler explains, 'leaves a mark that is no mark' (36). This is a matter of the systematic erasure of those who do not qualify as fully human, an erasure which makes violence invisible to us, which convinces us that 'there never was a human, there never was a life, and no murder has, therefore, ever taken place' (147). In this sense, the prohibition on grieving prolongs the violence of killing, adding a new layer of brutality to the original brutality, so that we are caught up in a vicious cycle where some lives are deemed ungrievable because they are considered less than human and where, conversely, some people are considered less than human because they are deemed ungrievable. On the one hand, the discourse of mourning 'our' losses can be exploited for nationalist purposes; on the other, the denial of 'their' losses aids in the dehumanisation of the other. The antidote to this is not just to shift our frames of perception so that we come to see those we do not usually see – and, then, perhaps, to mourn those we do not usually mourn – but also to alter the modalities of representation that portray some types of individuals (or groups) as inherently good and others as inherently evil. After all, when an individual is presented to us as a personification of evil, we find it difficult to identify with him or her, let alone recognise any trace of precariousness in him or her, which is why Butler argues that no understanding of humanisation can take place 'without a consideration of the conditions and meanings of identification and disidentification' (145).

III

Basing an ethics on our capacity to identify with the suffering of others rather than, say, on *a priori* principles of human rights, carries some risks, the first of which is that the failings of identification are so endemic that such an ethics might end up being unacceptably erratic. Though I wholeheartedly agree with Butler's contention that global power imbalances make it hard for Westerners to acknowledge the equal humanity of non-Westerners, I do not think that the matter is quite this simple, for if Americans have a hard time mourning the Iraqis and Afghans killed by the United States military, Iraqis and Afghans might also have a hard time mourning those who are far away from them, including each other. Butler suggests that we identify with the suffering of some people more than others because their names and faces are familiar to us in the sense of being culturally and ethnically similar to us, and undoubtedly this is true. But there are other ways that alliances based on familiarity are forged, ways that cut across cultural and ethnic differences. For instance, that my friend is black, my colleague is Chinese and my downstairs neighbour is Muslim does not change the fact that if this friend, colleague or neighbour is harmed or killed, I – a white atheist woman – will mourn more intensely than I would mourn another white atheist woman harmed or killed somewhere in Sweden. In other words, there seems to be an important link between familiarity (and thus our ability to mourn), on the one hand, and intimacy, proximity and shared history, on the other, that is not necessarily in any way based on similarity of culture or ethnicity. From this perspective, the ability to mourn the other may be too haphazard, too random a basis for ethics.

The second risk that accompanies an ethics based on our ability to identify with the suffering of others is that it can replace political action with paralysing grief. Grief can be privatising, and thus potentially depoliticising, because it tends to result in a retreat from the social world. This retreat may, in part at least, be a defence against our own vulnerability, for grief reminds us of the immensity of our dependence on others: the fact that we can be undone by the loss of others highlights the flimsiness of our fantasies of sovereignty. Indeed, besides acute bodily suffering, there are few things in life that 'interrupt' the coherence of our being more than the anguish we feel when we have lost someone who feels irreplaceable to us. If desire, intimacy and sexuality already challenge our aspirations of autonomy, grief often results – at least momentarily – in the utter dissolution of the self. As Butler correctly remarks, we 'cannot invoke the Protestant ethic when it comes to loss' (*Precarious Life* 21); we cannot decide how the task of grieving is to be performed or when it is going to come to an end. Rather, we are forced to ride waves of sadness that mock our attempts at self-mastery, that call us back to prior experiences of dispossession. Some of these experiences relate to losses we can name, but, ultimately, what grief touches is the unnameable core of melancholia that connects us to our constitutive inability to attain closure (to disavow our dependence on others). Butler describes such melancholia as a kind of timeless enigma that 'hides' in each loss we mourn, as an indelible trace of a primary vulnerability that we can no longer access directly but that our losses touch indirectly. In a more Lacanian vein, one could say that every loss reanimates the primary loss – the loss of *das Ding* (the primordial non-object of desire) – that constitutes the melancholy core of our being. That is, when we lose another person, we not only mourn that loss but we also mourn, with renewed energy, our own incompleteness, our own helplessness, even if we are not aware that this is what we are doing.

Butler asserts: 'On one level, I think I have lost "you" only to discover that "I" have gone missing as well' (22). This can be understood to mean that when I lose you, I no longer know who I am because who I am is so intimately tied to you that losing you makes me unintelligible to myself. But it can also be understood to mean that in losing you I have come up against melancholy realms of my being that I usually keep at bay through my efforts to lead a self-sufficient and reasonably organised existence. Butler implies that there are ethical lessons to be learned from such an encounter with the melancholy foundations of my being in the sense that my heightened sensitivity to my own precariousness leads (or should lead) to my heightened sensitivity to the precariousness of others. As she posits: 'Despite our differences in location and history, my guess is that it is possible to appeal to a "we," for all of us have some notion of what it is to have lost somebody. Loss has made a tenuous "we" of us all' (20).

Unquestionably, this is a poignant way to characterise the solidarity of suffering. But would it not be equally possible to argue that melancholia might lead to the kind of preoccupation with the self – the kind of solipsistic turning inwards that excludes all others from the self's sacred crypt of sadness – that represents the very antithesis of ethical accountability? Melancholia, even more than mourning, fends off others; it sacrifices present and future objects for the sake of the one that has been lost. As Sigmund Freud already argued, the melancholic copes with his or her loss by incorporating the lost object into his or her psyche, thereby translating a loss in the external world into an internal possession, with the result that this psyche, for the time being, becomes closed to other objects. The memory of the lost object, as it were, crowds out the possibility of new affective ties, which is why, for instance, we find it hard to cathect to a new love object when we are still mourning a lost one. In this sense, while grief may well function as an ethical resource in the way that Butler suggests, the melancholia that grief awakens may pull us in the opposite direction, away from others, from alterity, from the stimulation of new bonds. In addition, melancholia is difficult to translate into the vocabulary of ethical intervention because it arrests action; it is hard to get a depressed person out of bed, let alone into a political rally.

IV

Though grief may be a potent source of indignation, as an ethical resource it may also be somewhat unreliable precisely in so far as it conjures up the melancholy ghosts of our constitutive despair. Moreover, it would be relatively easy to stage a critique of Butler's ethics of mourning akin to the one that Wendy Brown stages in relation to Western notions of tolerance, namely that mourning – like tolerance – can function as a distraction from political and economic solutions to global problems. In the same way that discourses of tolerance make us feel that we are accomplishing something when in fact nothing has changed in concrete terms, the ethics of mourning can obscure the fact that mourning by itself does not transform things. If anything, as long as we get to focus on our grief, we do not actually need to *do* anything; we can feel good about ourselves because we experience ourselves as benevolent Western subjects who feel the appropriate remorse about the suffering and death of those far away from us. One could even propose that Brown's argument about tolerance being what the powerful extend to the disempowered – about how tolerance merely debases the tolerated even further – applies to grief as well in the sense that the objects of our grief may become all the more disempowered (pitiable, pathetic) by that grief.

Along similar lines, there might be an argument to be made about the potentially patronising implications of Butler's insistence that Western subjects are somehow uniquely responsible for grieving those who are less fortunate. Though she does not state the matter in these terms exactly, the implication of much of her discussion of shared precarity is that it is the Western subject in particular who must develop the capacity to mourn the violated other. The non-Western subject is, in this model, invariably the one who is the more violated, the more victimised and therefore in need of 'our' grief, while we, the Westerners, do not deserve the grief of non-Westerners but should, first and foremost, feel our guilt. There are of course excellent historical reasons for this line of reasoning. Obviously, the West should feel guilty about the colonial past and about the ways in which its ongoing aspirations of empire-building contribute directly to the suffering of non-Westerners. Yet there is also something questionable about the branding of the Western subject as one who is supposed to be racked by grief while it is the lot of the non-Westerner to be the suffering object of this grief. One could even say that, within this model, grief becomes the way in which Western subjects suffer. Does that mean that other forms of suffering have, once again, been relegated to the rest of the world (so that, say, they have their poverty while we have our grief)?

Yet Butler is also right in insisting that, under certain circumstances, grief can furnish a sense of political community, and that it can furthermore do so on a basis that is both more fundamental and more complex than mere identitarian identifications. If our goal is to transcend identity politics without thereby discarding our understanding of the reasons why various individuals and populations have sought shelter under identitarian labels (black, Muslim, queer and so on), then shared grief is a potentially powerful place to start. If I can get to the point where the other's grief becomes my grief, then the other's outrage about her oppression also becomes my outrage, with the consequence that I may be willing to overlook the differences between self and other to act on behalf of this other. There are alternative ways to arrive at the same place, and these include my rational assessment that the other has been unjustly treated, but Butler is correct in suggesting that there is something viscerally powerful about the grief we feel when the other's vulnerability, particularly the other's bodily vulnerability, has been exploited. Accounts of genocide, torture and rape, for instance, tend to move us even when we have no personal connection to the victims, which is precisely why Butler's call for a rethinking of grievability as a foundation for alleviating the power imbalances of the global order strikes a chord, why her ethics of precarity makes such intuitive sense, why it is hard to deny her basic insight that 'there can be no equal treatment without a prior understanding that all lives have an equal right to be protected from violence and destruction' (*Parting Ways* 21).

This is precisely why public acts of grieving are so important, why it is essential to see the pictures, to apprehend the names and faces of those who have been wounded even when these names and faces are not immediately familiar to us. Butler is right that the prohibition against mourning is the flipside of the derealisation of loss, of the indifference we are asked to display with respect to the other's suffering or even death. Furthermore, even when it comes to losses that are avowed, that 'count', we are encouraged to mourn as expediently as we can, so as to leave no debilitating residue of sadness that might impede the nation's general robustness, let alone interfere with capitalism's demand for efficiency; we are urged to grieve quickly, to get back on our feet, to brush ourselves off, to get back on track, to get 'back to business'. After a catastrophe, such as 9/11, there is a haste to return the world to its previous order, whether by sending people back to work, by resorting to nationalist slogans of renewed prowess, or by staging flamboyant architectural competitions to prove technological (and, by implication, military) invincibility. In the Western world, money, the Protestant work ethic and extravagant displays of power are used to bandage the wounds of violence, to re-establish the fantasy of being inviolable, beyond the reach of dangerous, 'irrational' others. This is one reason Butler maintains that there might be 'something to be gained from grieving, from tarrying with grief, from remaining exposed to its unbearability and not endeavoring to seek a resolution for grief through violence' (*Precarious Life* 30).

V

I appreciate Butler's claim that overcoming grief too quickly might eradicate one of our most important ethical resources. But I also want to note the masochistic tendencies of her ethics of precarity because these, in my view, complicate the task of theorising (not to mention attaining) social justice. Butler has always been quick to equate subjectivity with subjection (disempowerment), but the masochistic strain of her outlook has become acutely pronounced with her turn to Levinas, who famously quotes Fyodor Dostoyevsky: 'We are all guilty for everything and everyone, and I more than all the others' (105). The obvious problem with this formulation is that it implies that I am responsible for the other regardless of what the other has done – that is, regardless of any normative considerations. This, indeed, is the crux of the Levinasian ethical attitude. However, Levinas does not stop here. He draws a clear distinction between ethics (where normative considerations have no place) and justice (which arbitrates between different 'faces' on the basis of *a priori* norms of right and wrong). Levinas, in short, recognises that justice places limits on our ethical accountability. Butler, in contrast, ignores for the most part the distinction between ethics and justice, attempting, as it were, to apply Levinasian ethics to questions of global justice. Moreover, undoubtedly in part because of her anti-Enlightenment poststructuralist predilections, she resists the ideal of *a priori* principles of justice, with the result that she sometimes speaks as if normative judgements had no place in her theory.

Levinas argues that our ethical responsibility for the other is unconditional and inescapable, that the other is inviolable and that, unfortunately for us, even the executioner, even the Nazi guard, has a face. We may feel tempted to attack such a face, but ethics demands that we resist this temptation. This seems reasonable: I do not take issue with the idea that I should not counter murder with murder, particularly given that, as I just stressed, Levinas maintains that it is the task of justice – as opposed to ethics – to mediate between different faces. The trouble begins when Butler translates this Levinasian (ethical) injunction into a general theoretical stance, which means that assigning responsibility – in the sense that normative justice strives to do – becomes virtually impossible. In this manner, Butler arguably – though no doubt unintentionally – shifts the burden of responsibility from the victimiser to the victim; after all, in the absence of normative judgements regarding the behaviour of the victimiser, what matters is not the content of this behaviour but rather the response (and responsibility) of the victim. As Butler, chillingly enough, writes in *Precarious Life*, 'our responsibility is heightened once we have been subjected to the violence of others' (16).

Consider also the following statement from *Parting Ways*: 'The responsibility that I must take for the Other proceeds directly from being persecuted and outraged by that Other. Thus there is violence in the relation from the start: I am claimed by the other *against my will*, and my responsibility for the Other emerges from this subjection' (59, emphasis added). The basic idea here is that because the other 'interrupts' the coherence of my being, impeding my self-closure, I am, in a sense, always 'persecuted' and 'outraged' by the other; yet because the other is always already an ingredient of my self, I cannot denounce my responsibility for this other. In this model, responsibility is the flipside of being impinged upon by the other in ways that sometimes feel persecuting and outrageous. As Butler reminds us, according to Levinas 'precisely the Other who persecutes me has a face' (*Giving an Account* 90). Consequently, 'I cannot disavow my relation to the Other, regardless of what the Other does, regardless of what I might will'. Responsibility, in this sense, is 'not a matter of cultivating a will, but of making use of an unwilled susceptibility as a resource for becoming responsive to the Other': 'Whatever the Other has done, the Other still makes an ethical demand upon me, has a "face" to which I am obliged to respond' (91).

I understand why Butler's appropriation of Levinasian ethics represents an effective critique of Enlightenment rationality, particularly of the individualistic pretensions of the autonomous subject, who – to borrow from Adriana Cavarero – is 'too preoccupied with praising the rights of the *I*' (in *Giving an Account* 32). This critique, for good reasons, is longstanding in posthumanist theory. But does Butler's version of it not swing too far to the other extreme, making a virtue out of masochism? Is there not, say, from a feminist perspective, something quite uncomfortable about the idea that I am responsible for others who violate me 'against my will'? Along related lines, Butler's critique of 'the rights of the I' tends to backfire whenever it comes up against accounts of extreme oppression, such as Frantz Fanon's *The Wretched of the Earth*, which voice the need of a traumatised collectivity to re-establish its autonomy and self-determination in the face of subordination. Likewise, individual trauma narratives – such as Holocaust memoirs or chronicles of rape – often emphasise that being able to recover a degree of agency is an essential part of surviving trauma. In other words, they reveal that the quest for sovereignty is not invariably a synonym for arrogant individualism. And they also illustrate the problematic nature of an ethics that operates wholly without norms, that asks us to sustain others indiscriminately, irrespective of how appallingly they might behave.

VI

More generally speaking, the problem with Butlerian theory is that it consistently sets up a rigid dichotomy between bad autonomy and good relationality. Indeed, one could say that this is an instance where a vehemently anti-essentialist thinker falls into the kind of poststructuralist essentialism where some possibilities – such as the idea that autonomy might sometimes be an important component of human life – become unthinkable. Butler often talks as if the fact that we are not fully autonomous creatures means that we have no capacity for autonomy whatsoever. Yet in the same way that having an unconscious does not erase the conscious mind but merely complicates its functioning, our lack of seamless autonomy does not render us completely devoid of it. Moreover, as Jessica Benjamin, among others, has illustrated, autonomy is not necessarily always the repugnant antithesis of relationality, so that Butler's depiction of autonomy as intrinsically violent comes off as overly simplistic. Butler asserts that there is 'no recentering of the subject without unleashing unacceptable sadism and cruelty': 'To remain decentered, interestingly, means to remain implicated in the death of the other and so at a distance from the unbridled cruelty ... in which the self seeks to separate from its constitutive sociality and annihilate the other' (*Giving an Account* 77).

I agree that self-assertion can take place at the expense of others. And I agree that the fantasy of sovereignty can promote contempt not only for others but also for alternative, more relational modalities of being. But I am not convinced that the subject who seeks to recentre itself is automatically sadistic and cruel, driven to annihilate the other. Indeed, looking back, one might ask whether feminism, the civil rights movement, anticolonial struggles and resistance to apartheid would have been possible if those involved had decided that autonomy and self-determination are inherently malevolent. Moreover, I wonder whether such initiatives would have been possible without *a priori* values such as freedom and equality – values that arguably hark back to the very Enlightenment that Butler tries so hard to bury.

Interestingly, Butler's resistance to *a priori* values, even ones derived from the Enlightenment, dissipates in the context of her critique of Israeli state violence against Palestinians, for she argues that Palestinians have the right to basic rights, such as not to be dispossessed of land, due to their membership in a global human community. Regarding Palestine's claim 'to the lands that rightfully are its own', Butler writes: 'One could formulate the right in light of international law or on the basis of moral and political arguments that may or may not be framed within a specific version of the nation-state' (*Parting Ways* 205). I agree with this stance: I also think that Palestinians should have basic human rights regardless of whether or not they belong to a nation-state. Yet there is nothing about Butler's Levinasian vision that supports her sudden turn to the kind of liberal rights-based cosmopolitanism that can be traced, through Hannah Arendt, all the way back to Immanuel Kant. If Butler stayed faithful to her Levinasian approach, she would not be calling for equal rights for Palestinians but rather saying that self-preservation should not be a priority for them, that, indeed, there might be something profoundly unethical about their quest for sovereignty and self-determination. Butler makes a valiant effort to show that her cosmopolitanism is not the same as that of Kant by arguing that it is precarity rather than the integrity of the autonomous self that is the foundation for equal rights. But this does not change the fact that, in this instance, she falls back on the very system of Enlightenment morality that she has spent much of her career criticising, so that all of a sudden equal rights are all the rage. One could of course argue that the Enlightenment does not own the ideal of equal rights, that it is possible to think about equal rights beyond their humanistic context, as Jacques Derrida does when he claims that 'what remains irreducible to any deconstruction' is 'an idea of justice – which we distinguish from law or right and even from human rights – and an idea of democracy – which we distinguish from its current concept and from its determined predicates today' (74). But Derrida's elusive definition of justice and democracy is not what Butler is working with when she, in a Kantian vein, calls for international laws that recognise the rights of individuals not on the basis of their attachment to nation-states but rather on the basis of their humanity.

It seems to me that Butler cannot have it both ways. If she is going to recoil from any mention of the Enlightenment, as she consistently does, then she cannot use its values whenever these happen to suit her political purposes. Nor is it true that we can simply just discard *a priori* normative limits. There are situations where all of our talk about human precariousness will not get us very far, where normative judgements are indispensable. One of the limitations of posthumanist theory is that it places so much emphasis on deconstructing normativity that it tends to forget that while there certainly are normative limits we need to criticise and transgress, there are others we need to endorse and treasure. As Dominick LaCapra explains with his characteristic levelheadedness, there are some normative limits 'you might want to place in question, some you may want to reform, and others you may want to test critically and perhaps validate' (154). That is, not all normative limits are diabolical: there are some that are by far the best (or even the only) way to check the abuses of power. There are times when we need to make decisions about right and wrong, and to act accordingly. Whether we are talking about a man aiming his gun at Norwegian youth, or about a dictator aiming his genocidal rage at segments of his own population, we need universally applicable principles – normative limits – and the fact that we might never be able to agree fully on their parameters does not diminish the urgency of our desperate need for them.

Nor is there any reason to reject *a priori* norms, as many poststructuralist thinkers seem to do, on the basis that they are metaphysically founded, for it is perfectly possible to derive a set of *a priori* principles from provisional social agreements – agreements that remain open to constant re-evaluation and revision. As the feminist philosopher Amy Allen has argued persuasively, *a priori* norms are always historically specific in the sense that they arise in particular social contexts. This, however, does not mean that they are invariably worthless; that is, the loss of metaphysical foundations for our normative systems does not automatically invalidate them but merely reveals their historicity. Any *a priori* set of principles, Allen explains, is by definition 'our historical a priori', yet rejecting such principles wholesale 'would mean surrendering intelligibility' (35).

VII

Butler's resistance to normative limits explains, in part at least, her conflicted attitude towards the universal implications of her ethics of precarity. As I have emphasised, one of the strengths of this ethics is that it offers a universally applicable ethical paradigm that is grounded not in Enlightenment notions of sovereignty but rather in a social ontology that foregrounds human relationality and vulnerability. As we have seen, Butler explicitly acknowledges the universal reach of her paradigm: the fact that precariousness is a generalisable condition of human life. Yet her relationship to this universality is ambivalent, even reluctant, no doubt because it is difficult to talk about universality in the context of ethics without raising the very spectres of Enlightenment rationality and Western imperialism that she is trying to outwit. This ambivalence is particularly manifest in *Parting Ways*, where Butler performs an awkward retraction of her earlier rhetoric of generalisability by claiming that her emphasis on shared human precariousness is a matter of pluralisation rather than universalisation. Under pluralisation, she writes, 'Equal protection or, indeed, equality is not a principle that homogenizes those to whom it applies; rather, the commitment to equality is a commitment to the process of differentiation itself' (126). Speaking of suffering specifically, Butler adds that, unlike universalisation, pluralisation recognises that even though all of us are defenceless against suffering, any given experience of suffering is so unique that the attempt to compare various forms of suffering is bound to founder. If, as I noted at the beginning of this chapter, Butler's earlier work included a sustained effort to navigate the tension between universality and singularity, she now presents this tension as more or less insurmountable: 'If we start with the presumption that one group's suffering is *like* another group's, we have not only assembled the groups into provisional monoliths – and so falsified them – but we have launched into a form of analogy building that *will invariably fail*' (128, emphases added).

Butler's ambivalence about using the trope of universalism in *Parting Ways* is understandable, for in this text – which includes the aforementioned critique of Israeli state violence against Palestinians – she is walking a tightrope between arguing, on the one hand, that the Jewish history of exile, violation and dispossession should yield insight into the experiences of exile, violation and dispossession of others, including the Palestinians, and insisting, on the other, that we should not conflate these two experiences. In other words, however critical Butler is of Israel's policies toward the Palestinians (and she is very critical), she wants to make absolutely sure that she cannot be accused of claiming that these policies are akin to Hitler's National Socialism; she obviously does not want to imply that 'Zionism is like Nazism or is its unconscious repetition with Palestinians standing in for the Jews' (29). One can certainly understand why the context of her discussion calls for repeated disclaimers about strict analogies, and why it therefore complicates the discourse of generalisability that she has used more freely in her earlier books. The rhetorical challenges of Butler's analysis in this text are formidable because she does not want to downplay the specificity of the Nazi genocide, yet she seeks to build a model of political responsibility that would recognise convergent modes of dispossession; she wishes to acknowledge that 'there are historically specific modalities of catastrophe that cannot be measured or compared by any common or neutral standard' (29), yet she also strives to leap from one history of oppression to another. As she maintains: 'In thinking about the history of the oppressed, it seems imperative to recognize that such a history can and does apply to any number of people in ways that are never strictly parallel and tend to disrupt easy analogies' (100). Butler, in short, wishes to translate divergent experiences of suffering into claims about justice without thereby implying that the experiences in question are equivalent.

THE ETHICS OF PRECARITY

I understand why Butler insists that histories of dispossession can be convergent without being equivalent. I agree with her resistance to the kind of universalisation that erases important distinctions. And I would never endorse an ethical model where one history of suffering would negate another, where the specificity of suffering would be lost. Yet there is also something unconvincing about Butler's sudden attempt to replace universalisation with pluralisation, and particularly about her claim that, when it comes to experiences of suffering, analogies will 'invariably fail'. Given that the ability to draw analogies between different forms of suffering constitutes the very crux of her ethics of precarity, it is difficult to see how this ethics can survive the collapse of this ability. If anything, it seems that this collapse would instantly undermine the most radical potential of Butler's ethics, namely its ability to compete with other universalising paradigms, such as transcendental Enlightenment ones. Nor does Butler's hesitation about universalism seem theoretically necessary, for drawing an analogy does not cancel out the distinctiveness of the entities being compared. As Butler herself postulates in *Precarious Life*: 'When analogies are offered, they presuppose the separability of the terms that are compared. But any analogy also assumes a common ground for comparability, and in this case the analogy functions to a certain degree by functioning metonymically' (72). Exactly. If I draw an analogy by saying that you and I both have two eyes, this does not mean that our eyes are therefore identical: my eyes will still be blue while yours will still be brown. But what is important is the understanding that if someone throws acid in our eyes, we will both scream. Likewise, if I say that bodily vulnerability is something that you and I share, I do not mean to suggest that we experience this vulnerability in the same way.

A universalist ethics of precarity does not demand a similarity of experiences but merely that we are able to recognise points of contact between different experiences. Let us recall that even the most banal forms of universalism, such as the liberal rhetoric of 'different but equal', do not ask that we all have the *same* experiences but merely that – as human beings – we possess the capacity to recognise the correspondences, the often quite abstract resemblances, between different experiences.

When it comes to suffering, for instance, universalism does not presume that my suffering is *like* yours but merely that I am able to draw a parallel between your suffering and mine. In this sense, Butler's fear that universalisation is *intrinsically* homogenising seems somewhat misplaced, and in fact directly contradicts her own statements elsewhere in *Parting Ways*, such as the following: 'It is only possible to struggle to alleviate the suffering of others if I am both motivated and dispossessed by my own suffering' (127). Likewise, Butler explicitly posits that one history of suffering provides 'the conditions of attunement to another such history', so that 'one finds the condition of one's own life in the life of another where there is dependency and differentiation, proximity and violence' (130). I have already expressed my reservations about the idea that ethics should be based on something as unreliable as my capacity to be moved by the suffering of others. But if such an ethics is going to work at all, we must presuppose that the common experience of precariousness provides a grounds for translating from one experience to another in ways that open to a degree of universalization, that though each human life is unique, there is a kernel of sameness that makes identification (and therefore ethical indignation, outrage and action) possible.

VIII

This attempt to sort out the relationship between the universal and the particular, the generalisable and the singular, the potentially equivalent and the unique, surfaces strongly in the context of the concept of global apartheid that the editors of this volume foreground in their introduction. Like the relationship between Israel and Palestine on which Butler focuses, South African apartheid is one of the sorest spots in recent world history, frequently discussed with an emphasis on its exceptionality. Can it, then, be raised to an emblem of racism, inequality, suffering and poverty outside its original context? Can analogies be drawn between its oppressions and more global oppressions without losing the distinctiveness of the South African experience? Achille Mbembe seems to believe so when he remarks that the student protests that have recently rocked South African campuses 'can be felt afar, in a different idiom, in those territories of abandonment where the violence of poverty and demoralization have become the norm'. Michael Hardt and Antonio Negri suggest the same when they assert, in *Multitude*, that in 'the global Empire today, as it was before in South Africa, apartheid is a productive system of hierarchical inclusion that perpetuates the wealth of the few through the labor and poverty of the many' (166–167).

The volume editors find much that is productive about such attempts to draw comparisons, not least because they recognise that insisting on the specificity of South African apartheid makes it all too easy for Western powers to disavow oppression on their own doorstep, to insist that systematic segregation is not a problem 'over here' – say, in the United States – in the same way as it is 'over there'. The emphasis on global apartheid is effective in rendering this type of disavowal impossible. At the same time, the editors point to an important pitfall in drawing the analogy between South Africa and global apartheid too carelessly, namely that this can enable the global West to use South Africa as a screen upon which to project its optimistic fantasy that since apartheid was dismantled in South Africa, it can also be easily dismantled globally. The editors note that such a fantasy is particularly pernicious in light of the fact that the end of South African apartheid coincided 'with South Africa's entry into the neoliberal order of global capitalism' (15). Even though this state of affairs merely rearticulates some of the very pillars of inequality upon which apartheid was built, it is expedient for supporters of neoliberalism who wish to promote global capitalism as an antidote to the world's problems, including the problems of 'global apartheid'. This is why the editors reject the kind of facile globalisation of apartheid that allows the West to engage in hypocritical gestures of self-critique without actually doing anything to alleviate global inequalities. Instead, the editors advance a concept of global apartheid that acknowledges that apartheid 'stretched back to the dawn of modernity and to the beginning of European colonialism'. In other words, if it is convenient for Western powers to think of apartheid as a malaise that started in South Africa and has now somehow suddenly spread to the rest of the world, the editors ask us to admit that global apartheid reaches back at least as far as René Descartes and 'the division, the separateness, the apartness, of mind and body, and the subjection of body to mind that he inaugurates' (18).

Though the volume editors find the Marxist approach of Hardt and Negri more palatable than its neoliberal counterpart, this approach is also not without its problems, for the image of the multitude that underpins it – the image of an unruly but potentially revolutionary swarm of people from all walks of life – could be accused of being falsely universalising in the sense that it appears more open to difference than it actually is. Hardt and Negri portray the multitude as a mesh of singularities that come together for political purposes. This is an inspiring vision. Unfortunately, in their haste to transcend the categorisation of people by race, class, gender and so on, Hardt and Negri do what other Marxist critics, such as Alain Badiou and Slavoj Žižek, have also done: they move directly from the level of singularity – the unique individual – to the level of universality without pausing at the level of the particular. In a different context (see Ruti), I have argued that the cost of doing so is to lose track of the fact that the particularity of subject positions can impede the access of certain individuals to the universal (in this case, the multitude). It is not that people necessarily *want* to be categorised according to race, class, gender and so on. But they cannot avoid external perceptions that insist on this categorisation, with the result that some of them may find it harder than others to enter the multitude. For instance, I can well imagine that the politicised multitude welcomes the figure of a male revolutionary (a familiar Marxist figure) more eagerly than the figure of a South African female farmer. This is why the editors are right to argue that it is not enough to posit, as Hardt and Negri do, that, when it comes to the composition of the multitude, 'no one is necessarily excluded but their inclusion is not guaranteed' (226). The editors are correct to insist that in the context of envisioning ways to defeat global apartheid, the inclusion of the subaltern is politically non-negotiable.

Because singularities always – and sometimes against their will – participate in particular groupings of identity, a theory of the multitude that fails to account for the ways in which some singularities are by default excluded from this multitude does not reach far enough. This, of course, is the reason Butler resists universalisation. As I hope to have demonstrated, I agree with her hesitation – to a point. I certainly agree that we need to remain keenly cognisant of the fact that some individuals and populations remain much more acutely precarious than others and therefore potentially marginalised by attempts to build generalisable platforms for collective action. Even so, I believe that remaining too cautious about drawing analogies between different sites of oppression leads to the kind of theoretical and political paralysis that today's world cannot afford. I suppose I would rather take the risk of levelling some distinctions than of not being able to discern any points of correspondence at all. The latter predicament makes it too easy for the world's powers that be – as well as for ordinary citizens – to deny oppressions that are taking place in their own backyard at the same time as it impedes the formation of global solidarities. The promise of such solidarities is why I find the concept of global apartheid theoretically and politically auspicious. It seems to me that the editors sum up the conundrum at hand perfectly when they state: 'The knot in the concept of global apartheid is that apartheid both *must* and yet *cannot* be detached from South Africa; it is *necessary* that apartheid be detached from South Africa and, at the same time, *impossible* to fully detach it, leaving an untranslatable remainder' (21–22). I view this impasse not as a site of paralysis but rather as a potential opening towards 'justice to come' (à la Derrida).

REFERENCES

Allen, Amy. *The Politics of Our Selves: Power, Autonomy, and Gender in Contemporary Critical Theory*. Columbia UP, 2008.

Badiou, Alain and Slavoj Žižek. *Philosophy in the Present*. Translated by Peter Thomas and Alberto Toscano, Polity Press, 2009.

Benjamin, Jessica. *Like Subjects, Love Objects: Essays on Recognition and Sexual Difference*. Yale UP, 1995.

—. *Shadow of the Other: Intersubjectivity and Gender in Psychoanalysis*. Routledge, 1998.

Brown, Wendy. *Regulating Aversion: Tolerance in the Age of Identity and Empire*. Princeton UP, 2006.

Butler, Judith. *Precarious Life: The Powers of Mourning and Violence*. Verso, 2004.

—. *Giving an Account of Oneself*. Fordham UP, 2005.

—. *Frames of War: When Is Life Grievable?* Verso, 2010.

—. *Parting Ways: Jewishness and the Critique of Zionism*. Columbia UP, 2012.

Cavarero, Adriana. *Relating Narratives: Storytelling and Selfhood*. Translated by Paul A. Kottman, Routledge, 2000.

Derrida, Jacques. *Specters of Marx: The State of the Debt, the Work of Mourning, and the New International*. Routledge, 2006.

Edelman, Lee. *No Future: Queer Theory and the Death Drive*. Duke UP, 2004.

Fanon, Frantz. *The Wretched of the Earth*. Translated by Constance Farrington, Penguin, 1961.

Hardt, Michael and Antonio Negri. *Multitude: War and Democracy in the Age of Empire*. Penguin, 2004.

LaCapra, Dominick. *Writing History, Writing Trauma*. Johns Hopkins UP, 2001.

Levinas, Emmanuel. *Entre Nous: Thinking-of-the-Other*. Translated by Michael B. Smith and Barbara Harshav, Columbia UP, 1998.

Mbembe, Achille. 'The State of South African Political Life.' *Africa Is a Country*, 19 September 2015, africasacountry.com/2015/09/achille-mbembe-on-the-state-of-south-african-politics/. Accessed 7 August 2016.

Ruti, Mari. *Between Levinas and Lacan: Self, Other, Ethics*. Bloomsbury Press, 2015.

CHAPTER 5
HANNAH ARENDT'S WORK OF MOURNING: THE POLITICS OF LOSS, 'THE RISE OF THE SOCIAL' AND THE ENDS OF APARTHEID

Jaco Barnard-Naudé

> No revolution has ever solved the 'social question' and liberated men from the predicament of want, but all revolutions ... have followed the example of the French Revolution and used and misused the mighty forces of misery and destitution in their struggle against tyranny and oppression (Arendt, *On Revolution* 112).

> Politicization, for example, is interminable, even if it cannot and should not ever be total (Derrida, 'Force of Law' 971).

The 'rise of the social' constitutes the demise of politics and yet there is a politics that rises from these ashes – a politics occasioned, precisely, by the emergence of the social question as inaugurating a particular kind of loss. This politics of loss is a politics of the social. Following the work of Hannah Arendt, I accept the twofold contention that 'loss is not only constituted by, but is constitutive of, the social' (Truscott, Van Bever Donker & Minkley 1). I begin with Arendt's definition of the social question as what 'we may better and more simply call the existence of poverty' (*On Revolution* 60). I continue to follow her in her argument that the loss at stake, as the constituted/constitutive loss that marks the 'rise of the social', is the loss of politics. However, I take my leave of Arendt to the extent that I argue that she, unwittingly perhaps, *politicises* the rise of the social precisely through her mourning for the loss of politics.

The thesis as regards the politics of loss as a politics of the social, read in the light of Arendt's definition of the social as the question of poverty, should not be taken to imply an argument that the loss of politics is somehow responsible for the existence of material poverty, for it is hardly the case that the factual existence of scarcity and poverty through the ages is or was caused by the loss of the particular kind of politics that Arendt considered invaluable. Yet, at the same time, in an age marked by what Jean-Luc Nancy and Philippe Lacoue-Labarthe have called the 'retreat of the political' (122) and Slavoj Žižek, with reference to Giorgio Agamben, 'post-political' biopolitics ('A Permanent Economic Emergency' 92), the possibility of a retrieval of politics depends, to an ever-increasing extent, on a concern with the factual existence of poverty.

In this regard, it seems that the supreme symptom of our postpolitical age, the rootstock of all social antagonisms of the era, lies ultimately in the fundamentally unequal distribution of this factual existence of poverty – a condition which is increasingly being (but has by no means only recently been) described as 'global apartheid' (Bond 5).[1] Already in 1978, Gernot Köhler published an article in which he showed that the structure of apartheid South Africa was markedly similar to that of global society. He thus defined 'global apartheid' as follows:

> a structure of world society which combines socioeconomic and racial antagonisms and in which (i) a minority of whites occupies the pole of affluence, while a majority composed of other races occupies the pole of poverty; (ii) social integration of the two groups is made extremely difficult by barriers of complexion, economic position, political boundaries, and other factors; (iii) economic development of the two groups is interdependent; (iv) the affluent white minority possesses a disproportionately large share of world society's political, economic, and military power (266).

Recently, Žižek drew attention to the segregationist dimension of globalisation when he pointed out with reference to Peter Sloterdijk that 'capitalist globalization not only stands for openness, conquest, but also for a self-enclosed globe separating the Inside from the Outside' (*Trouble in Paradise* 63). 'Global apartheid', however, does not simply refer to increasing levels of welfare inequality in our 'postmodern' societies. Rather, it is the name of a very specific (post-)*political* system of rule at the level of the planetary – a system which incorporates the newly authoritarian political conditions (dictated by supra-sovereign institutions like the World Bank, European Commission and International Monetary Fund) by way of which the hegemony of neoliberal market consumerism, the so-called great 'leveller', is perpetuated and entrenched in these societies (see Aitkenhead).

It is against this backdrop that Jacques Derrida could open his seminal *Specters of Marx* with the following words:

> One name for another, a part for the whole: the historic violence of Apartheid can always be treated as a metonymy. In its past as well as in its present. By diverse paths (condensation, displacement, expression, or representation), one can always decipher through its singularity so many other kinds of violence going on in the world. At once part, cause, effect, example, what is happening there translates what *takes place* here, always here, wherever one is and wherever one looks, closest to home (xv).

Taken with Derrida's earlier insistence in 'Racism's Last Word' that apartheid is untranslatable, the elevation of 'Apartheid' to the level of a signifier that pertains to a 'global' condition means that it has nevertheless moved beyond the irreducible territorial specificity of its coinage. In this sense 'Apartheid' always will have been an exemplar of what Georg W.F. Hegel called a concrete universal. It is in recognition of the losses that humanity as a whole suffers, as well as in the hope of a retrieval of what has been lost as a result of this concrete 'universality' of 'apartheid', that I revisit Arendt's critique of the social question.

My argument holds that Arendt's *identification* of poverty *as*, specifically, the social question should be of primary concern to us (see *On Revolution*). It is Arendt's argument that the social question encroached detrimentally upon the terrain of politics 'proper' when its solution became a matter of politics, when we attempted 'to liberate mankind from poverty by political means' (114). This, she argues in *The Human Condition*, is the case because the social question struck at what she considered to be the very heart of politics: plurality. The social question struck politics in this way by changing the imagery of the historical process as a revolving motion, to the biological imagery which sees 'a multitude – the factual plurality of a nation or a people or society – in the image of one supernatural body driven by one superhuman, irresistible, "general will"' (60).

I will make the case for an understanding that Arendt's work *does* mourn for the loss of this politics grounded in plurality. In this sense alone can it be said that Arendt's position on the social is melancholic or 'nostalgic'. I continue to argue that Arendt's position on the social is, nevertheless, a *political* one, one that still makes politics responsive to and responsible for the social question, and this means that her position is not simply or 'properly' melancholic. In short, by way of the very 'political' antagonism that Arendt adopts towards the social question, she politicises the latter. This leads to the conclusion that Arendt adopts a *transformative position* in relation to politics. As such, her political philosophy on the subject is better characterised as its own particular *work of mourning*. I use the word 'mourning' here in its Derridean sense, as opposed to the sense in which Sigmund Freud used it in his early work to signify the overcoming of melancholia.

Following Andrew Schaap's assertion that 'how politics is distinguished from the non-political is always a political question' (167), I argue that, precisely because Arendt's philosophy of the social is its own work of *politics*, it is unnecessarily reductive to read her work as no more than a nostalgic yearning for politics in the ancient sense. I particularly oppose Emilios Christodoulidis's contention that Arendt's work on the social leaves the political 'gloriously vacuous' (515). Arendt certainly describes very carefully a certain loss in relation to the political – a loss that occurred contemporaneously with the 'rise of the social'. But far from a glorious evacuation, I claim that this description, this genealogy of loss, constitutes itself politically as a work of mourning. While Arendt certainly does not use the term 'mourning' explicitly, the very fact that she takes up the decline of politics as correspondent with the rise of the social means that she constitutes the rise of the social as a *political* work of mourning.

In the late thought of Derrida, there repeatedly occurs an argument that mourning is an intensely political activity. As a result, an encounter with Derrida's thinking on the work of mourning becomes indispensable, both in terms of approaching Arendt's work on the social *and* characterising it as political work. One of the key features of Derrida's work on mourning is its disruption of the early Freudian distinction between mourning and melancholia (see 'Fors' and *Memoires for Paul de Man*). This disruption, I will argue, is what enables Derrida to arrive at the conclusion that mourning is political through and through. The implication of this reading of Derrida alongside Arendt will be an understanding that Arendt's mourning for politics engages politics, as I've already mentioned, in a transformative way. What this means, in essence, is that Arendt keeps intact the ontological distinction between the realm of politics and the domain of the social, while she recognises the admission of the social to political consideration – though without positing the (to her mind inappropriate) *solution* of the social question as such – as a task for politics. It is at the level of the 'solution' that Arendt was always sceptical about what politics can or should be asked to do. Arendt believed politics to be entirely incapable of resolving the existence of poverty. But contrary to how some commentators have read her, she also did not believe that politics could somehow be kept insulated from the social question. That is why she distinguishes, in the epigraph quoted above, between solution, 'use' and 'misuse'. In the end, Arendt redraws the social as a work of politics *and* as a work of mourning. I will conclude by briefly relating the implications of this work of mourning to the question of transformation in 'postapartheid' South Africa.

The rise of the social and the loss(es) of politics

Arendt characterises the emergence of society as the 'rise of housekeeping'. With the 'emergence' of society she means the passing of matters of the household – 'the activities of sheer survival' (*The Human Condition* 46) – from the private sphere into the 'light of the public sphere' (38). Her contention is that this passage has blurred the distinction between the private and the political and thereby has changed the meanings of the terms as well as their significance for the life of 'the individual and the citizen': 'Since the rise of society, since the admission of the household and housekeeping activities to the public realm, an irresistible tendency to grow, to devour the older realms of the political and private as well as the more recently established sphere of intimacy, has been one of the most outstanding characteristics of the new realm' (45).

It is important for our purposes to emphasise that Arendt explicitly distinguished the homogenising or 'levelling' imperatives of the social from the political principle of 'equality among peers' (40). The difference between the two lies in the views they take on plurality. Whereas the principle of political equality among peers continues to value and protect plurality, society insists on conformist action and homogeneity of opinion – an insistence that was originally based in the patriarchal household. The decline of this family arrangement caused the absorption of the family unit into the social and its groupings, characterised by a 'kind of no-man rule' (39) and a principle of equality based on uniformity of interest and opinion.

The form of government that emerges from this shift of the family to society is bureaucracy – a form of mass administration and rule by nobody. In the context of the French Revolution, Arendt remarks:

> Since the revolution had opened the gates of the political realm to the poor, this realm had indeed become 'social'. It was overwhelmed by the cares and worries which actually belonged in the sphere of the household and which, even if they were permitted to enter the public realm, *could not be solved* by political means, since they were matters of

administration, to be put into the hands of experts, rather than issues which could be settled by the twofold process of decision and persuasion (91, emphasis added).

The rise of mass society, in turn, signifies that 'the social rather than the political' (43) now constituted the public realm, and this movement corresponded with the victory of equality-as-uniformity in the modern world where distinction and difference have become matters of the 'intimate' and the individual. This equality is 'in every respect different from equality in antiquity' (41) where the public realm was permeated by an agonistic spirit among equals according to which everybody constantly had to distinguish themselves from their peers through action and speech.[2] It was in the public realm that men could exhibit their individuality and irreplaceability and, for such a public realm to exist, men had initially to come together as equals in their difference.

If bureaucracy marked the victory of the social in governmental affairs, the rise of economics and statistics (the study of 'behaviour') marked that victory in the realm of the social sciences. For Arendt, economics by its very nature could only emerge as a science when individuals became social beings 'and unanimously followed certain patterns of behavior' (42), so that the exception could be characterised as asocial or abnormal. And this application of the law of large numbers and long periods marked the 'wilful obliteration' (42) of the very thing that makes the study of history and politics meaningful: acts and events. In the end, the victory of economics, statistics and behavioural sciences indicates that man's animality as a species-being (his 'one-ness') has paradoxically and alarmingly been elevated to the level of distinction: 'through society it is the life process itself which in one form or another has been channeled into the public realm' (45).[3]

It should be clear from the above that for Arendt, the social, when it 'burst' into the public realm, constituted a series of losses from the point of view of authentic politics. The most significant of these was, from the ontological point of view, 'the conditio sine qua non and the conditio per quam' of all politics – plurality – as the expression of the principle that 'we are all the same, that is human, in such a way that nobody is ever the same as anyone else' (8). At the experiential level, the loss of plurality triggered the decline of the experience of action, an experience that embodied par excellence the principle of spontaneity and distinction through excellence. The loss of plurality and action, then, meant for Arendt a decline in the very worldliness of Man.

In Arendtian terms, the rise of the social as a loss of plurality and of action necessarily meant a loss of freedom (as opposed to liberty). This is the case, because Arendt harboured a deeply positive notion of freedom. By linking freedom to appearance and the public realm, Arendt insisted that 'the raison d'etre of politics is freedom and its field of experience is action' (in Arendt & Kohn 145). From this point of view, Arendt's conception of freedom is positive in that it posits the presence of the human being with others (appearance) as the precondition for action, in contradistinction to the negative idea of freedom as an absence, namely of constraint (which others represent). Arendt makes it clear in her meditation on revolution that the French Revolution started out in the name of freedom but, because it came to consider liberation from the necessity and want of the life process as the overarching end of the revolution, it ended in the supreme violence of terror, which in itself marked a profound loss of the political concept of power as acting-in-concert.

But Arendt did not simply describe or report these losses that were occasioned by the existence of poverty politically formulated as the social question. My claim is that she *mourned* these losses and that this mourning itself constituted a politics or a political work. As Hanna Pitkin puts it with reference to the political experiences that Arendt held dear: 'She regarded these experiences and activities as the most valuable available to human beings, called them our "lost treasure", and tried to restore our access to the full significance of these words so that we might also recover the corresponding forms of life' (1). If Pitkin's description is taken as valid, then a certain diagnosis imposes itself: Arendt argued that humanity suffered a tremendous loss at the hands of the rise of the social. Yet it is precisely by recognising and accepting this loss ('moving on' from it) that she was able to work towards a certain 'restoration' of our access to the political experiences and activities that were lost. By taking up that task again and again, she mourned the loss of politics *politically*. It is to such politics as the work of mourning that I turn below.

Mourning and melancholia

The argument of this chapter depends to a critical extent on an understanding that politics 'is' the work of mourning (for the social). I want to attempt now to justify this contention with reference to the 'traditional' psychoanalytic account of the relationship between melancholia and mourning, questioned as it is by Derrida's rereading of Freudian mourning.

In the early work of Freud, the distinction between melancholia and mourning takes place by way of an identification of melancholia as a pathology and mourning as a 'normal affect' (203). Melancholia and mourning describe psychic responses and/or reactions to the experiences of loss: 'of a beloved person or an abstraction taking the place of the person, such as fatherland, freedom, an ideal and so on' (203). Freud thus describes melancholia as 'a profoundly painful depression, a loss of interest in the outside world, the loss of the ability to love, the inhibition of any kind of performance and a reduction in the sense of self' (204). Mourning is distinguished from melancholia by one trait, namely that the 'disorder of self-esteem is absent' (204). And this is the case because, as Freud famously puts it: 'In mourning, the world has become poor and empty, in melancholia it is the ego that has become so' (206). Melancholia, quite simply, represents a loss of ego, mourning a loss of the love object.

Melancholia corresponds with the process of incorporation: I identify with the object lost in reality in such a way that I deny its loss. I interiorise it in such a way that I keep it alive in me, refuse to release my libidinal investment in it and, consequently, refuse to mourn the lost object as lost because, for me, it is not 'really' lost. Moreover, the paradox of incorporation is that, by refusing to accept the actual death of the lost love object, I do not keep the dead alive in me. In other words, the tragedy of incorporation is that the ego refuses to mourn: 'I pretend to keep the dead alive, intact, safe (save) inside me, *but it is only in order to refuse, in a necessarily equivocal way, to love the dead as a living part of me*, dead save in me, through the process of introjection, as happens in so-called "normal" mourning' (Derrida, 'Fors' 71, emphasis added). As Derrida so pointedly remarks: 'Incorporation is a kind of theft to reappropriate the pleasure-object' (72).

Whereas melancholic incorporation, then, is failed introjection, introjection proper is associated with mourning, because in introjection the libidinal investment in the object is withdrawn and the object is interiorised in such a way that it does not become a living part of the ego. 'Where the process of mourning works through loss and allows us to move on to form new attachments and re-engage with life, melancholia thwarts our re-engagement with life; it leaves us paralysed in the loss, closes off the future and prevents us from moving on' (Walker 116). The melancholic state is accompanied by grief, nostalgia and always 'the feeling of loss – a loss of direction ensuing from the collapse of a project or horizon for action' (Arditi 81).

In his later work, Freud thought of melancholia as the resurrection of the lost object within the ego as a signal contribution to ego formation. As Tammy Clewell puts it, Freud comes to realise that it is only through internalisation of the lost object through 'bereaved identification' that the subject becomes as such: 'Freud collapses the strict opposition between mourning and melancholia, making melancholy identification integral to the work of mourning' (61). The outcome of this revision of the distinction between melancholia and mourning is that grief work may well be interminable.

In the wake of this shift in Freud's thinking, Derrida's rereading of Freud and of Nicolas Abraham and Maria Torok departs from and further complicates the original distinction between mourning and melancholia, introjection and incorporation. Whereas the change that Freud made to the original distinction addresses the fundamental (and possibly interminable) nature of melancholic incorporation, his theory still relies on the incorporation of the lost object into the self through identification. In other words, melancholic incorporation has the effect of a denial of the otherness of the Other (Clewell). In his foreword to Abraham and Torok (*The Wolf Man's Magic Word*), Derrida writes:

> the question could of course be raised as to whether or not 'normal' mourning preserves the object as other (a living person dead) inside me. This question – of the general appropriation and safekeeping of the other *as other* – can always be raised as the deciding factor, but does it not at the same time blur the very line it draws between introjection and incorporation, through an essential and irreducible ambiguity ('Fors' 71)?

In his approach to mourning, Derrida retains the later Freudian notion that mourning is constitutive of the self, but he adds that mourning *also* constitutes the relation with the Other (Kirkby). This leads Derrida to adopt a different idea of incorporation, one in which, in order to mourn the Other as such, incorporation must always fail: 'The incorporation should not be total, and in that case, of course, the Other remains foreign in myself, it remains Other, it doesn't become part of myself' (in Kirkby 466). And this means that mourning proper is impossible.

Mourning, if there is such a thing, is always failed mourning (impossible) and as such interminable. There is no mourning that is not always already also melancholic. One of the implications of this addition of the relation with the Other through failed incorporation is that the nature of mourning involves necessary failure, because for Derrida, without such a failure there can be no relationship to the Other. Mourning is impossible because the one (the Other) who is lost is both within us but also beyond us, unreachable – 'nothing we say of or to them can touch them in their infinite alterity' (Derrida, *The Work of Mourning* 11). Yet, fidelity to the Other consists in mourning and so is worked out – at least initially – in the interiorisation of the dead Other, in the *necessity* of an interiorisation that is at once impossible. In this sense, 'the possibility of the impossible commands here the whole rhetoric of mourning' (Derrida, *Memoires for Paul de Man* 34). Inevitably and according to this logic, the interiorisation of loss must fail and, as Derrida puts it, interiorisation must 'fail well' in order for mourning to be successful (*The Work of Mourning*

144), in order to be faithful to the Other. If mourning is simply successful it would amount to an introjection-incorporation of the Other, which would deny both the otherness of the Other and the otherness of death.

The work of mourning, then – the active taking up – of this infinite responsibility reveals the political aspect of mourning. As Derrida puts it in *Aporias*: 'I would say that there is no politics without an organization of the time and space of mourning, without a topolitology of the sepulcher, without an anamnesic and thematic relation of the spirit as ghost [revenant], without an open hospitality to the guest as ghost' (61). Joan Kirkby argues that Derrida's reconstruction of Freudian incorporation means that the politics of mourning resides in 'an ongoing dialogue with the other' (470): 'At the death of the other a conversation is initiated, it is a time of reading and thinking' (471). The ethical imperative of mourning is that it remains and remains as impossible. It suggests an undeniable responsibility – an *infinite* responsibility which cannot and does not leave us with 'any form of good conscience' (Derrida, *Specters of Marx* xv).

Kirkby suggests that the politics of mourning resides in the openness to be transformed by the Other, 'a provocation to think new paths, new ways through apparent impasses' (470). As Derrida puts it in *Adieu to Emmanuel Levinas*: '*It is necessary* to deduce a politics and a law from ethics. This deduction is necessary in order to determine the "better" or the "less bad"' (115, emphasis added). Politics, as Derrida taught and Žižek recently affirmed (see *Demanding the Impossible*), is the realm of responsible decisions. Simon Critchley argues that it suggests a 'realm of risk and danger. Such danger calls for decisions or ... "political invention", an invention taken in the name of the other' (271).

Arendt's reading of the social as a Derridean 'work of mourning'

Reading Arendt's essay 'We Refugees', Samantha Hill suggests that there is a dimension or undercurrent in Arendt's work that is deeply concerned with the problem of loss. This remark read with Freud's description of mourning, according to which it is the *world* that has become poor, and Arendt's description of the social as the existence of poverty, raises the provocation to surmise that Arendt's definition of the social is ultimately a definition that calls for or engages the kind of mourning of which Derrida writes. To be sure, while the social is a definition of material poverty, 'the rise of the social' is a description of the poverty that 'the world' (which for Arendt is inescapably the public sphere and, as such, the political) has come to suffer. In other words, the definition of the social as the existence of poverty occasions for Arendt the mourning *for* what was lost with the emergence of the social and for Arendt, as we know, this loss was politics; politics as, to put it succinctly, the conditions for what Nancy has called 'the experience of freedom'.

However, if we consider closely the way in which Arendt engaged the loss of politics, we might certainly see that the 'interiorisation' of this loss in her work passed through the 'melancholic identification' to which Freud subscribed in his later work. But in the final instance, such a close consideration will reveal that Arendt's position corresponds to, or can be better rendered as, the necessarily failed incorporation that characterises the Derridean politics of mourning. For, as Pitkin indicates, Arendt never ceased her conversation with the 'lost treasure', and for her the 'perpetrator' of the loss of this treasure was undeniably the 'rise of the social'. In fact, if the work of mourning is the work of necessary failure, then although Arendt might not have realised it, her mourning for politics in the wake of the emergence of the social question caused her to set up a veritable politics of the failure of politics. This is the politics of loss, the politics of the social. It is this politics of the necessary failure of politics, this politics of the social, which amounted to her work of mourning (at least as regards this aspect of her work).

The fact that Arendt did not change her position, but relentlessly and unyieldingly held on to the argument that the emergence of the social question coincided with the loss of politics and, correspondingly, the experiences 'most valuable' (Pitkin 1) to human beings, can be read from the consistency with which she argues the matter, from *The Human Condition* (first published in 1958) to *On Revolution* (published in 1963) right up until an interview from 1970 collected in *Crises of the Republic* (1972) in which she comments that the revolutionary student movement in the United States achieved enormous success 'so long as it was a question of purely legal and political matters' (202) but 'accomplished nothing' (202) when it collided with the 'enormous social needs' (202) of the city ghettos in the north.

This insistence on the loss/failure of politics when it confronted the social question or when the social question became a 'political' question started, as we have seen, in *The Human Condition*, where Arendt carefully traces the 'unconscious substitution' of the 'social' for the 'political' from the Greek to the Roman heritage and comments that such a substitution betrayed 'the extent to which the original Greek understanding of politics had been lost' (23). For Arendt this loss of politics meant the loss of the two activities that constituted the *bios politikos* – action (deeds) that is, as she famously says, 'not brutal', and speech (words) that is 'not empty' (200) – and these were the only activities within the *vita activa* that could constitute 'an autonomous and authentically human way of life' (13) because it took place directly between human beings.

But it is crucial to note that the rise of the social did not for Arendt imply the permanent and irretrievable loss or total eclipse of politics as action and speech (Pitkin). Julia Kristeva remarked in a lecture on Arendt that the idea of a 'refoundation as survival' of politics for our age was central to Arendt's work and it implies the duty to 'modify and augment old foundations in accordance with new discoveries that now lend meaning to diverse lives' ('Refoundation as Survival' 354). What this would imply, as I read Kristeva, is that in Arendt's work the 'libidinal' investiture in the possibility of politics could never have been and never was withdrawn, yet the relationship to the 'old foundations' could not simply be 'incorporated' either. In other words, this modification and augmentation of which Kristeva writes indicates a *transformative* relation to the 'lost treasure' and, as such, the posture of necessary failure or infidelity that characterises mourning.

Thus, already in the conclusion to *The Human Condition*, Arendt writes that the capacity for action is still with us, although (referring to 'the scientists') it 'has become an experience for the privileged few' (324). And in the 1970 interview, she unequivocally recognised the political initiative of the revolutionary student movements as action and commented that what 'really distinguishes this generation in all countries from earlier generations ... is its determination to act, its joy in action, the assurance of being able to change things by one's own efforts' (*Crises of the Republic* 202). Moreover, with the student movements 'another experience new for our time entered the game of politics: It turned out that acting is fun' (203). In these comments, Arendt also gives us a very important clue regarding what made it possible to recognise these movements as authentic politics. She writes: 'The basic question is: What really did happen? As I see it, for the first time in a very long while a spontaneous political movement arose which not only did not simply carry on propaganda, but acted, and, moreover, acted almost exclusively from *moral motives*' (203, emphasis added).

From these comments it is possible to conclude that Arendt's diagnosis of the social as coinciding with the loss of politics did not amount to the early Freudian melancholic or 'nostalgic' yearning for what was supposedly irretrievably lost in politics, nor to such a melancholic's denial of this loss. Yet, in a theoretical posture characteristic of the later Freud's view of mourning, there is a 'melancholic identification' in Arendt's work with the 'lost treasure', which caused her to engage with the traces that remained of politics.[4] This generated in her work 'sites for memory and history, for the rewriting of the past as well as the reimagining of the future' (Arditi 81). Indeed, I want to suggest that Arendt's work of mourning for politics allowed her to identify those experiences in the post-war era that resembled the (lost) principle of action and therefore allowed her to honour the memory of politics in its ancient sense. In this sense, she did not deny the loss of politics or yearn for it nostalgically. She soberly and realistically engaged with the loss by describing the historical process that led to it, and she actively and tirelessly took up the infinite responsibility that this loss left us with.

To summarise, Arendt's work of mourning for the loss of politics is a work that disrupts the clean distinctions between incorporation and introjection, melancholia and mourning as it was conceived by the early Freud and later elaborated upon by Abraham and Torok. As such, its closest psychoanalytical 'fit' is the Derridean idea of failed incorporation. This is the case because Arendt realised that the recognition of action in the modern age depended on a certain interiorisation of, or identification with, action as it existed in the Greek *polis*, while refusing a dogmatic fidelity to – or a successful incorporation of – it. In other words, and conforming to Derrida's account of mourning, a certain reappropriation of the lost tradition *was* crucial in order for modern politics to maintain a relation of *resemblance* with what was lost, in order for it to be *recognised* as authentic politics when it did occur.

In Arendt's work, the loss of politics occasioned a mourning process of *necessary failure or impossibility*: it was necessarily impossible to return to politics in the ancient sense, because Man and the world he inhabits had changed fundamentally and permanently. Yet it was impossibly necessary that, with the rise of the social, those exceptional instances of action and freedom in the modern age be recognised and memorialised as such, so as not to succumb to the temptation to dismiss such moments as mere aberrations in accordance with an ideology that would have the general progress of History be the emergence of the uniformly behaving masses or One Man of society. Such an ideology, as she argued in *The Origins of Totalitarianism*, was proto-totalitarian and, as such, utterly destructive of the politics she held dear and worked to restore.

The theoretical consequence of this unfaithful/faithful mourning for politics was that Arendt did not exclude the emergence of social matters from political processes such as action and speech: she acknowledged that the rise of the social necessarily meant that social problems would form part of political processes, that, for instance, revolution as the political event par excellence would 'use and misuse' the social question. In her discussion of the labour movement in *The Human Condition* she notes, quite frankly, that the difference between premodern slave labour and modern, free labour is that the labourer 'is admitted to the political realm and fully emancipated as a citizen' (217). In addition, she recognises 'the sudden and frequently extraordinarily productive role' this movement has played in modern politics when it appeared that the labourers, 'if not led by official party programs and ideologies, had their own ideas about the possibilities of democratic government under modern conditions' (216).[5] What these remarks reveal is that the overwhelming concern for Arendt was the restoration of the experiences to which politics granted access: appearance, action, freedom. It is for this reason that, years later, in answering a question put to her by her friend Mary McCarthy at a conference dedicated to her work, as regards what a person is supposed to do in the public space if he does not concern himself with the social question, she admitted that social matters have a 'double face', one of which should not be subject to political debate (because it is a question of administration) and one which should be (or, at least, could be) (see Benhabib).

In this way, by admitting the social to political consideration, Arendt was 'unfaithful' to the tradition and thus willing to mourn it as lost (Other). In the 1970 interview, she commented that 'this new assurance that one can change things one doesn't like is conspicuous especially in small matters. A typical instance was a comparatively harmless confrontation some years ago. When students learned that the service employees of their university were not receiving standard wages, they struck – with success' (*Crises of the Republic*). She regards this instance as 'positive' action 'exclusively from moral motives' (203) and thus clearly regards and recognises the political action taken in consequence of and in solidarity with this social issue as authentic and worthwhile *political* action in the name of the Other. Why would her comment here not amount to Arendt contradicting her earlier refusal of a political solution for the social? Because, as Schaap points out with reference to James Clarke (and this is the crucial point about the 'politics of the social' that I have been talking about), in Arendt social matters become political when 'others recognize it as a shared reality ... when it can become the basis for solidarity and action' (165).

In a short passage in *On Revolution* in which Arendt discusses the principle of solidarity, she moreover intimates that politics can 'out of solidarity' establish 'deliberately and, as it were, dispassionately a community of interest with the oppressed and exploited' (88) and concludes that 'solidarity is a principle that can inspire and guide action' (89). Why this emphasis on 'solidarity' through which social matters are admitted to the political realm? I think that the answer lies in solidarity's disclosure of a plurality acting in concert and, as such, revealing the possibility of the action as political and, therefore, as holding open the space for an experience of freedom.

In addition, solidarity arises out of respect, which Arendt held to be a crucial condition of politics since it was grounded in 'a kind of "friendship" without intimacy and without closeness', a 'regard for the person from the distance which the space of the world puts between us' (*The Human Condition* 243). It is, in this regard, important to point out that Arendt considered the modern loss of respect as a 'clear symptom of the increasing depersonalisation of public and social life' (243); in other words, the loss of respect was a symptom of the emergence of the social. By the same token, one could argue that the re-emergence of respect in the way Arendt defines it, and coincidental with solidarity, would mark for her a political moment in the treatment of a social issue. And as noted above, she acknowledged that this was indeed an actuality that came to pass in the face of the emergence of the social. To put it differently, this was the 'face' of social matters that could be subjected to political debate: the extent to which they could and should give rise to solidarity and action.

Quite apart from this, Vanya Gastrow has argued that Arendt's use of the term 'social question' as the given existence of poverty carries 'a narrow meaning, and is only intended to refer to the administrative and bureaucratic question of meeting the physical needs of the poor, as opposed to all questions and matters of debate relating to poverty' (10). What Arendt thus relentlessly resisted was the idea that politics could *solve* the mere existence of poverty, that is, the social question: 'For Arendt the bare fact of poverty alone in the form of scarcity does not equate to political oppression, and the technical processes of alleviating it cannot be achieved by deliberation in the political realm' (59). But, as Gastrow argues, where poverty was the result of exploitation and oppression, there would be no reason to exclude deliberation on and action against the way in which such exploitation and oppression contributed to the social question, since in these cases the 'common interest' would be something akin to 'the dignity of man' and action would arise out of the solidarity generated by such common interest (Arendt, *On Revolution* 88).

In this sense, it could be argued that while Arendt did not believe that mankind could be 'liberated' from poverty through political means, she certainly thought that politics could contribute to the *relief* of poverty where such poverty was the result of exploitation and oppression in general. The inclusion of 'social' issues as viable for consideration in politics as such indicates that Arendt did not adopt a stance towards politics in which she was simply unable truly to mourn the loss of politics in the ancient sense at the same time as she lamented, in a paralysed way, the 'rise of the social'. It is for this reason that Christodoulidis's analysis is inaccurate in its conclusion that Arendt leaves the political 'gloriously vacuous'. Arendt realised that her work of mourning for the loss that politics sustained with the rise of the social would have had to be alive, henceforth, to the concerns of the day, and in the modern age those relating to 'the social' irrevocably infiltrated politics. As she remarks in the famous interview with Günter Gaus: 'I live in the modern world, and obviously my experience is in and of the modern world' (*Essays in Understanding* 52).

It was, however, her reverence for the original or premodern principles and practices of politics, as well as her acute awareness of the history of the fate of politics when it attempted to solve the social question (that is, terror and collapse), that left in her thinking a resistant melancholic trace, one which caused her to adopt a rigid political stance towards the social question and, as Gastrow indicates, caused her to underestimate the extent to which debate can exist over seemingly private, or then 'social', matters. Put in a different register, it was her very fidelity to the tradition which she was mourning that generated an inability to appreciate fully how much the social question would become the burden of the sphere of politics. But even in this aspect, the Derridean character of her mourning stands in full view: Arendt's mourning for the loss of politics was unfaithful to the loss, by virtue of the very fidelity to what was lost. We can thus see why Kristeva (*Hannah Arendt* 19), in her biography of Arendt, could write as follows: ' "Faithful and unfaithful." That is precisely how we find Hannah all throughout our reading of her intellectual experience.' Such are the paradoxes and pitfalls, Derrida counsels, of any process of mourning: we must mourn, we cannot mourn (enough).

The work of mourning in postapartheid South Africa

Christodoulidis implored South African readers to question 'conventional conceptions' (501) of the social and the political and of their separation, specifically Arendt's. In the course of his formulation, Arendt's *description* of the way in which the rise of the social eclipsed the scene of politics, how the revolutions 'used and misused the mighty forces of misery and destitution in their struggle against tyranny and oppression', becomes her normative theory of 'the political as a denial of the social' (501).[6] Questionable as such a formulation of Arendt's project might be (she hardly 'denied' the social politically; her point is precisely that politics *couldn't deny* the onset of the social, while she still insisted on an ontological distinction between politics as freedom and the social as necessity), Christodoulidis insists that Arendt depoliticised poverty and aimed at undercutting our 'ability to understand and redress' it as a political issue (501). I hope that my argument thus far has shown that Arendt not only admitted 'the social' to political consideration, she also thought that, under certain conditions, political action in the name of social issues was possible and necessary. What Arendt remains ultimately concerned about is the extent to which politics *misuses* the social question and ends up denying its *conditio sine qua non* and *conditio per quam*: plurality. And this is why she held that it is dangerous to attempt to 'liberate mankind from poverty by political means' (*On Revolution* 114). I will return to this point in conclusion.

Be that as it may, Christodoulidis identifies in postapartheid South Africa an 'Arendtian' separation of the political and the social that has generated an elevation of the political above the social, which, in turn, has resulted in a neoliberal, market-driven (as opposed to politics-driven) structural adjustment programme that has failed to address the social devastation left in South Africa in the wake of the disastrous politics of apartheid: 'In this disturbing conjunction the political having been so successfully separated off from the social is made to yield to market imperatives, and the whole cohort of "natality", "worldliness", "acting-in-concert" and the rest, become hollowed out to the point where "democratic experimentalism" means nothing but market adjustment, and delivers nothing but the reproduction of privilege' (503). He concludes by urging us to resist 'analytical exercises that separate the social from the political, the ' "sphere" of social equality from the "sphere" of political participation' because such exercises are 'from the point of view of the plight for social justice nothing short of catastrophic for those who find their life-chances increasingly sacrificed to the false necessities of markets' (520).

As far as Christodoulidis's diagnosis goes – and while I remain sceptical of the very rosy *political* picture he draws, in Arendtian terms, of the early years of South Africa's political transition – there is much in it with which I agree. It is certainly the case that the political moment in South Africa came at the cost of politically *addressing* the social question adequately and that a certain social–political divide disconcertingly lies 'at the very heart of South Africa's constitutional settlement' (Christodoulidis 516), irksome as Arendt might have found such a formulation ('at the very heart'). However, the divide that Christodoulidis claims for the postapartheid transition is not Arendt's. This is the case because Arendt's identification of the existence of material poverty as the social question is not, without more, a definition of the grossly skewed/unequal/racialised *distribution* of poverty that South Africa inherits from apartheid and that structurally corresponds to the condition of global apartheid. To be sure, *this* inequality in the distribution of material resources, opportunities and welfare in general is the *political* dimension or 'face' of the social question, and there is absolutely nothing in Arendt that militates against or is targeted to prevent the political consideration of this aspect of the social question. On the contrary, if one takes the view that it is this inequality that prevents or reduces political plurality, then there is everything to suggest that the matter would be as political for Arendt as it is for us today.

But what is even more troubling about Christodoulidis's argument is how he ignores his own plea to avoid 'analytical exercises that separate the social from the political' (517–518) when he argues that the inclusion of justiciable socioeconomic rights in a constitution (such as ours) redraws the social–political divide and thus depoliticises poverty, because the transformative potential of such social rights constitutionalism inevitably ends up, under conditions of global capitalism, yielding to the market. Apart from the point that today *all* institutionalised politics appear to ultimately end up yielding to the market – this is the point of the critique of the 'postpolitical' condition – Christodoulidis fails to take into account the postpositivist point that the argument could certainly be made that to include socioeconomic rights in a constitution (as law) and to make them justiciable is necessarily to *repoliticise* them, is perhaps even to defer their depoliticisation *indefinitely*.

Rather than a dogmatic adherence to an ontological distinction between the social as necessity and the political as freedom, the unprecedented inclusion of these 'social' rights in a constitution in postcolonial Africa is surely to *undercut* the very distinction between the political and the social. And to make their meaning and interpretation at least partially a matter for the judiciary (as a branch of government) is at the very least to intensify, not reduce, their politicisation. This conclusion holds as long as one is prepared to admit to a view of constitutionalism that sees the judiciary and judicial review as a necessary and irreducible site of politics and the political process (see Michelman).

The inclusion and justiciability of socioeconomic rights under a constitution in fact holds the potential for political action that does not always already end up yielding to the market. This has been illustrated repeatedly in our socioeconomic rights jurisprudence where the Constitutional Court has ordered realisation of socioeconomic rights (and thus has deployed the social in a *political* fashion) against the dictates of the market and has thereby served as the focal point of an extraparliamentary politics of the social. The best example of such a politicisation is probably the Constitutional Court's judgment in the famous Treatment Action Campaign case in which the Court held that restrictions on the availability of the antiretroviral drug Nevirapine to HIV-positive pregnant women in the public health sector were unreasonable and, as such, violated unjustifiably the right to access to healthcare in the Constitution.[7] In the course of the judgment, the Court held that state policy must take account of the existence of poverty and that the limitations on the availability of Nevirapine disproportionately affect the poor. It further held that while it is an 'extraordinarily difficult' task to realise the socioeconomic rights in the Constitution, they nonetheless impose constitutional obligations on the state, which means that it 'has to find the resources' to satisfy a court order in this regard.[8]

For the sake of plurality

Arendt's work of mourning the loss of politics is ultimately motivated by an overriding concern for the experience of freedom. In Arendt's account, the experience of such freedom is possible only under conditions of a public sphere not overwhelmed by the society of uniform and uniformly behaving mass men, but vibrant with the plurality of the human condition. As she writes: 'What is at stake is the revelatory character without which action and speech would lose all human relevance' (*The Human Condition* 182), and such revelatory character cannot exist in the absence of plurality.

Arendt's worry about the 'society' of labour and consumption was that the togetherness one could find in it 'has none of the distinctive marks of true plurality' (212) because it requires 'the actual loss of all awareness of individuality and identity' (213); it rests 'not on equality but on sameness'. Under conditions of vast socioeconomic inequality (in which the 'sameness' and 'conformity' of labour prevails), plurality and, consequently, an experience of freedom stand little chance, for under such conditions man is entirely thrown back unto himself – lonely – in the darkness of the household and unable to distinguish himself, to disclose a world, from the homogenous society of 'behaving' masses. Under such conditions, as Arendt speculates, 'the withering of the public realm, so conspicuous throughout the modern age, may well find its consummation' (220).

Aletta Norval has argued that if, in postapartheid South Africa, 'the conception of the people as homogenous unity is to predominate, then the prospects for a truly plural, open process of nation-building would seem to be limited' (297). In other words, if the social is to predominate, the prospects of authentic politics would be limited. However, argues Norval, if non-racialism and the impossibility of nationhood could become a 'central articulating principle', South Africa could avoid the pitfalls that have beset the postcolonial process of nation-building. However, Norval readily admits that for the latter to come true, a series of conditions will have to be met, and she includes crucially among these 'the elimination of gross material inequalities' (298).

Considerations of time and space do not allow me to pursue Norval's argument any further, save to say that it simply cannot admit of any doubt that in postapartheid South Africa 'the social question', the existence of poverty, is, to an undeniably great extent, a consequence of the political misuse of the social during apartheid. For what is 'apartheid' if not the untranslatable political name of an imposed set of *social* conditions, of the imposition of inequality? What is it if not a homogenising logic that attempted to deny at all cost the plurality of the human condition? Without addressing the social question in South Africa *as* a political question, the equality and plurality that are the very condition of politics and the experience of freedom remain as a loss that the social will have mourned. Arendt herself wrote in the Preface to *The Origins of Totalitarianism* that 'to turn our backs on the destructive forces of the century is of little avail' (viii) and that efforts to escape from 'the grimness of the present into nostalgia for a still intact past' (ix) would be utterly in vain.

In our own context, I doubt that Arendt would have counselled us to turn a blind eye to the loss of equality and plurality in the wake of the *misuse* of the social question by the 'politics' of the apartheid and the early postapartheid eras. In other words, I doubt that her work carries the message that politics in (post)modernity can dispense with (as in 'be finished with' or, as I have argued, 'resolve') the social question. Her work certainly seemed unable to do so at the same time as it never fails to converse with the spectre of the 'lost treasure'. In this way Arendt inaugurated a politics of the social as her work of mourning for the loss of politics, incomplete and imperfect as it invariably was and has to be as a work of mourning.

As Kristeva remarks, Arendt 'advocates neither the nostalgic conservatism of the past, nor a destructive dismantling. There is no instructions manual for this new world and its new politics' ('Hannah Arendt Prize'). It is high time that not only the 'new world' of postapartheid South Africa, but also and indeed the whole world situated as it now firmly is in a new millennium, learns from Arendt that a politics of the social is an inevitable part of the work of mourning for the devastating losses perpetrated by the 'destructive forces' that History collects under the signifier 'apartheid'. As a Kantian, Arendt was well aware that 'it is in the power of freedom to pass beyond any and every specified limit' (Kant 312). It is on this possibility of the experience of freedom, inseparable as it is from plurality, that Arendt refused to give up. It is on this possibility that we should continue to resolutely insist at the same time as we soberly mourn the loss of politics that the 'rise of the social' inaugurated.

NOTES

1. If there was any doubt that 'austerity', as applied to fiscal spending, is a term that emerged only recently, say after the 2008 global financial meltdown, Patrick Bond's book makes it clear that the postcolony has long been the victim of 'fiscal austerity' (vii). Imposed by the international financial system in the early stages of South Africa's reintegration into the global political economy, this 'austerity' lies arguably at the root of postapartheid South Africa's intractable inability to overcome its social ills.
2. Arendt describes the Greek *polis* as 'the most individualistic and least conformable body politic known to us' (*The Human Condition* 43).
3. To this extent, Arendt is certainly one of the earliest thinkers of what Michel Foucault would later describe as 'biopolitics'.
4. Ranjana Khanna describes the trace as 'that supplement that has become remaindered but insists on its presence covertly' (76).
5. We have certainly seen in our own time how protest over a seemingly insignificant social issue, such as a small increase in metro fares (Brazil),

can result in large-scale political protest and the demand either for a new government or even for an entirely new form of government. As regards the latter, I am thinking of the case of Tunisia, where Mohammed Bouazizi's self-immolation in protesting unemployment unleashed the wave of protest that would eventually lead to the ousting of a president that had been in power for 23 years and a democratisation of the country that culminated in free and fair elections.

6. Christodoulidis makes much of the often quoted passage in *On Revolution* where Arendt writes that 'nothing could be more futile and more dangerous' than the attempt to 'liberate mankind from poverty by political means' (114). Arendt was of course concerned by the fact that the history of revolution has revealed that such a 'futile' attempt unleashes violence and eventually terror, all while leaving the social question as prevalent as ever.

7. *Minister of Health and Others* v *Treatment Action Campaign and Others* (No. 2) 2002 (5) SA 721 (CC).

8. Ibid., para. 99.

REFERENCES

Abraham, Nicolas and Maria Torok. *The Shell and the Kernel: Renewals of Psychoanalysis, Volume I*. U of Chicago P, 1994.

———. *The Wolf Man's Magic Word: A Cryptonymy*. U of Minnesota P, 2005.

Aitkenhead, Decca. 'Slavoj Žižek: "Humanity Is OK, but 99% of People Are Boring Idiots".' *The Guardian*, 10 June 2012, www.theguardian.com/culture/2012/jun/10/slavoj-zizek-humanity-ok-people-boring. Accessed 7 August 2016.

Arditi, Benjamin. 'Talkin' 'bout a Revolution: The End of Mourning.' *Parallax*, vol. 9, no. 2, 2003, pp. 81–95.

Arendt, Hannah. *Crises of the Republic: Lying in Politics, Civil Disobedience, on Violence, Thoughts on Politics and Revolution*. Harcourt, 1972.

———. *On Revolution*. Penguin, 1990.

———. *Essays in Understanding 1930–1954: Formation, Exile and Totalitarianism*. Edited by Jerome Kohn, Schocken Books, 1994a.

———. *The Origins of Totalitarianism*. Harcourt, 1994b.

———. *The Human Condition*. U of Chicago P, 1998.

Arendt, Hannah and Jerome Kohn. *Between Past and Future*. Penguin, 2006.

Benhabib, Seyla. *The Reluctant Modernism of Hannah Arendt*. Rowman & Littlefield, 2000.

Bond, Patrick. *Against Global Apartheid: South Africa Meets the World Bank, IMF and International Finance*. University of Cape Town P, 2003.

Christodoulidis, Emilios. 'Depoliticising Poverty: Arendt in South Africa.' *Stellenbosch Law Review*, vol. 22, no. 3, 2011, pp. 501–520.

Clarke, James P. 'Social Justice and Political Freedom: Revisiting Hannah Arendt's Conception of Need.' *Philosophy and Social Criticism*, vol. 19, no. 3/4, 1993, pp. 333–347.

Clewell, Tammy. 'Mourning beyond Melancholia: Freud's Psychoanalysis of Loss.' *Journal of the American Psychoanalytical Association*, vol. 52, no. 1, 2004, pp. 43–67.

Critchley, Simon. 'The Other's Decision in Me (What Are the Politics of Friendship?).' *European Journal of Social Theory*, vol. 1, no. 2, 1998, pp. 259–279.

Derrida, Jacques. 'Fors: The Anglish Words of Nicholas Abraham and Maria Torok.' Translated by Barbara Johnson, *The Georgia Review*, vol. 31, no. 1, 1977, pp. 64–116.

———. 'Racism's Last Word.' Translated by Peggy Kamuf, *Critical Inquiry*, vol. 12, no. 1, 1985, pp. 290–299.

———. *Memoires for Paul de Man*. Translations edited by Avital Ronell and Eduardo Cadava, Columbia UP, 1988.

———. 'Force of Law: The "Mystical Foundation of Authority".' Translated by Mary Quaintance, *Cardozo Law Review*, vol. 11, 1990, pp. 920–1045.

———. *Aporias*. Translated by Thomas Dutoit, Stanford UP, 1993.

———. *Specters of Marx: The State of the Debt, the Work of Mourning, and the New International*. Translated by Peggy Kamuf, Routledge, 1994.

———. *Adieu to Emmanuel Levinas*. Translated by Pascale-Anne Brault and Michael Naas, Stanford UP, 1999.

———. *The Work of Mourning*. Edited and translated by Pascale-Anne Brault and Michael Naas, U of Chicago P, 2003.

Freud, Sigmund. *On Murder, Mourning and Melancholia*. Translated by Shaun Whiteside, Penguin, 2005.

Gastrow, Vanya. 'The Demise of Revolutionary Politics and the Rise of Terror? Assessing Hannah Arendt's Hypothesis of the "Social Question" in Post-Apartheid South Africa.' MPhil diss., University of Cape Town, 2011. open. uct.ac.za/bitstream/item/4570/thesis_law_2012_gastrow_v.pdf?sequence=1. Accessed 16 August 2016.

Hill, Samantha. 'Accounting for Loss: Hannah Arendt's "We Refugees".' 2010, www.researchgate.net/publication/228277416_Accounting_for_Loss_Hannah_Arendt's 'We_Refugees'.

Kant, Immanuel. *Immanuel Kant's Critique of Pure Reason*. Translated by Norman K. Smith, Macmillan and Company, 1929.

Khanna, Ranjana. 'Signatures of the Impossible.' *Duke Journal of Gender, Law and Policy*, vol. 11, no. 1, Spring 2004, pp. 69–91.

Kirkby, Joan. 'Remembrance of the Future: Derrida on Mourning.' *Social Semiotics*, vol. 16, no. 3, 2006, pp. 461–472.

Köhler, Gernot. 'Global Apartheid.' *Alternatives: Global, Local, Political*, vol. 4, no. 2, 1978, pp. 263–275.

Kristeva, Julia. *Hannah Arendt*. Translated by Ross Guberman, Columbia UP, 2001.

–––. 'Hannah Arendt Prize for Political Thought.' 15–16 December 2006, Bremen, www.kristeva.fr/Arendt_en.html. Accessed 7 August 2016.

–––. 'Refoundation as Survival: An Interrogation of Hannah Arendt.' *Common Knowledge*, vol. 14, no. 3, 2008, pp. 353–364.

Michelman, Frank. 'Law's Republic.' *Yale Law Journal*, vol. 97, no. 8, 1988, pp. 1493–1537.

Nancy, Jean-Luc. *The Experience of Freedom*. Translated by Bridget McDonald, Stanford UP, 1993.

Nancy, Jean-Luc and Philippe Lacoue-Labarthe. *Retreating the Political*. Edited by Simon Sparks, Routledge, 1997.

Norval, Aletta. *Deconstructing Apartheid Discourse*. Verso, 1996.

Pitkin, Hanna F. *The Attack of the Blob: Hannah Arendt's Concept of the Social*. U of Chicago P, 1998.

Schaap, Andrew. 'The Politics of Need.' *Power, Judgment and Political Evil*, edited by Andrew Schaap, Danielle Celermajer and Vrasidas Karalis, Ashgate, 2010, pp. 157–170.

Truscott, Ross, Maurits van Bever Donker and Gary Minkley. 'The SARChI Social Change Papers: The Remains of the Social.' Internal document distributed by the editors to potential contributors to this collection, 2013.

Walker, Kathryn. 'The Tragedy of Interruption.' *Critical Sense*, Spring 2004, pp. 115–145.

Žižek, Slavoj. 'A Permanent Economic Emergency.' *New Left Review*, vol. 64, July/August 2010, pp. 85–95.

———. *Demanding the Impossible*. Edited by Yong-june Park, Polity Press, 2013.

———. *Trouble in Paradise: From the End of History to the End of Capitalism*. Allen Lane, 2014.

CHAPTER 6
SOUVENIR
Annemarie Lawless

> The key figure in early allegory is the corpse. In late allegory, it is the 'souvenir' [*Andenken*]. The 'souvenir' is the schema of the commodity's transformation into an object for the collector. The *correspondences* are, objectively, the endlessly varied resonances between one souvenir and the others (Benjamin, *Selected Writings* 4: 190).

In *Trust*, the American philosopher Alphonso Lingis explains how he never liked to travel with a camera. He had the usual objections of a conscientious tourist: 'It objectifies people with whom I wanted to interact ... there is something false and delusive in trying to fix and stock up images and situations from the past ... it was the changes in my heart I brought back home that were alone real' (49). However, when he was given a camera as a gift, he decided to try it out. At first he only shot images of buildings and landscapes, but one day, while focusing on some willows fringing a lake in Kashmir, he accidentally snapped some men bathing. To his surprise, the men smiled and called out, 'Thank you!' Lingis writes that he then realised that taking photographs of people, especially those 'who have no, and never will have, possessions, is the most innocent gift I could give them'.

There is much to feel uneasy about here: the implication that those without possessions are to be pitied; that they are the passive recipients of a gift, even though the gift in question is a photograph that will not in fact be given, but kept by the one who has transformed these people into an image for his own use and pleasure; and, perhaps above all, the claim that this exchange between perceiver and perceived, tourist and native, rich and poor, is 'innocent'. This kind of discomfort accompanies the reader through many of Lingis's recent books, which are part travel memoirs and part philosophical meditations about encounters with strangers and the strange.[1] It is evident that Lingis wants to cut through socioeconomic and political determinisms and subjectivations in order to get at what it is for one thinking, feeling, breathing body to encounter another thinking, feeling, breathing body – not a subject-to-subject encounter, still less a human-to-human one, but rather a creaturely one, epidermis to epidermis.[2] In a different register, that of Gilles Deleuze and Félix Guattari, who inform much of Lingis's thinking, a person precedes and exceeds all markers of subjectivity: he/she/they/it is a site of pure expressivity that cannot be forced to represent, a singularity that cannot be made to signify, a rhizome that cannot be arborified.

Fine, one might say – but the discomfort remains, stubbornly. While Lingis often seems quite deliberate in soliciting such discomfort in his readers, this is not simply the discomfort of those he dismisses as 'tight-assed liberals' who, out of 'respect' (*Body Transformations* 96) for the people they deem Other, refuse to engage in the most basic and simple forms of social interaction, such as bodily contact, erotic innuendo, dirty jokes and slapstick humour. Rather, the discomfort that Lingis activates for us – that is, for those whom Pierre Bourdieu famously describes as 'the dominated fraction of the dominant class' (196) – is the collective guilt of those who possess enormous privilege over those who have none and who are historically implicated by that possession. Guilt stems from a sense of responsibility, from the knowledge of the social and economic injustices that create privilege and distribute power, and this sense of responsibility is necessary for the exercise of ethical caution, a bulwark against further injustices. But guilt can also become a protective device for the guilty, operating on the principle that the more you feel bad, the less you are bad. It can lead to a smug sense of righteousness through which one resists certain feelings, such as the sorrow or pity or love one might feel for the plight of a stranger, because those feelings stem from self-indulgent sentiment, they betray a moral narcissism, a lack of social awareness and sophistication; they are self-serving, trite and embarrassing. In the ultimate extension of this thought, empathy itself becomes an ethical transgression. It is precisely this assumption that Lingis targets. At a fundamental level, his work asserts, people need to care about each other, to love each other, and even if the ways in which this love is expressed can seem self-serving, trite or embarrassing, it is vitally important that we feel it.

There is another photograph discussed in *Trust*. Lingis recounts a day in Ethiopia when he had to pay a visit to the bank in Addis Ababa. As he approaches the building, he sees a woman lying on the sidewalk with her two children. She is evidently dying of Aids: her body is emaciated, her breasts shrivelled, her skin pocked with dark blotches. When Lingis finishes his business at the bank and exits it, he slips between two cars and surreptitiously snaps a photograph of her. On his return to the United States, he develops the film roll and writes the following:

> There was only the thin bent smear of black on the silent paper of the photographic print. Yet I looked at the print and saw her and her children too as though she were there in front of me, in the aisle of the mall. I see her blinded by the midday Ethiopian sun, not seeing me, her wasted hand supporting her child in the last extremities of love. In writing this I know I am returning to her, though she is dead by now. This inability to depart from her, this desperate weakness, is perhaps also love (106).

Love, or simply another way that the first world feeds off the third, a hearty chicken soup for the soul made out of the suffering of others? This chapter will follow a rather counterintuitive route and take the claim to love as sincere. My subject is not the work of Lingis, but love: love as a form of 'desperate weakness' and its relation to the aesthetic image. It is true that Lingis makes his claim to love from the safe distance of an American shopping mall and that the woman in the photograph most likely did not benefit much from his trip to the bank. For this reason, it is easy to dismiss this claim. But perhaps it is a little too easy: the default mode of the conscientious tourist, that good liberal, is to perform respect for the Other by reducing the Other to the context in which they are viewed, to avoid creaturely contact, to cause no offence, and, at the extreme, to uphold the isolation that maintains caste separation. But Lingis pointedly refuses context. He refuses to make the photograph of the woman and her child, and his own position in relation to her, representative of the larger issues that have converged in the conditions that allow such a photograph to exist in the first place. What interests him is not, to use Roland Barthes's term, the photograph's *studium*, but only the personal, wounding quality of the photograph, its *punctum*.[3] The *punctum* of a photograph can be so strong that Barthes goes on to suggest that it emits 'a kind of little simulacrum ... which I should like to call the *Spectrum* of the Photograph, because this word retains, through its root, a relation to "spectacle" and adds to it that rather terrible thing which is there in every photograph: the return of the dead' (*Camera Lucida* 9).

For Walter Benjamin, that feeling of haunting is the symptom of the allegorical condition: in symbol, the relation of life to its image is seamlessly reciprocal; but in allegory, image and life are profoundly, disturbingly fused. The figure for early allegory is the corpse because in the corpse the image and that of which it is an image are riveted to one another in mute bondage; the figure for modern allegory is the souvenir because it presents an image of life at the same time as it presents life as an image – like the commodity, it is essentially ungraspable and distant. In his essay on Goethe's *Elective Affinities*, Benjamin relates this distant quality to love. He argues that earthly love cannot be fulfilled, it cannot complete itself; rather, it is marked by its perpetual striving, which 'is not a naked foundering but rather a true ransoming of the deepest imperfection which belongs to the nature of man himself' (*Selected Writings* 1: 345). For Benjamin, reinstating weakness as the principal characteristic of man is of utmost political importance: in the 'Theologico-Political Fragment', he writes that redemption and the 'coming of the Messianic kingdom' depend on the intensification of creaturely experience, and that the 'profane, therefore, though not itself a category of this Kingdom, is a decisive category of its quietest approach' (*Reflections* 312–314). The sacred can only be broached through a deepening of the profane. It is therefore a 'question of dialectics', not of striking a balance between the two elements, but going so deeply into one element that a second element is drawn out and redeems the first: 'Just as a force can, through acting, increase another that is acting in the opposite direction, so the order of the profane assists, through being profane, the coming of the Messianic Kingdom' (314). This movement between two extremes is again invoked in his essay on surrealism where, writing on the tendency of the surrealists to veer towards a kind of Romantic intoxication, he argues that the purpose of such intoxication is to win 'the energies of intoxication for revolution' (*Selected Writings* 2: 215), because 'all ecstasy in *one* world [is] humiliating sobriety in the world complementary to it' (210). When Lingis writes of a 'desperate weakness [which] is perhaps also love' (*Trust* 106), he is articulating a dialectical operation: out of the sense of desperate weakness love is produced and becomes its redeeming force. This kind of love is not a self-valorising Absolutism, but rather a 'sober' Absolute; that is, an Absolute that has 'forfeited its transcendence' and establishes itself instead amid the ordinary folds of immanence.[4]

In what follows, I first compare Barthes's statements about the photographic image to Benjamin's concept of the 'dialectical image'. According to Benjamin, the dialectical image opens up a specific mode of cognition whereby understanding is reached by way of a 'flash' that arrests thought. In order to consider how this flash of the dialectical image can be understood as an experience that produces love, I then turn to Baruch Spinoza's concept of the third kind of knowledge, and in particular to Deleuze's reading of Spinoza, in order to suggest that the dialectical image can be understood as a conduit for the third kind of knowledge, and since the affect of the third kind of knowledge is love, the dialectical image can likewise be understood as the redemptive force that Benjamin argued it was. Both Spinoza's third kind of knowledge and Benjamin's dialectical image depend on a specific experience of temporality in which the past collides with the present and the present becomes saturated with time. Benjamin articulates this idea in his concept of allegory and the flash of Messianic time in the dialectical image; in Spinoza, the apprehension of the total face of nature (*facies totius naturae*) can only take place under a species of eternity (*sub species aeternitatis*). In the final section I try to draw together these several strands through a reading of Deleuze's concept of *a life* as pure immanence: *a life* is the common skin we share, a creaturely skin that is the mark of our 'desperate weakness, which is perhaps also love'.

I. The photograph and the dialectical image: Barthes and Benjamin

The connection between love and photography has been explored by Eduardo Cadava and Paola Cortés-Rocca in their article 'Notes on Love and Photography', which is primarily a reading of Barthes's *Camera Lucida*. Since both love and photography transform their object into an image, they contend that for Barthes 'the law' governing both photography and love is that which 'interrupts identity by marking it with the sign of difference and transformations' (10). But more fundamentally, I would argue, what unites Barthes's discussions of both photography and love is the problem of the image, for it is indeed a problem. In *The Lover's Discourse*, the amorous subject attaches his desire to an array of different images, which together form a vast structure that Barthes calls the 'Image-repertoire'. The heart is 'held, enchanted, within the domain of the Image-repertoire' (52), and if this Image-repertoire could have a language (that is, if it could be made to signify successfully), then it would 'be precisely the utopia of language; an entirely original, paradisiac language, the language of Adam' (99).

In Benjamin's register, this 'utopia of language' is the 'language of Adam'; that is, the pre-Fall, pre-allegorical state in which words and things were locked in the luminous fusion of the symbol, and the word was both creative and the thing created.[5] Post-Fall, words no longer share natural correspondence to things, and we thereby enter into the condition of 'overnaming', which is the condition of allegory and 'the deepest linguistic reason for all melancholy' (*Selected Writings* 1: 73). For Barthes, as for Benjamin, it is precisely due to this overnaming that love cannot be signified as such and thus cannot be fulfilled. As Barthes writes, the Image-repertoire may be forced into writing, but only at a cost: 'What writing demands, and what any lover cannot grant it without laceration, is to sacrifice a little of his Image-repertoire, and to assure thereby, through his language, the assumption of a little reality. All I might produce, at best, is a writing of the Image-repertoire; and for that I would have to renounce the Image-repertoire of writing' (*The Lover's Discourse* 98–99). Writing, in other words, although produced by the Image-repertoire, cannot reproduce that from whence it came. It always somehow says both too much and too little, confined to everything that has already been said and named. The lover is trapped by the platitudes of love just as the photograph is confined to its platitudinous surface: sign and signified are irretrievably riveted to one another and yet the sign seems inadequate, inexpressive, mute. In the 'Winter Garden' photograph, a photograph of Barthes's mother taken when she was a child, the peculiar 'air' that characterised his mother seems to have been transported intact unto the photograph's surface, and it manifests only at the level of that surface: the 'air' 'flows back from presentation to retention' and must be experienced entirely 'on the level of the image's finitude' (90).

This is why Barthes asserts that one cannot *read* a photograph and that the photograph is therefore essentially undialectical, at least if one understands the dialectic as 'that thought which masters the incorruptible and converts the negation of death into the power to work' (90). In his writings on photography, Benjamin also invokes the connection between readability and photographs.[6] But, in contrast to Barthes, who understands the dialectic in terms of completion or fulfilment, Benjamin understands the dialectic as the irreconcilable separation of two elements, which, through their separation, create a charged flashpoint between each other. The dialectic, understood in Barthes's sense, is compatible with Benjamin's idea of symbol, but in Benjamin's sense the dialectic belongs to allegory. In *The Origin of German Tragic Drama*, symbol is that wherein 'the beautiful is supposed to merge with the divine in an unbroken whole' (160), in a 'mystical instant' (178). Allegory, on the other hand, is dialectical: it is 'accomplished in the movement between two extremes' (178), and these extremes are nature and history.⁷ In Convolute N of *The Arcades Project*, the mystical instant of symbol is the bud of 'mythic time'; its ideal form is the epic. The historical materialist must renounce the epic element of mythic time and expose history as that which is composed of 'images, not stories' [N11, 4]: not the story of man's serene progression through time in a continuous and unbroken narrative, in other words, but snapshots and souvenirs ripped from the context that would catalogue and explain them. History is the ruin of time, and its ideal form is citation: 'To write history ... means to cite history. It belongs to the concept of citation ... that the historical object in each case is torn from its context'.

However, for Benjamin allegory is specifically a form of writing. History is denatured time in the same way that the inscription is denatured speech. The inscription is like fossilised speech, marooned in historical time from the mystical instant of its utterance. It is a fragment, and by themselves fragments are 'quite incapable of emanating any meaning or significance on their own'; but in the hands of the allegorist, they can be transformed into a constellation or schema, and through this 'he speaks of something different and for him it becomes a key to the realm of hidden knowledge; and he reverses it as emblem of this. This is what determines the character of allegory as a form of writing' (*German Tragic Drama* 184).⁸ In other words, the inscription is not the key to knowledge, but the image – the pattern that the constellation or schema forms – of the key to knowledge. In inscription, speech is petrified in the image of the word.

It is due to this slippage between image and inscription that a quarrel exists in Benjamin studies as to whether or not the 'dialectical image' – which is the name that Benjamin gives to the allegorical schema or constellation in *The Arcades Project* and 'On the Concept of History' (in *Selected Writings* 4) – designates an actual image or if it is something that should be understood solely in linguistic terms.⁹ However, this distinction, simple as it is, obscures things: the dialectical image is an image, but an image of words. Benjamin makes this very point when he quotes from a 'monologue-like essay' by 'the brilliant Johann Wilhelm Ritter': 'The letter alone speaks, or rather: word and script are, at source, one, and neither is possible without the other' (*German Tragic Drama* 214). For Benjamin, Ritter gets to 'the very heart of the allegorical attitude' (214) with the theory that *'alles Bild sei nur Schriftbild'* – every image is only a word-image or, as in the common German use of this word, a typeface.[10] In allegory, the image 'is only a signature, only the monogram of essence, not the essence itself in a mask' (214). Not essence itself, but a monogram of essence, and allegory is a kind of monogram: it is 'a schema; and as a schema it is an object of knowledge, but it is not securely possessed until it becomes a fixed schema: at one and the same time a fixed image and a fixing sign' (184).[11]

With some justification, Anselm Haverkamp complains of the 'ongoing misreading' of the dialectical image in Benjamin, particularly the tendency to interpret the 'flash' and 'shock' of the dialectical image as some mystical recognition scene and to interpret the dialectical image as simply an image.[12] For Haverkamp, the dialectical image is, rather, a 'readable citation' (72). He argues that 'image' is the metaphor for citation and that the word 'dialectical' has to be taken as reading: 'Language is citation: language reused and reread' (71). According to Haverkamp, Benjamin used the term 'image' in accordance with 'a fashion of the time' (72), though he resisted the 'mainstream application of the term', and Benjamin draws attention to that distinction in *The Arcades Project* when he delineates between his idea of the dialectical image and the 'archaic' image [N3, 1]. The dialectical image, unlike the archaic image, is not essence in a mask but the monogram of essence. The difference between a dialectical image and an archaic image may be further characterised in the same terms in which we have discussed historical time and mythic time: the archaic image is a symbol or representation, whereas the dialectical image is produced through a historical perspective. Benjamin argues that what distinguishes 'images from the "essences" of phenomenology is their historical index', and this historical index 'not only says that they belong to a particular time; it says, above all, that they attain to legibility only at a particular time'. This 'now' depends on the moment of legibility, which is a moment that is also marked by the 'death of *intentio*' because it brings 'dialectics to a standstill': deciphering the world according to the signs and meanings with which we have endowed it is possible only up to a point. The moment at which reading is brought up against the limit of readability is the moment at which inscription passes into image and becomes something that we can no longer read but only see: 'image is dialectics at a standstill' [N2a, 3]. The inscription thus becomes an image.

In *The Origin of German Tragic Drama*, Benjamin famously states: 'Ideas are to objects as constellations are to stars' (34), meaning that ideas, as verbal concepts, are as separate from the objects they seek to represent as the individual stars are from the patterns we read in them.[13] In 'The Doctrine of the Similar', he writes again about the concept of the constellation:

> The perception of similarity is in every case bound to a flashing up. It flits past, can possibly be won again, but cannot really be held fast as can other perceptions. It offers itself to the eye as fleetingly and transitorily as a constellation of stars. The perception of similarities thus seems to be bound to a moment in time. It is like the addition of a third element – the astrologer – to the conjunction of two stars; it must be grasped in an instant (*Selected Writings* 2.2: 695–696).

Perceiving the image – or reading the inscription – depends on the perception of similarities, what Benjamin will later call, in the essays on Charles Baudelaire and Marcel Proust, correspondences. This perception is bound to a specific moment in time, an instant that cannot be wilfully prolonged, a *flash*.

In *Camera Lucida*, Barthes argues that it is through light that the photographic image is produced and through light that the viewing subject is touched or wounded by the image. Light becomes a 'carnal medium', a shared skin, and this carnality accounts for the 'pangs of love' that some photographs impart to their viewers; not those pangs of a lover's sentiment, but 'another music ... its name oddly old-fashioned:

Pity' (116).¹⁴ These emotions are not provoked by every photograph, but when it happens, it happens in a flash: the 'reading of the punctum (of the pricked photograph, so to speak) is at once brief and active' (49). For Barthes, the photograph is therefore close to the haiku, for 'the notation of a haiku, too, is undevelopable: everything is given, without provoking the desire for or even the possibility of a rhetorical expansion' (49). The haiku and the photograph are schematic images: constellations. The constellation cannot be read star by star but only through the pattern that the stars form when viewed together all at once. We are thus in the realm of Benjamin's dialectical image: 'Where thinking comes to a standstill in a constellation saturated with tensions – there the dialectical image appears. It is the caesura in the movement of thought' [N10a, 3]. The power of the dialectical image cannot be reduced merely to its parts. It depends, rather, on the imperceptible element that creates the concatenation between things, just as the brilliance of a mosaic depends more 'on the quality of the glass paste' than it does on its individual pieces (*German Tragic Drama* 29). The flash occurs on the horizon of thought, a horizon, as Deleuze and Guattari write, from which 'we return with bloodshot eyes' (*What Is Philosophy?* 41): bloodshot because the horizon is real – it takes place between bodies, in time and space. Yet, they continue, the bloodshot eyes that witnessed and saw 'are the eyes of the mind' (41).

II. Deleuze's book of light

It is a well-known but underappreciated fact that Spinoza was a lens grinder by profession. This daily activity may have influenced his understanding of the human mind – Spinoza approaches the mind as a kind of lens, a material device that can be manipulated to move beyond the capacity of merely human perception. In *Ethics*, Spinoza distinguishes between conceptions (*conceptus*) and perceptions, asserting that the 'word "perception" seems to indicate that the mind is in a passive relation to an object; but "conception" seems to express an action of the mind' (2Def3Exp).¹⁵ Later, he reiterates the point, cautioning against confusing thinking with mere 'picturing': 'I understand by ideas, not images, such as those which are formed in the bottom of the eye and, if you wish, in the middle of the brain, but under conceptions of thought' (2P48S). These conceptions of thought are ideas, and all ideas, according to Spinoza, are adequate and true if they are related to God: that is, if they are derived from and express the *facies totius naturae* or *rerum concatenatio* (the concatenation of all things).[16] If the ideas are related solely to the individual mind alone, then they will be false and inadequate.

The subtitle of Book V of *Ethics* is 'On the Power of the Intellect, or, On Human Freedom', and Deleuze describes it in 'Spinoza and the Three "Ethics"' as an 'aerial book of light, which proceeds by flashes' (32–33). He arrives at this conclusion after working through the three forms of knowledge as presented by Spinoza in *Ethics*. The first form of knowledge is that of signs and affects (*affectio*), and these pertain to one's physical situation in a particular moment in time. They constitute a 'slice of duration (*durée*)' (22). Signs are effects of the affects, 'shadows that play on the surfaces of bodies, always between two bodies ... effects of light in a space filled with things colliding into each other at random' (24). However, the kind of knowledge produced from signs and affects 'is hardly a knowledge but an experience in which one randomly encounters the confused ideas of bodily mixtures, brute imperatives to avoid this mixture and seek another, and more or less delirious interpretations of these situations'. When Spinoza speaks of the affect-images produced by this first form of knowledge, says Deleuze, it is 'only to be severely criticized, denounced, and sent back to their night, out of which light either reappears or in which it perishes' (26).

The second kind of knowledge, what Spinoza calls 'common notions', are concepts of bodies or objects and constitute the 'second aspect of light' (26). With the first kind of knowledge, light is reflected or absorbed by bodies that produce shadows, and the imagination grasps only those shadows. In the second kind of knowledge the intellect can apprehend the intimate structure (*fabrica*) of those shadows, and thereby the relation between bodies. A common notion is the concept of the structure that is formed by at least two bodies; common notions are thus universals, but they are 'more or less' universals depending on whether their concept takes in just two bodies or that of all possible bodies (*facies totius naturae*) (25). Deleuze then makes the following claim:

> Understood in this way, modes are projections. Or rather, the variations of an object are projections that envelop a relation of movement and rest as their invariant (involution). And since each relation involves all the others to infinity, following an order that varies with each case, this order is the profile or projection that in each case envelops the face of Nature in its entirety, or the relation of all relations (25).

Modes are projections or extrinsic individuations. But these projections *envelop* the relation of movement and rest that brought those projections into existence: in other words, they envelop their cause, which is God. Every projection is therefore an invariant (something that is unaltered by transformation) and an involution (a function that is its own inverse) and is connected to every other relation and on to infinity to comprise 'the relation of all relations' or the *facies totius naturae*. Hence, Deleuze refers to Spinoza's philosophy as an 'optical geometry': each relation is formed by at least two bodies, each of which, in turn, is formed by two or more bodies and so on into infinity. When we encounter a body that agrees with our own, joyful passive affections are produced, which become joyful active affections when we can form an idea of the intrinsic structure that we share with that other body. A common notion is a relation, in this sense, and the accumulation of joyful affections helps us form that initial relation. Modes are 'projections of light', and therefore also *'coloring causes'* (25), which at their limit would merge with every other colour as an infinite mode.

It is towards this kind of knowledge, the kind capable of taking in the *facies totius naturae*, which Spinoza calls the third kind of knowledge and Deleuze the 'third state of light', that the whole of the *Ethics* moves.[17] According to Deleuze, this knowledge is composed 'no longer [of] signs of shadow or of light as color, but light in and of itself' (29). Deleuze argues that common notions, 'insofar as they are projections, are already optical figures' (30) because they are *concepts* of relations. The first kind of knowledge presents a 'logic of the sign', the second a 'logic of the concept', the third 'a logic of essence': Shadow, Colour and Light, respectively (33). One cannot begin with Light, but 'one must reach it as quickly as possible' (29).

For Deleuze, Book V is 'a method of invention that will proceed by intervals and leaps, hiatuses and contractions, somewhat like a dog searching rather than a reasonable man explaining' (31). Its form is different from the other books because what Spinoza points to is the direct knowledge of essences: *'absolute and no longer relative speed, figures of light and no longer geometric figures revealed by light'* (32, original emphasis). Where common notions always refer to relations of movement and rest (relative speeds), essences make themselves understood in flashes: 'Essences on the contrary are absolute speeds that do not compose space by projection, but occupy it all at once in a single stroke' (30).

However, as Deleuze admits, the chain of reasoning that leads to the third kind of knowledge is less self-evident than the others. The first kind of knowledge is derived from an associative chain of signs and affects. The second kind is produced by an automatic chain of concepts and causes. But the chain for the third kind of knowledge, the final link, is missing: as Deleuze writes, it leads to a 'double interval'.[18] Deleuze takes proposition 10 as an example. Quoting Spinoza: 'As long as we are not torn by affects contrary to our nature, we have the power of ordering and connecting the affections of the body according to the order of the intellect' (32). Deleuze points out that the subordinate clause (bodies that agree with our own and thus increase our power or joy) and the principle (that through this power we can form a common notion and from there we can ultimately move to an apprehension of the *facies totius naturae*) actually open up a rift: we are required to fill in the gap ourselves, and unless we do so, we will be 'undecided about the fundamental question: How do we come to form any common notion at all? And why is it a question of the least universal of notions (common to our body and *one* other)' (32)?

Deleuze does not answer his question, but instead argues that Book V surpasses demonstration and decidability because its method depends on a form of thought that operates at absolute speed. With this kind of thought, leaps, lacunae and cuts are positive characteristics. He compares the style of Book V to the thought of certain mathematicians:

> When mathematicians are not given over to the constitution of an axiomatic, their style of invention takes on strange powers, and the deductive links are broken by large discontinuities or on the contrary are violently contracted. No one denies Desargues's genius, but mathematicians like Huygens or Descartes had difficulty understanding him. His demonstration that every plane is the 'polar' of a point, and every point the 'pole' of a plane, is so rapid that one has to fill in everything it skips over. No one has described this jolting, jumping, and colliding thought better than Evariste Galois, who himself encountered a good deal of incomprehension from his peers: analysts 'do not deduce, they combine, they compose; when they arrive at the truth, it is by crashing in from all sides that they happen to stumble on it'. Once again, these characteristics do not appear as simple imperfections in the exposition, so that it can be done 'more quickly', but as powers of a new order of thought that conquers at absolute speed (31).

This new order of thought depends on the interval to function and on a 'speed of absolute survey' (*survol*) to draw together to the maximum degree terms that are distant as such (32). The double interval in Spinoza thus invites a double reading: 'on the one hand, a systematic reading in pursuit of the general idea and at the same time, the affective reading, without an idea of the whole, where one is carried along or set down, put in motion or at rest, shaken or calmed according to the philosophy of this or that part' (*Spinoza* 129).

Deleuze compares the expressionist philosophy of Spinoza and Leibniz in terms of light and dark: Leibniz is said to be closer to the Baroque, to darkness, his *'fuscum subnigrum'* is a matrix out of which colour and light emanate, but in Spinoza all is light. He is therefore closer to the Byzantine, where 'everything is light, and the Dark is only a shadow, a simple effect of light on the bodies that reflect it (affection) or absorb it (affect)' (24). In his book on Leibniz, *The Fold*, Deleuze compares the camera obscura to the dark and windowless monad. The Leibnizian monad and the Spinozan mode are similar: both are individual centres of expression. But for Leibniz, the world that each monad expresses does not exist outside the monad that expresses it. Furthermore, Leibnizian expression is tied to concepts of creation and emanation, and expression is inseparable from signs. It is thus a 'symbolic' philosophy, and equating signs to expression means that at times expression is confused and at other times it is distinct: '*Such a symbolic philosophy is necessarily a philosophy of equivocal expressions*' (Deleuze, *Expressionism* 29, original emphasis). Spinoza, however, separates signs from expression. The type of knowledge that comes from signs is inherently inadequate. However, we are capable of forming an adequate idea, which is to say 'a distinct idea that has freed itself from the obscure and confused background from which in Leibniz it was inseparable' (330). Where Leibniz operates in the realm of symbolism, harmony and analogy, Spinoza's language,

> on the other hand, hinges on univocity: first of all, the univocity of attributes (in that attributes are, in the same form, both what constitute the essence of substance, and what contain modes and their essences); second, univocity of causation (in that God is the cause of all things in the same sense that he is cause of himself); then univocity of ideas (in that common notions are the same in a part as in a whole). Univocity of being, univocity of production, univocity of knowing; common form, common cause, common notion – these are the three figures of the Univocal that combine absolutely in an idea of the third kind (332).

To take this in, a special perception is required – absolute survey or overview. It is the momentary glimpse capable of taking in the *facies totius naturae* or immanence, the *flash* of the dialectical image. Indeed, Deleuze uses this very language: Spinoza's philosophy 'is the quintessential object of an immediate, unprepared encounter, such that a nonphilosopher, or even someone without any formal education, can receive a sudden illumination from him, a "flash"' (*Spinoza* 29).

Curiously, in *The Origin of German Tragic Drama*, Benjamin attributes his understanding of the Idea to Leibniz:

> The idea is a monad. The being that enters into it, with its past and subsequent history, brings – concealed in its own form – an indistinct abbreviation of the rest of the world of idea, just as, according to Leibniz's *Discourse on Metaphysics* (1686), every single monad – the pre-stabilized representation [*Repräsentation*] of phenomena resides within it, as in their objective interpretation. The higher the order of the ideas, the more perfect the representation [*Repräsentation*] contained within them. And so the real world could well constitute a task, in the sense that it would be a question of penetrating so deeply into everything real as to reveal thereby an objective interpretation of the world. In the light of such a task of penetration it is not surprising that the philosopher of the monadology was also the founder of infinitesimal calculus. The idea is a monad – that means briefly: every idea contains an image of the world. The purpose of the representation [*Darstellung*] of the idea is nothing less than an abbreviated outline [*Verkürzung*] of this image of the world (47–48, translation modified).

The original German words are telling: the monad-Idea is a stabilised re-presentation. Deleuze agrees: in *The Fold*, he describes how Leibniz puts a great screen between the Many and the One, between chaos and order. This screen is the *fuscum subnigrum*, and 'is like the infinitely refined machine that is the basis of Nature' (87). If chaos is the 'sum of all possibles', a 'universal giddiness', then it is the screen that makes it possible to 'extract differentials [to be] integrated in ordered perceptions' (87). For Benjamin, the idea is an 'image of the world', but it is not a dialectical image, because a dialectical image is marked by time, whereas Ideas are 'timeless constellations' (*German Tragic Drama* 34). However, the *Darstellung* of the idea is a 'contraction' (*Verkürzung*) of that image – it is what produces the dialectical image, which is the *image of an image*, or a citation of a citation. As Haverkamp argues with marvellous succinctness, '"Legibility" is what cuts [the dialectical image] off from mere *imagerie* and mere imagination and turns it, dialectically, from what it contains, fossil-like, into the schema of what this fossil, flash-like, reveals' (74). The flash occurs at the collision of affect and concept. It emerges like the sudden apparition of a ghost that haunts the remains. One can never be sure of what it is that one has seen, but only that one has seen, that one has *felt* that one has seen, and in its wake this spectrum leaves a trace in eyes that are now bloodshot.

III. A life
Considered in allegorical terms ... the profane world is both elevated and devalued (Benjamin, *German Tragic Drama* 175).

In *Difference and Repetition,* Deleuze states that paradox is 'the pathos or the passion of philosophy' (227). Paradox is always opposed to the order of common sense. It breaks up the faculties and 'places each before its own limit, before its incomparable: thought before the unthinkable which it alone is nevertheless capable of thinking; memory before the forgotten which is also its immemorial, sensibility before the imperceptible which is indistinguishable from its intensive' (227). It is what, in Benjamin's language, brings dialectics to a standstill. However, at the same time, says Deleuze, paradox 'communicates to the broken faculties that relation which is far from good sense, aligning them along a volcanic line which allows one to ignite the other, leaping from one limit to the next' (227). One part igniting the other, like the glass paste of a mosaic, or the jagged strokes of lightning. 'Objectively,' Deleuze continues, 'paradox displays the element which cannot be totalized within a common element, along with the difference which cannot be equalized or cancelled at the direction of good sense' (227). This element is singular essence, which is to say, immanence itself.

In one of his final texts, Deleuze defines immanence as 'A LIFE' (*Pure Immanence*). The indefinite article is of crucial importance: it is 'the mark of the person only because it is determination of the singular' (30). Immanence is pure expression expressing. It is life itself, we might say; but it is, more importantly, *a* life. We must pay attention to the articles in this statement: 'The transcendental field is defined by a plane of immanence, and the plane of immanence by a life' (28). The transcendental field is defined by *a* plane of immanence, which is to say the transcendental field is singular essence, the difference that cannot be equalised, the element that cannot be totalised; *the* plane of immanence is defined by *a* life, which is to say, *a* mode. Through its singular essence, through its difference that cannot be equalised, through an element that cannot be totalised, a mode expresses substance. But in order to express substance, one must not 'faithfully rest in the contemplation of bones' (233), as Benjamin states in *The Origin of German Tragic Drama*: the leap forward to redemption, to beatitude, means, for Deleuze, 'to become active; to express God's essence, to be oneself an idea through which the essence of God explicates itself, to have affections that are explained by our own essence and express God's essence' (*Expressionism* 320). 'If we take the indefinite article as an index of the transcendental', Deleuze argues, then no one 'has described better what *a* life is than Charles Dickens':

> A disreputable man, a rogue, held in contempt by everyone, is found as he lies dying. Suddenly, those taking care of him manifest an eagerness, respect, even love for the slightest signs of life. Everybody bustles about to save him, to the point where, in his deepest coma, this wicked man himself senses something soft and sweet penetrating him. But to the degree that he comes back to life, his saviors turn colder, and he becomes once again mean and crude. Between his life and his death, there is a moment that is only that of *a* life playing with death. The life of the individual gives way to an impersonal and yet singular life that releases a pure event freed from the accidents of internal and external life, that is, from the subjectivity and objectivity of what happens: a 'Homo tantum' with whom everyone empathizes and who attains a sort of beatitude. It is a haecceity no longer of individuation but of singularization: a life of pure immanence, neutral, beyond good and evil, for it was only the subject that incarnated it in the midst of things that made it good or bad. The life of such an individuality fades away in favor of the singular life immanent to a man who no longer has a name, though he can be mistaken for no other. A singular essence, a life ... (*Pure Immanence* 28–29).

Shorn of the markers that would individuate him, the man becomes – momentarily – pure intensity. It is no longer *his* life, but *a* life: pure event, the absolute speed of a light that reveals in its flash the *facies totius naturae* in *a* life. It is a moment that is lost as quickly as it arrives: returning to health, to waking life and reality, to context, he is reminded of who he is and of life as it has already been defined for him. Deleuze takes care to say that this experience of *a* life does not happen only in extreme situations that dramatise the passage between life and death: it can happen at any time, but only 'between-times, between-moments' – empty time, in other words, time not claimed by the individual, or by the demands of 'internal and external life', or by 'the subjectivity and objectivity of what happens', time in which one is no longer the subject but an indefinite article, *a life*. In the realisation of *a life*, life coincides with life, a momentary collision of presence with the present, pure event: 'It doesn't just come about before or come after but offers the immensity of an empty time where one sees the event yet to come and already happened in the absolute of an immediate consciousness' (29).

The intellectual understanding of a paradox does not lead to the beatific state. One must abide in paradox. What the man experiences as a stage towards his momentary encounter with beatitude is this: 'thought before the unthinkable which it alone is nevertheless capable of thinking; memory before the forgotten which is also its immemorial; sensibility before the imperceptible which is indistinguishable from its intensive' (29). In the very next moment, a 'volcanic line' seems to ignite one relation to another, 'leaping from one limit to the next', and finally, though *at an absolute speed* that makes everything appear to have happened all at once, the relation of all relations, the *facies totius naturae*. This image, in Benjamin's words, 'flashes up at the moment of its recognisability, and is never seen again' (*Selected Writings* 4: 390). In a moment of acute physical weakness, desperate weakness, a sweetness and a softness opens up in him, which is perhaps also love.

NOTES

1. See, for example, the following works by Lingis: *The Community; Foreign Bodies; Abuses; The Imperative; Trust; Body Transformations; Dangerous Emotions; First Person Singular*.
2. I understand a 'creaturely' encounter as one that is not mediated through the representations and symbolic structures of consciousness and self-consciousness, which would position a person as subject over and against the world as object. For extended discussions of this idea, see Weigel's *Walter Benjamin* and Santner's *On Creaturely Life*.
3. The *studium* of a photograph is all of its historical, political and socioeconomic significations, but the *punctum* is something less easily readable: it is what 'breaks' or disturbs the *studium* by 'wounding' the viewer. With the *studium*, one may view photographs 'as political testimony or enjoy them as good historical scenes'; with the *punctum*, what one sees is 'that accident which pricks me (but also bruises me, is poignant to me)' (*Camera Lucida* 26–27). Like Lingis, Barthes is not especially interested in the *studium* of a photograph, but rather in its *punctum*: 'I am a primitive, a child – or a maniac; I dismiss all knowledge, all culture, I refuse to inherit anything from another eye than my own' (51).
4. The 'sober Absolute', as Rudolphe Gashé notes, is the Absolute as the profane, the creaturely: it is that which has been 'de-sacralized, de-divinized', an 'Absolute that has forfeited its transcendence' (65).
5. See the fragment 'On Language as Such and the Language of Man', which was composed in 1916, the same year he began thinking about his *Trauerspiel* study (*Selected Writings* 1).
6. See, in particular, 'A Little History of Photography'. This is one of the first essays in which Benjamin mentions the 'aura', a concept that seems to correspond (at first blush, at least) to Barthes's conception of the 'air'. After naming the aura a few times in the essay, Benjamin pauses to ask, 'What is aura actually?' and answers that it is a 'strange weave of space and time: the unique appearance or semblance of a distance, no matter how close it may be' (*Selected Writings* 2: 518). Just as Barthes asserts that he cannot read a photograph, Benjamin makes a photograph's readability germane to the loss of its aura. The subjects of early portrait photographs had their aura intact, he argues, because newspapers were still a luxury item, 'photography had

not yet become a journalistic tool, and ordinary people had yet to see their names in print' (512). The first people to be reproduced as images therefore 'entered the visual space of photography with their innocence intact – or rather, without inscription' (512). While the gaze of the subjects of early portraiture instilled a sense of their enduring presence and caused viewers to feel a sense of sudden proximity, the post-aura photograph, with its accompanying inscription, effects a temporal disjunction.

7. It is 'by virtue of a strange combination of nature and history that the allegorical mode of expression is born' (Benjamin, *German Tragic Drama* 167).

8. In the original German, the last sentence of this citation reads: 'Das macht den Schriftcharakter der Allegorie' (161).

9. In *Dialectical Images*, Michael W. Jennings argues that Benjamin's dialectical image is the result of a nihilist combination of mysticism and Marxism. In *Walter Benjamin*, Sigrid Weigel focuses on the figure of the 'detail' to establish a connection between *The Origin of German Tragic Drama* and 'A 'Little History of Photography'. She argues that Benjamin 'develops his method of reading as a saving critique in nuce: as the gaze of a philosophical critique that perceives the historical charge in the detail and is able to decipher the traces of history in remnants and fragments' (243). Susan Buck-Morss, in *Dialectics of Seeing*, and Eduardo Cadava, in *Words of Light*, both have produced readings that tend to 'perform' Benjamin's understanding of the dialectical image. Cadava attempts 'to understand Benjamin's concept of history by analyzing his persistent recourse to the language of photography in his discussions of history' (xix). Unlike Cadava's book, which produces a set of 'photographs in prose' (xix), Buck-Morss reproduces actual photographs in her book, and comes under considerable censure from Anselm Haverkamp for doing so. Haverkamp is of the view that the dialectical image is primarily a readable image. Samuel Weber makes a similar argument but focuses on the 'ability' or potentiality of the dialectical image.

10. See Benjamin's *Ursprung des deutschen Trauerspiels* (190). Disappointingly, John Osborne's translation renders this phrase as 'every image is only a form of writing' (214).

11. This word 'schema', the Latin for figure, is important. It appears in my epigraph, where Benjamin describes the souvenir as marking 'the schema

of the commodity's transformation into an object for the collector', while Barthes invokes the word 'schema' in the preface to *The Lover's Discourse*: 'These fragments of discourse can be called figures. The word is to be understood, not in its rhetorical sense, but rather in its gymnastic or choreographic acceptation; in short, in the Greek meaning: σχῆμα is not the "schema", but, in a much livelier way, the body's gesture caught in action and nor contemplated in repose: the body of athletes, orators, statues: what in the straining body can be immobilized. So it is with the lover at grips with his figures: he struggles in a kind of lunatic sport, he spends himself, like an athlete; he "phrases", like an orator; he is caught, stuffed into a role, like a statue. The figure is the lover at work' (3–4). Barthes suggests here that, at least in his understanding, schema is different from figure: schema is something frozen, petrified if you will, while figure is physical, active, dynamic. It is not clear if this distinction between figure and schema exists for Benjamin. About the inscription, he states at one point: '*Ins Gelesene geht sie ein als >Figur<*' (the inscription enters into the read as its figure), which does not suggest that he considers 'figure' as either passive or active. But of schema, he writes that it is both fixed and fixing, and this apparent contradiction is resolved in his concept of the dialectical image.

12. He is particularly critical of Buck-Morss's book in this respect: 'Without more than the evidence of suitable pictures, Buck-Morss solves the mystery of the "dialectical image" much as Alexander solved another problem in cutting the Gordian knot. Why untie an obviously overcomplex theory if one can demonstrate so easily what it is about, and thus avoid the detour of too much thinking?' (Haverkamp 72)

13. Benjamin states that Ideas are 'something linguistic', and in support of this point, he quotes Hermann Güntert: 'Plato's "Ideas" are – if, for once, they might be considered from this one-sided viewpoint – nothing but deified words and verbal concepts' (*German Tragic Drama* 36).

14. As Cadava and Cortés-Rocca explain, Barthes here plays on the proximity between the French words for film and for skin: 'From *pellis*, the skin, *pellicule* and "film" originally have the same meaning: a small or thin skin, a kind of membrane' (26, n17). Barthes himself draws on this connection in *Roland*

Barthes by Roland Barthes when he describes the *pellicule* as a 'skin without puncture' (54–55).

15. As George H.R. Parkinson notes in his translation, 'Spinoza may here be distancing himself from Descartes, who said that he took the word "idea" to mean "whatever is immediately perceived by the mind"' (Spinoza 330, n4).
16. For full discussion of this, see Cesare Casarino's 'Marx before Spinoza'.
17. In Henri Bergson, there is a similar idea. In *The Creative Mind*, he distinguishes between two kinds of knowledge: 'The first implies going all around it, the second entering into it. The first depends on the viewpoint chosen and the symbols employed, while the second is taken from no viewpoint and rests on no symbol. Of the first kind of knowledge we shall say that it stops at the *relative*; of the second that, wherever possible, it attains the *absolute*' (133).
18. The term 'double interval' comes from Plato's *Timaeus*: in the midst of creating the Soul of the world, God needs to neutralise differences between divisible and indivisible Sameness, Difference and Being, so he forges two separate chains, one marked by a double interval (1, 2, 4, 8), the other by a triple interval (1, 3, 9, 27) (*Timaeus* 35–37). In his commentary on this passage in *Difference and Repetition*, Deleuze remarks that in his effort to 'draw from the depths of an intensive *spatium* a serene and docile extensity, and to dispel a Difference which subsists in itself even when it is cancelled outside itself', Plato's God 'dances upon a volcano' (234). Difference is singular essence, the multiple inequalities and differences that rumble beneath and threaten to fracture the auratic façade of the One. When the term 'double interval' resurfaces in Deleuze's discussion of Spinoza, it is to mark a specific point at which the pathway to the third kind of knowledge suddenly falls away.

REFERENCES

Barthes, Roland. *Roland Barthes by Roland Barthes*. Translated by Richard Howard, U of California P, 1977.

———. *The Lover's Discourse*. Translated by Richard Howard, Farrar, Straus & Giroux, 1978.

———. *Camera Lucida*. Translated by Richard Howard, Farrar, Straus & Giroux, 1981.

Benjamin, Walter. *Ursprung des deutschen Trauerspiels*. Suhrkamp Verlag, 1955.

———. *Reflections: Essays, Aphorisms, Autobiographical Writings*. Translated by Edmund Jephcott, edited by Peter Demetz, Schocken Books, 1986.

———. *The Origin of German Tragic Drama*. Translated by John Osborne, Verso, 1998.

———. *The Arcades Project*. Translated by Howard Eiland and Kevin McLaughlin, The Belknap Press of Harvard UP, 1999.

———. *Selected Writings*, 4 vols. Edited by Howard Eiland and Michael W. Jennings, Harvard UP, 2006.

Bergson, Henri. *The Creative Mind: An Introduction to Metaphysics*. Dover Books, 2010.

Bourdieu, Pierre. *The Field of Cultural Production: Essays on Art and Literature*. Edited by Randal Johnson, Columbia UP, 1993.

Buck-Morss, Susan. *The Dialectics of Seeing: Walter Benjamin and the Arcades Project*. MIT Press, 1989.

Cadava, Eduardo. *Words of Light: Theses on the Photography of History*. Princeton UP, 1997.

Cadava, Eduardo and Paola Cortés-Rocca. 'Notes on Love and Photography.' *October*, vol. 1, no. 116, 2006, pp. 3–34.

Casarino, Cesare. 'Marx before Spinoza: Notes toward an Investigation.' *Spinoza Now*, edited by Dimitris Vardoulakis, U of Minnesota P, 2011, pp. 179–234.

Deleuze, Gilles. *Spinoza: Practical Philosophy*. Translated by Robert Hurley, City Lights Books, 1988.

———. *Difference and Repetition*. Translated by Paul Patton, Columbia UP, 1994.

———. *Pure Immanence: Essays on a Life*. Translated by Anne Boyman, Zone Books, 2001.

———. *Expressionism in Philosophy: Spinoza*. Translated by Martin Joughin, Zone Books, 2005.

———. *The Fold: Leibniz and the Baroque*. Translated by Tom Conley, Continuum, 2006.

Deleuze, Gilles and Félix Guattari. *A Thousand Plateaus: Capitalism and Schizophrenia*. Translated by Brian Massumi, The Athlone Press, 1988.

———. *What Is Philosophy?* Translated by Hugh Tomlinson, Columbia UP, 1991.

———. 'Spinoza and the "Three Ethics."' *The New Spinoza*. Edited by Warren Montag and Ted Stolze. Minneapolis: U of Minnesota P, 1997, pp. 21–37.

Gashé, Rudolphe. 'The Sober Absolute.' *Walter Benjamin and Romanticism*, edited by Beatrice Hanssen and Andrew Benjamin, Continuum, 2002, pp. 51–69.

Haverkamp, Anselm. 'Notes on the Dialectical Image.' *Diacritics*, vol. 22, no. 3/4, 1992, pp. 69–80.

Jennings, Michael W. *Dialectical Images: Walter Benjamin's Theory of Literary Criticism*. Cornell UP, 1987.

Lingis, Alphonso. *The Community of Those Who Have Nothing in Common*. Indiana UP, 1994a.

———. *Foreign Bodies*. Routledge, 1994b.

———. *Abuses*. U of California P, 1995.

———. *The Imperative*. Indiana UP, 1998.

———. *Trust*. U of Minnesota P, 2004.

———. *Body Transformations*. Routledge, 2005a.

———. *Dangerous Emotions*. U of California P, 2005b.

———. *The First Person Singular*. Northwestern UP, 2007.

Santner, Eric L. *On Creaturely Life: Rilke, Benjamin, Sebald*. U of Chicago P, 2006.

Spinoza, Baruch. *Ethics*. Translated and edited by George H.R. Parkinson, Oxford UP, 2000.

Weber, Samuel. *Benjamin's -abilities*. Harvard UP, 2008.

Weigel, Sigrid. *Walter Benjamin: Images, the Creaturely, and the Holy*. Translated by Chadwick Truscott Smith, Stanford UP, 2013.

CHAPTER 7
RE-COVER: AFRIKAANS ROCK, APARTHEID'S CHILDREN AND THE WORK OF THE COVER
Aidan Erasmus

Ek's 'n agtergeblewende
op die grasvelde van my kinderdae[1]

(Fokofpolisiekar, 'Kyk noord')

In an eight-part series of short videos released on their website chronicling the recording of their latest album, *Bloed, sweet en trane*, the lead vocalist, Francois van Coke, from the Afrikaans rock band Van Coke Kartel (VCK) explained what he deemed was the inspiration for the lyrics on the album:

> I think it's like ... that obviously comes across in the lyrics is like just, where life is at the moment. I think that's probably my main goal with the lyrics on this album is just to write about normal, everyday things ... like what I'm experiencing ... Ja, I think *Bloed, sweet en trane* is a collection of songs about a new chapter for me and the band, and the realisation that things like love and playing music with others and music makes you part of ... something, even if you're very insignificant in the greater scheme of things (*Eendag op 'n slag*).

VCK emerged after the break-up of the Afrikaans punk-rock outfit Fokofpolisiekar.[2] Fokofpolisiekar's 2003 EP, entitled *As jy met vuur speel sal jy brand*,[3] caused an uproar in conservative Afrikaans-speaking communities because of songs, such as 'Hemel op die platteland',[4] which openly expressed an antireligious sentiment, so distancing the band from a fundamental tenet of Afrikaner nationalism (see Badprop; De Olim; Herholdt; Nel). Given the ways in which their music challenges the subject position of white South Africans in particular – specifically, Afrikaans-speaking white youth – after the democratic transition of 1994, the group has also been linked with a certain articulation of what it means to be white in a postapartheid South Africa constituted against the racialised apartheid past. Fokofpolisiekar, their music and their lyrics have been seen as marking an important moment in this shift in this set of debates, and their 'contribution to the South African music scene with their questioning of white patriarchal South African values as well as their visceral and poetic use of the Afrikaans language, paved the way for a fresh alternative movement within South African music' (Smit 2). Fokofpolisiekar has been seen by Sonja Smit as a direct antecedent of both the hip hop artist Jack Parow and the debate around whiteness in post-1994 South Africa. She notes that Jack Parow 'emerges from within a context in which (some) young alternative Afrikaans [speaking] musicians are processing and reclaiming their Afrikaans-ness as something that is not always associated with apartheid... before Fokofpolisiekar made it popular and acceptable, singing in Afrikaans was not popular among white alternative bands in South Africa' (2). The band became a popular cultural sensation, giving rise to a documentary film, *Fokofpolisiekar: Forgive Them*, a full-page newspaper advert condemning their actions, as well as a 224-page published biography (see Klopper).

As Fokofpolisiekar was well known for giving the Afrikaans music scene 'a good kick in the balls' (*Weekly Mail & Guardian*, 13 May 2004), the expectation that VCK would protest in the same brash manner was not unwarranted. Contrary to these expectations, Van Coke's thoughts on the album seem subdued, and instead of expressing frustration with the apparatuses of cultural and political power that were the object of Fokofpolisiekar's protest, Van Coke acknowledges that perhaps protest need not be voiced as explicitly as before; perhaps being a musician is in and of itself protest enough. According to Van Coke, it 'makes you part of ... something, even if you're very insignificant in the greater scheme of things' (*Eendag op 'n slag*). In a recent review of *Bloed, sweet en trane*, a critic's impatience with a song entitled 'In die agtergrond'[5] is audible:

> Most of all I just don't get the album. Since when do they sing about shitty jobs and being content on the weekends with an *'uitsig en 'n ligte bries om in af te koel, son sak in die agtergrond'*?[6] When I listen to VCK, I want to escape the lousy whirlpool that is my reality, not be reminded of it. I want to be inspired to go out and break shit and be able to blame it on the music. But with this album I just kind of, you know, can't (Van der Spuy).

Other reviewers, while not echoing this frustration as dismissively, also refer to VCK's engagement in *Bloed, sweet en trane* with a sense of disillusionment. They also note VCK's espousal of excessive alcohol consumption, substance abuse and a subculture of destructive habits, practices synonymous with 'Afrikaans-rock junkies':

> With Bloed, Sweet & Trane [VCK] spits in the face of terms like 'hitting the ceiling' and 'circling the creative cul-de-sac' on their hardest-hitting album yet. They've conjured up enough fresh, fist-pumping riffs here to last Afrikaans-rock junkies a lifetime. There's barbed-wire garage-rock tumbleweeds about gazing te diep in die bottel ('Die dag').[7] There's slow walking power anthems knowing that you know nothing ('Môregloed').[8] There are regular intoxicated liaisons with violence and friends with bad habits ('Here, man'[9]) (Welfare).

In this chapter, I interpret this frustration with *Bloed, sweet en trane* that manifests in its inability to inspire its listeners to 'go out and break shit and be able to blame it on the music' (as Fokofpolisiekar may have done) as an invitation to take VCK's supposedly absent, reactionary gesture seriously. By reading VCK and Fokofpolisiekar alongside earlier examples of Afrikaans popular music – specifically the 'cover versions' or new performances by VCK of previously recorded songs by other artists – as well as the historical narrative of white protest music within which they are inserted, I argue that the expectations placed upon VCK to protest are not unwarranted.

In fact, these expectations are the constitutive grounds upon which VCK (and, by extension, Fokofpolisiekar) can engage the postapartheid social. Moreover, in addition to the investment in dissent that marks the music of both groups, the work of VCK involves a covering, re-covering and a recovery of the everyday as constituted by apartheid's difference. The 'cover' or way in which VCK articulates the unstable terms of the social – as it emerges in the wake of apartheid – echoes insistently in their music, and I suggest that attention to these echoes renders the cover as the form constitutive of the remains that haunt rock and roll after apartheid.[10]

A season in paradise[11]

In 1988, the Afrikaans pop singer Carike Keuzenkamp released *Ek sing*, a compilation of ballads about South Africa. At the time of its release, South Africa was visibly at war, with the Internal Security Act of 1982 granting police greater powers to respond to the growing unrest and resistance in the country. In 1986 and 1987 alone, security forces detained 26 000 people, the majority of whom were under the age of 18 (see Webster). Despite the country being in a state of emergency, the South Africa that Keuzenkamp presented in her album was utopian, pastoral and romanticised. The album – with tracks like 'Bartolomeu Dias', 'As die suidoos gaan lê'[12] and 'Dom diedelie dom' – was one of many recordings at the time that expressed 'the escapist, fantasy nature of ... mainstream Afrikaans pop', and was 'noteworthy for its almost complete denial of the realities of the social realm' (Jury 100).[13] One song in particular, 'Dis 'n land',[14] demonstrates this in content as much as in form. The ballad's chorus speaks of an incredibly diverse and inclusive country, one animated by a common goal.

In her references to a country which affords all its people a sense of belonging and which faces a hopeful and bountiful future, Keuzenkamp ascribes to South Africa (both as political and geographic formation) a historical trajectory that will produce a distinctly modern state that 'works for the people' and acknowledges the right to self-determination of all its diverse constituencies. This devotion to futurity is encapsulated in Keuzenkamp's evocation that South Africa is a country of dreams and progressive sentiment, and the emphatic request that we allow the future to entirely envelope us.

The future that Keuzenkamp offers is one that renders absent the violent, fraught and complex history that South Africa at war presents, and is almost desperate in its repeated recourse to the claim that South Africa will cater for all people within its borders, granting all the right to both a cultural and a political life. While we may attribute this to the tradition of Afrikaans balladry in South Africa, or to the very obvious manner in which Keuzenkamp's project is the project of apartheid and its ideology of good neighbourliness, we should be aware of other reverberations of its content. Indeed, her lyrics implicitly echo Prime Minister P.W. Botha's well-known warning to white South Africans of 1979, amid growing unrest, unemployment and looming economic failure, that 'we are moving into a changing world [and] we must adapt otherwise we shall die'(Giliomee 586). The repeated questions in the third verse about parental responsibility – of the protection of minors, the securing of possibility for the next generation, and the child as South Africa's locus of potentiality for the nation – resonate with the themes of reform, change and the South African state's 'overriding consideration' in the 1980s that survival was key (587).

What is particularly resonant here is the figure of the child, which appears in various, often contradictory guises throughout 'Dis 'n land'. In one sense, the child is the detained protester, fighting *against* the state (emblematic of youth involvement in anti-apartheid activities from the time of the Soweto Uprising of 1976 to the township unrest and resistance of the 1980s). In another sense, he is the soldier, fighting *for* the state (emblematic of the young white conscripts sent to fight in the border wars and to patrol the townships). Lee Edelman argues that within the child, as constituted in Lacanian psychoanalysis, lies the 'perpetual horizon of every acknowledged politics, the fantasmatic beneficiary of every political intervention' (3), and that to elaborate a politics without the child at its centre is to deny an investment in futurism, or its 'unquestioned good' (7). In the case of 'Dis 'n land', the figure of the child carries Keuzenkamp's vision of the future. The child must produce the heteronormativity that apartheid demands, for 'the fantasy subtending the image of the Child invariably shapes the logic within which the political itself must be thought' (2). By invoking the child (who, as social actor within Afrikaner patriarchal society, must be male), and invoking him also *through* both mother and father as a rhetorical question, Keuzenkamp situates the child as both product and producer of the particular politics of Afrikaner society, a subject that is ensured and protected by the terms of apartheid as well as positioned as its condition of possibility.[15] 'Dis 'n Land' is prescriptive for the generation that will follow Keuzenkamp, and renders the future of South Africa as dependent not only on the child, but also on the continuation of an unsustainable present. Similarly, ending the song with a repetition of the first two lines of the third verse — which speak specifically about the responsibility of the male and female parent — articulates the commitment to this reproductive futurity; to a politics that cannot account for a future without the child as its locus. Put differently, the children of apartheid must produce apartheid's future or a future that is apartheid. It is a loop that resembles the rhythmic sympathy and tonal resonance of the cover – that which produces, that which determines the terms upon which what follows it will rest, and *is* that which follows it.

Apartheid's children

>bly en leef
>
>want jou dood sal ek nooit verwerk nie[16] (Van Coke Kartel, 'Dankie, ek is veilig hier')

In 2011, as the second single off their fourth album, *Wie's bang*,[17] VCK released their own song 'Dis 'n land'. While not described explicitly as a cover of 'tannie' Carike's version,[18] it transforms her composition into what has been called a 'fist-pumping requiem for a lost dream' (see Keylock). VCK's melding of violence and satire in their re-playing detracts from and denies the nostalgic anxiety of place and belonging that Keuzenkamp expresses, preferring instead a sombre and barren reading of the terms of the social set in motion by apartheid. Instead of replicating the chorus verbatim, VCK invoke elements of discord, disillusionment and disunity that are in stark contrast to the yearning for togetherness-in-difference that Keuzenkamp articulates:

> Dis 'n land van kleure en klank
> Dis 'n land van liefde vir drank
> Jy is nie ek nie, ek's jaloers op jou
> Dis 'n land van korrupsie en goddank
> Dis 'n land van liefde vir drank
> Jy is nie ek nie, ek's jaloers op jou.[19]

This reappearance of Keuzenkamp's work in that of VCK can easily be read as parody – aligning VCK, Fokofpolisiekar and other post-1994 white musical groups with the heritage of protest through rock and roll, which has largely been one of parody – but this would obscure the VCK version's relation to the anxieties of Keuzenkamp's original. One line that evokes this anxiety (which is elaborated more explicitly than in Keuzenkamp) is the mention of 'murderers greeting each other with a hi-five', alongside snide commentary on the postcolonial state, corruption and the complexities of power:

> In die land van die blindes is een-oog koning
> Koning loop met die losprys weg
> En moordenaars groet mekaar met 'n hi-five
> Ek wou my krane stadig afdraai
> Maar die lotery is klaar gewen
> met 'n skoot deur die kop van 'n magnaat.[20]

One could say that anxiety about control – whether in the sense of a stability of self that pervades everyday life or a stability of the social – governs both Keuzenkamp's and VCK's renditions. While Keuzenkamp might not render the anxieties of a state at war explicit, it emerges through the investment in futurity that marks her composition. In fact, it is the future promised by apartheid (according to Keuzenkamp) – a future deferred in the wake of apartheid – that prevents any possibility of VCK covering her work verbatim.[21] VCK express worry about the present after the fall of the apartheid regime, but with an inflection that registers an earlier moment of engagement as a familiar failure – seen in the mention of the 'king walk[ing] away with the ransom' – and one that is (almost inevitably) interrupted by violence in the midst of an attempt to retain control: 'I wanted to slowly turn my taps off/but the lottery has already been won/with a shot through the head of a magnate'. What is revealing is that in the following verse the anxieties of this moment are claimed *by* VCK, by self-consciously including themselves in the first person within a narrative of what could be referred to as 'unrest' (to use the terms of Keuzenkamp's South Africa):

Blameer die duiwel
Lippe bewe morsig en die spoeg spat
Oorgehaal maar beheer verloor
En ons vier dit met 'n hi-five
Ek wou my krane regtig afdraai
Maar die lotery is klaar gewen
Met skote deur die bors van die magnaat.[22]

In their claiming ownership of land, their complacency and their depiction of post-1994 politics as well as through the line 'and we celebrate it with a hi-five', VCK – unlike Keuzenkamp's song, where such a direct line does not appear – name themselves as part of something that is chaotic, divided and desperate. Preceding this affirmation is statement of being 'prepared but [having] lost control', which should be interpreted as the expression of the fulfilment of Keuzenkamp's anxieties in her original 'Dis 'n land'. In some sense, the figure of the child that has disappeared in VCK's cover is represented by VCK themselves, who as the 'children of apartheid' must – and do – rearticulate Keuzenkamp's politics. In the moment when VCK progress from observer in verse one to participant in verse two and, perhaps most prominently, to agent in the shift from 'this is a land' to 'it is *our* land' before the final chorus, VCK's version of 'Dis 'n land' moves from a mere repetition and amplification of Keuzenkamp through the cover, to recovery, in the form of embodying the resonant loop that the cover enables; through becoming the children of apartheid, VCK must cover and re-cover.

To elaborate the work of the cover in inaugurating a different state of emergency more carefully, we need to return to Fokofpolisiekar, not only as musical progenitors of VCK, but also to establish VCK as the inheritors of Fokofpolisiekar's gesture of protest. In this sense, we can locate VCK within a discourse about whiteness after apartheid. According to Ross Truscott and others, South Africa's 1996 Constitution – which asks that the 'injustices of the past' be recognised – bears 'the mark of authenticity' (17), for it represents '[the] gaze towards the past of injustice and its legacy, from the "liberated" position of the present'. While the disavowal of any relation to or culpability for apartheid as a political project can be thought of as the constitutive act by which the notion of the postapartheid is inaugurated, the legacies of apartheid are still apparent in the cultural, social and psychological configurations of white South Africans in particular. This suggests that a complete rejection of apartheid would mean disentangling the white subject as produced by apartheid. To become a South African in the fullest sense of the term, one needs to disavow the past in a way that recognises it but does not repeat it. 'The *absence* of a radical rupture with the past' (196, emphasis added), as Gavin Steingo suggests, is what refuses a gesture of denunciation.

In a series of interviews by Cornel Verwey and Michael Quayle with white, middle-class Afrikaners, this specific tension becomes clear. While many 'did much discursive work to discard certain visible aspects of Afrikaner identity', they also 'maintained whiteness as central to [this] identity, thus maintaining their claim to white privilege' (552).[23] As recent protest marches and allegations of a 'white genocide' by white groups such as Red October and other 'minority advocacy groups' have shown,[24] this results in the production (in the public as well as private sphere) of a 'ghettoized Afrikaner identity based on racial exclusivity, racist notions of inherent black inferiority, and out-group threat' (560). Commenting on this paranoia,[25] Francois van Coke speaks, as if in a completely different temporal context – perhaps a state of emergency – about this fear that persists into the postapartheid:

> 'I think there are a lot of scared people in South Africa at the moment' explains Francois, and that fear is expressed succinctly in songs like 'Einde van die wêreld'[26] ... with lines like 'Dis oor almal wat al jare vrees/ Altyd gereed vir die ongelukkige einde/Ons hoor dit oor en oor ... (It's about everyone that's been afraid for years/Always ready for the unlucky end/we hear about it over and over) (Walker).

VCK's cover of 'Dis 'n land' could be thought of as inaugurating a state of emergency around whiteness after the end of apartheid, as well as replaying the politics of an earlier moment of disquiet, as heard through 'tannie' Carike. The line 'you are not me/I am jealous of you' renders VCK (and, in some ways, their fans) proponents or embodiments of Verwey and Quayle's threatened whiteness, but it is also an act of dissociation, exacerbated by a distortion of Keuzenkamp through the dismembered chorus that VCK delivers. In much the same way as Keuzenkamp animates white fears by resorting to an insulated space where diversity reinscribes racial difference, VCK's rendition, in both content and form, performs a similar incomplete gesture. By claiming 'it is *our* land', VCK refuse to relinquish 'the land of colours and sounds' (the only line from Keuzenkamp's chorus that is reiterated unchanged) which they, as the 'children of apartheid', must yield. The state of emergency is precisely that the cover cannot escape that which it is covering, nor can it transcend it. It is the act of living in a space where the angst of a community forms the script through which whiteness is worked through. Indeed, we must hear it over and over again.

Total onslaught

> Let the simulation of ravening commence. Mechanisation means never having to wonder what to pretend to desire next (Daniels).

Francois van Coke's allusion to the centrality of music to everyday life needs to be taken seriously. In his writings on punk rock and its relation with race, Stephen Duncombe provides an apt point of departure for understanding how VCK's protest is textured by the work of rock and roll:

> My personal alienation was given social expression. In punk I found the outsider identity I desired, without borrowing a (Black) culture and a history that was so evidently not my own. As ridiculous as this might now sound, as a punk I imagined I could be White and not-White at the same time. White Noise [a band] was both a recognition of my race and an imaginary rejection of it (in Duncombe & Tremblay 3).

Duncombe views the relation between punk and race as one that allowed whiteness to be both questioned and affirmed through certain experiences in California in the 1960s in which he was involved. It was in this space that inhabiting the category of white became problematic, as for many the changing social circumstances made race very prominent: 'Whether through legal restriction, social exclusion or physical violence, non-Whites in the West were ... continually reminded of their race' (1–2). Duncombe stresses that what characterised this particular moment was a deliberate immersion in what he terms a '(Black) culture'. But instead of appropriating 'black' expressive forms, what is crucial about Duncombe's articulation of the permeation of race is that through punk there is a negotiation of the category that, while already in question before it could be inhabited, had to be inhabited in order to inhabit punk. In a manner of speaking, punk's condition of habitation *is* contestation. In this way punk can both highlight the issues pertaining to a certain articulation of whiteness and at the same time affirm it, despite what those issues may mean for a broader discourse about race. It comes as no surprise that as a student in the 1960s Duncombe played in a band named White Noise.

In the discursive space that punk offers (and it is important to read this discursive space as strongly determined by the genre of punk and the broader genre of rock and roll), whiteness is named as that which no longer constitutes the universal but which haunts any move beyond it.

As Duncombe notes, while whiteness was a subject positioning that many adopted openly, punk 'forc[ed] … this subject positioning into popular consciousness'; 'you had to name yourself as White … and figure out what the hell this meant' (4). It is here that the affirmation of whiteness inherent in the first instances of punk's racial politics takes on a particularly dissonant tone, one that celebrates difference while it reinforces the very categories it has posited as uncomfortable and contestable. In these terms, the presence of Nazi symbolism and the resounding calls of 'White Power', which have become synonymous with the genre, become irredeemable under the banner of something like postmodern pastiche or merely a collection of signifiers haphazardly thrown together.[27] This occurrence is not confined to the US or Europe and can be seen in the name of what is considered the first punk group in South Africa, The Third Reich (Lucey interview). Punk allowed a white riot of a different kind, and it is a white riot that the cover enables.

To return to the point made earlier about inheritance, it is important to note that VCK is hardwired to produce music that must deliver some form of protest not only because of its parentage in Fokofpolisiekar, but because of rock and roll's rendering as protest music in South Africa. The conflation of rock and roll and protest in South Africa comes to a head through punk, and it is no surprise that Fokofpolisiekar, through their protest, are referred to as a punk band.[28] In her thesis on rock music in Durban from 1963 to 1985, Lindy van der Meulen highlights the connection between rock and roll as music and culture and protest, both in a broader sense and in the context of apartheid South Africa, suggesting that 'the fact that rock has been linked to protest and defiance throughout its history is important, and that this feature of rock cannot be excluded from its definition' (16–17). Given this conflation, the function that rock and roll may have within the broader configuration of whiteness after apartheid cannot be anything but protest, and protest in all its ambivalence, particularly as it emerges in South Africa. This not only permeates the sounds that VCK and Fokofpolisiekar produce, but is present in other creative forms as well. The design and layout of Fokofpolisiekar's biography by Annie Klopper repeat this conflation through subtle aesthetic references to what is known as punk's DIY ethos, by the smudged fingerprints on the edges of the pages, and by what looks like handwritten corrections over certain paragraphs. A gesture of defiance is clearly visible on the title page with the words 'Die Bende' (The Gang) superimposed with adhesive tape onto the graphic of a Jägermeister brand logo. While this may reference punk rock's DIY ethos as well as the practice of drinking that has a history alongside the genre, specifically in South Africa in the 1990s,[29] this particular palimpsestic image signifies dysfunction, alcoholism and rebellion in the mind of the reader, setting the *'bende'* on a journey towards dystopia.[30]

Although VCK deny any real alignment with punk or punk rock, with bassist Wynand Myburgh commenting on the ambiguity of the genre allocation by referring to the fact that 'commercial guys call us punks, and punks call us commercial',[31] it is important to listen to the practice of naming at work here. In the same ways as punk rock as a set of practices *seems* to engage with whiteness in constructive ways but within that engagement complicates its own relationship with race, VCK and Fokofpolisiekar play to the same tune. While there is a visceral protest against visceral conditions, it is a protest that cannot be completed precisely because it affirms what it is attempting to reject. As Duncombe suggested in his own experience with his group White Noise, the gesture must imagine being both white and non-white at the same time, or reject race as well as affirm it. Fokofpolisiekar and VCK play out a rejection of whiteness after 1994 through the scripts of punk rock, which must return to another, familiar articulation of whiteness as reified by apartheid. It must cover in the guise of re-covering.

Lawrence Grossberg's concept of the rock apparatus is helpful as a way of unpacking the work of genre alongside what punk enables. Grossberg constructs a theory of rock and roll as a lens of empowerment, locating 'the effects of rock and roll at the level of an (at least potentially) oppositional politics which produces a rupture between the rock-and-roll audience (in their everyday life) and the larger hegemonic context within which it necessarily exists' (55). Grossberg attempts to define those effects through a definition of rock and roll as a strategy of survival and empowerment in everyday life. The rock apparatus 'locates what sorts of "pleasures" or energising possibilities are available to its fans [and] restructures social life by rearranging the sites at which pleasure can be found and energy derived, at which desire and power are invested and operative' (54). For rock and roll fans, everything is desirable and deniable. The conditions for this reinvestment of energies and the reconstitution of what may be thought of as 'possibilities' derive from the youth experience of society – 'the rock and roll culture transforms many of the structures of contemporary boredom (e.g. repetition and noise) into the structures and pleasures of its musical and listening practices'. Grossberg notes the historical implications of using the term 'youth' here in relation to rock and roll, pointing out that 'rock-and-roll celebrates youth, not merely as a chronological measure but as a difference defined by the rejection of the boredom of the "straight" [heteronormative] world'. The boredom that he refers to is directly related to the ways in which 'the politics of youth celebrate change, risk and instability', and 'the very structures of boredom become the sites of new forms of empowerment'.

Grossberg's reminder that rock and roll must always reduce its surfaces to pleasure, but only in the terms of covering, is productive to hold on to. If we listen to VCK and Fokofpolisiekar through Grossberg, and if we take Francois van Coke's words seriously, the protest that VCK and Fokofpolisiekar may make is largely a practice of ex-corporation, of reinvesting the boredom of the postapartheid into a rock apparatus that provides some sort of pleasure. Rock and roll and protest become a mechanism through which to *survive*, to adapt rather than die, as P.W. Botha exhorted.

Another review of *Wie's bang* reads as follows:

Ek is een van daai pretentious faggots wat prentjies sien in hulle kop as hulle musiek luister. Wanneer ek na 'Wie's Bang' luister, sien ek vir Francois, Wynand, Jed en Jason op 'n krans staan. Voor hulle is die einde. Die honger, lee maag van die duisternis, die vrees, die leemtes van die gate in ons kultuur. Voor hulle is die dinge, watookal dit mag wees, wat jou bang maak. Dit dreig om hulle in te sluk. Maar die vier lede van VCK staan regop, en skree harder as nog ooit tevore dat hulle fokken WEIER om dit te laat gebeur[32] (Zirkie).

A verse by the singer and songwriter Koos du Plessis from 'Skadu's teen die muur'[33] demonstrates the very real sense of change in the 1980s in South Africa. With the apartheid state failing, the speaker recognised that bygone visions are now grave and ominous, and that apartheid has had its designated moment. What is interesting, however, is that 'Skadu's teen die muur' is also covered verbatim by VCK in their version with the same name, on their third studio album, *Skop, skiet en donner*, released in 2010.[34] Ironically, the term *'skop, skiet en donner'* – while colloquially used in Afrikaans to describe a violent beating – was also used to describe the last whites-only general election in 1987, which was overshadowed by the National Party's campaign slogan 'Reform yes, Surrender no' and was accompanied by widespread stayaway action by trade unions and opposition movements.

Simply through the practice of the cover, VCK repeat Du Plessis's invocation of desperation, as well as the nonchalant manner in which he presents the dreams that have died. It is similarly fitting that the title of the album invokes violence, while the album that follows it (*Wie's bang*) reiterates paranoia and fear as its framework, along with other references to war and dystopia found in Fokofpolisiekar album titles (*As jy met vuur speel sal jy brand, Lugsteuring, Brand Suid-Afrika, Antibiotika*).[35] One reviewer described *Skop, skiet en donner* as 'exhibit[ing] such a beautiful balance between angst, playfulness and attitude that it can't help but *feel* like liberation' (Young). What the work of the cover amplifies in the cases of 'Skadu's teen die muur' and 'Dis 'n land' is not only the feeling of liberation, but the point that Fokofpolisiekar raises in a track titled 'Verklaar' off their first album with the line 'en ons sing al jare saam/aan ons doodslied'.[36] Put differently, VCK cannot renounce difference, which it must bring into being after those 'dreams have died'. Subsequently, they (and their fans too) stand on the edge of what is constituted as a perpetual and temporal end that never happens, whether out of choice or not, and scream loudly.

NOTES

1. 'I am the one who stayed behind (or, I was left behind)/on the pastures of my childhood.'
2. 'Fuck off police car.'
3. 'If you play with fire, you will burn.'
4. 'Heaven in the countryside.'
5. 'In the background.'
6. 'being content on the weekends with a view and a light breeze to cool off in, sunset in the background'.
7. 'gazing too deep into the bottle' ('The Day').
8. 'Morning Glow'.
9. Literally, 'Lord, man'; colloquially, 'goddammit'.
10. An attendant question here is whether a postapartheid rock and roll that does not protest is possible. The answer, I argue, is that the cover is the only form in which dissent might be disavowed. I elaborate upon this later.
11. The title of a Breyten Breytenbach work.
12. 'When the southeaster abates'.
13. Brendan Jury cites Hanneli van Staden and the way in which she describes Afrikaans popular music and its function: 'By singing about beaches, seagulls, puppy love and rugby, society's attention is taken away from socio-political issues – that ... in South Africa are most relevant. In this way, Afrikaans light music artists help to create and promote a false consciousness' (100).
14. 'It's a land'. The lyrics of 'Dis 'n Land' by Keuzenkamp could not be reproduced in this chapter due to licensing complications, but it is easily accessible online. The album in which the song first appears, Ek Sing (1987), is readily available on iTunes and other online music stores. The lyrics (in Afrikaans) can be read here: http://www.lyricsbox.com/carike-keuzenkamp-dis-n-land-lyrics-pzww9jq.html
15. The child in Keuzenkamp's ballad is caught up in a larger configuration of gender stereotypes espoused by Afrikaner nationalism that allow Afrikaans ballads such as 'Dis 'n land' and *'liefdesliedjies'* (love songs) to render women 'passive, acquiescent, and the victims of unrequited love', and 'conversely men ... as active manipulators of space and time, usually as farmers, soldiers or men of courage who engage in heroic struggles and quests' (Jury 101).

16. 'stay and live/because I could never work through your death'.
17. 'Who's Scared?'
18. *'Tannie'* can be translated as 'aunty'. Particularly in white Afrikaans-speaking communities, it is used to show respect to older women. Similarly, the word *'oom'*, 'uncle', is its masculine form. On being asked in relation to the music video for 'Dis 'n land', where VCK donned clothing associated with elderly Afrikaner women, whether their attire in the video was inspired by Carike Keuzenkamp in the 1980s, bassist Wynand Myburgh responded, 'Die idee was om op tannie Karike en 80's tannies te speel [the idea was to play on Aunty Karike and '80s aunties]' (Griffin).
19. 'It's a land of colour and sound/it's a land with a love for alcohol/you are not me, I'm jealous of you/it's a land of corruption and immorality/it's a land with a love for alcohol/you are not me, I'm jealous of you.'
20. 'In the land of the blind being one eyed is king/king walks away with the ransom/and murderers greet each other with a hi-five/I wanted to slowly turn my taps off/but the lottery has already been won/with a shot through the head of a magnate.'
21. We see this embodied in the five-track EP *Energie* released in 2015 by VCK, of which all tracks are covers, ranging from the Beatles' 'Help' to 'Got to Give It Up' by Thin Lizzy. Striking here is that the only South African and Afrikaans cover is that of 'Energie' by Johannes Kerkorrel, a figure renowned for his position within the white Afrikaans-speaking anti-apartheid cultural collective or protest movement Voëlvry of the 1980s. We see the foreclosure represented in the fact that the pop singer Keuzenkamp can only be perverted, while the protest musician Kerkorrel must emerge as close as possible to the original, with obvious punk rock inflections.
22. 'Blame the devil/lips shake messily and the spit splatters/prepared but lost control/and we celebrate it with a hi-five/I really wanted to turn off my taps/but the lottery has been won/with shots through the chest of the magnate.'
23. The use of the term 'Afrikaner' here mirrors that of the text cited in this case for the sake of conceptual clarity. There are obvious debates (especially in the postapartheid era and specifically referenced by Verwey and Quayle in their discussion) surrounding whether or not people associate

with or use the term 'Afrikaner' or prefer the term 'Afrikaans-speaking', and what exactly both the use of the terms and the terms themselves actually mean.

24. On 10 October 2013, a group of protesters representing white rights in South Africa marched to the Union Buildings in Pretoria as part of 'Red October', and 'despite arguments that the event was intended to advance minority rights in general, the focus was very much on the rape and murder of white people by black people, something organisers did not shy away from characterising as genocide' (De Wet).

25. In 2014, Fokofpolisiekar released a single track titled 'Paranoia' as a precursor to a new album. Hunter Kennedy (rhythm guitarist and lyricist) noted that Fokofpolisiekar's intent was always to change Afrikaner identity by deconstructing known opinions and stereotypes, and 'that identity is not fully formed yet and [they] think a big part of forming that identity will be for Afrikaners to accept their "Africanness" ... Afrikaners are the ones alienating themselves ... Paranoia is one of the side-effects of not understanding who you are and where you fit in' (in Inggs). At the time of writing, this promised album has yet to be released.

26. 'End of the world'.

27. Duncombe characterises the adoption by the Ramones and others of Nazi regalia and terms such as 'blitzkrieg' as being part and parcel of 'an attempt by young Whites, dissatisfied with the world they were born into, to grab and forge a new ethnicity for themselves' (Duncombe & Tremblay 5).

28. From the 1970s onwards, culminating in the late 1980s, there was a significant increase in the nature of cultural resistance, musical protest and involvement from specifically white English-speaking South Africans (later Afrikaans-speaking in the form of the Voëlvry Movement) against the apartheid government and its policies through the musical idiom of rock and roll. Before the 1970s, what was considered rock and roll engaged in playing covers, or 'hit parade material', particularly in Durban. However, by the early 1970s, rock and roll had become a veritable white middle-class youth culture, with more and more 'progressive' rock, or 'rock with a message', beginning to take hold. This growth was paralleled by a noticeable boom in South African popular music in general in the 1970s and 1980s, specifically

with regard to jazz – said to represent a 'discourse closest to an international musical vernacular of the oppressed' (Ballantine 309) – and groups combining Western and African musical idioms, like Johnny Clegg with Juluka and Savuka, among others. The first punk bands emerged in Durban, and sprouted a plethora of bands over the period from 1977 to around 1982 alone, with some trailing into the mid- to late 1980s as well. Nasan Pather argues that 'since its inception in this country, the idea of the punk rock ... song lyric as a space within which social issues could be addressed then evolved into the highly politicised articulations of the alternative bands in the 1980s' (2).

29. Lauren Basson highlights this in the context of the punk scene specifically, when she notes: 'At every Fuzigish gig that I have been to, including the ones at Woodstock (30 September 2005) and Violent Femmes (5 November 2005), the trumpeter whose stage name is Big Willy will suspend a beer funnel from the stage so that the skankers can refresh themselves as they run by. The photograph of Fuzigish in a *Stage* magazine that was analysed has all four members holding a beer (*Stage* 2005: 29). A quick quantitative analysis of how many times the words beer, alcohol and drunk are used in any of the Hog Hoggidy Hog interviews on their website reveals that these words appear in twelve of the twenty interviews that are provided. The words beer and drunk are also used extensively in Hog Hoggidy Hog lyrics, for example, in the songs "Sad Goodbye" and "The Incident". The address of Half Price's website is www.drunkpunk.co.za. In fact, when the punk bands were starting out in the country they would get drunk and play terribly. A few of them developed serious reputations for being out of control. Half Price has been banned from three Cape Town venues for their drunken behaviour. Half Price's drinking habits are reflected in their lyrics as well. For example, the song "I Drink All Day" starts with five word repetition of the word beer, which is shortly followed by a list of their favourite local beers: I drink a Castle and an Amstel and a Black Label. I drink as long as I am able. Their songs "Real Men" and "Can-O-Beer" follow a similar theme pattern' (51).

30. The epigraph at the beginning of the biography, taken from 'Evening' by Frederic Prokosch, also creates an image of the band as disturbing, uncomfortable, introducing 'wildness' and 'terror and desire' (Klopper 5).
31. This was to highlight the response of one reviewer on www.punk.co.za who referred to them as sounding much like Avril Lavigne, an American pop singer (see Badprop).
32. 'I'm one of those pretentious faggots who see pictures in their head when they listen to music. When I listen to "Wie's bang", I see Francois, Wynand, Jed and Jason standing on a cliff. In front of them is the end. The hungry, empty stomach of the wilderness, the fear, the emptiness of the holes in our culture. In front of them are the things, whatever they may be, that make you scared. It threatens to swallow them. But the four members of VCK stand up straight, and scream louder than ever before that they fucking REFUSE to let it happen.'
33. 'Shadows against the wall'.
34. 'Kick, Shoot, and Beat Up'.
35. Translation: If you play with fire you will be burnt, Air Disturbance, Burn South Africa, Antibiotics.
36. 'and we have been singing together for years/our song of death'.

REFERENCES

Badprop, Angola. 'Wat kan 'n polisiekar doen?' *Die Burger*, 22 March 2004.

Ballantine, Christopher. 'A Brief History of South African Popular Music.' *Popular Music*, vol. 8, no. 3, 1989, pp. 305–310.

Basson, Lauren. 'Punk Identities in Post-Apartheid South Africa.' Minor dissertation submitted in partial fulfilment of an MA, University of Johannesburg, 2007.

Breytenbach, Breyten. *A Season in Paradise*. Faber and Faber, 1980.

Daniels, J.D. 'Clocking Out.' *N+1 Magazine*, 6 December 2010, nplusonemag.com/online-only/paper-monument/clocking-out/. Accessed 18 August 2016.

De Olim, Charles. 'Punk Afrikaans Band Suffers Christians' Wrath.' *Saturday Weekend Argus*, 11 March 2006, www.iol.co.za/news/south-africa/punk-afrikaans-band-suffers-christians-wrath-269061. Accessed 13 October 2012.

De Wet, Phillip. 'Red October March Calls for End to Black-on-White Violence.' *Mail & Guardian*, 10 October 2013, mg.co.za/article/2013-10-10-red-october-march-steve-hofmeyr. Accessed 12 May 2014.

Duncombe, Stephen and Maxwell Tremblay. *White Riot: Punk Rock and the Politics of Race*. Verso, 2011.

Du Plessis, Koos. 'Skadu's teen die muur.' *Skadu's teen die muur*, Warner Bros. Records, 1980.

Edelman, Lee. *No Future: Queer Theory and the Death Drive*. Duke UP, 2004.

Eendag op 'n slag, Part 1. Produced by Freakscene, 2013.

Fokofpolisiekar. 'Kyk noord.' *Antibiotika*, Rhythm Records, 2006.

———. 'Verklaar.' *As jy met vuur speel sal jy brand*, Rhythm Records, 2003.

Fokofpolisiekar: Forgive Them for They Know Not What They Do. Directed by Bryan Little, Fly on the Wall Productions, 2009.

Giliomee, Hermann. *The Afrikaners: Biography of a People*. Tafelberg, 2003.

Griffin. 'Van Coke Kartel – "Dis 'n Land" Music Video & Interview.' *Wat kyk jy?* 24 January 2012, www.watkykjy.co.za/2012/01/van-coke-kartel-dis-n-land-music-video-interview/. Accessed 8 August 2016.

Grossberg, Lawrence. 'Is There Rock after Punk?' *Critical Studies in Mass Communication*, vol. 3, no. 1, 1986, pp. 50–74.

Herholdt, Faan. 'As jy met vuur speel, sal jy brand.' *Die Burger*, 22 March 2004.

Inggs, A. 'Fokofpolisiekar Release New Single, "Paranoia".' *Rolling Stone*, 28 February 2014, www.rollingstone.co.za/musicrev/item/3145-fokofpolisiekar-release-new-single-paranoia. Accessed 2 March 2014.

Jury, Brendan. 'Boys to Men: Afrikaans Alternative Popular Music 1986–1990.' *African Languages and Cultures*, vol. 9, no. 2, 1996, pp. 99–109.

Keuzenkamp, Carike. 'Dis 'n land.' *Ek sing*, Decibel, 1988a.

———. *Ek sing*, Decibel, 1988b.

Keylock, Miles. 'Van Coke Kartel: Wie's Bang Album Review.' *Rolling Stone*, 2012, www.rollingstone.co.za/albumsrev/174-van-coke-kartel. Accessed 20 November 2013.

Klopper, Annie. *'n Biografie van 'n bende: Die storie van Fokofpolisiekar*. Protea Boekhuis, 2011.

Nel, Jaco. 'Polisiekar in pekel nadat lid God vloek.' *Beeld*, 17 February 2006.

———. 'Woede oor skool leerlinge vra om Polisiekar-groep te boikot.' *Beeld*, 3 March 2006.

Pather, Nasan M. 'South African Punk Rock, New Wave and Alternative Music 1977–1989.' Dissertation submitted in partial fulfilment of an MA, University of Durban-Westville, 2000.

Smit, Sonja. 'Jack Parow: Reinventing Representations of White Male Identity in Post-Apartheid Popular Performance Practices.' Paper presented at the conference 'Images of Whiteness: Exploring Critical Issues', Mansfield College, Oxford, 12–14 July 2011, www.inter-disciplinary.net/wp-content/uploads/2011/06/smitwpaper.pdf. Accessed 8 August 2016.

Steingo, Gavin. 'I Am Proud to Be South African Because I Am South African': Reflections on "White Pride" in Post-Apartheid South Africa.' *African Identities*, vol. 3, no. 2, 2005, pp. 195–210.

Truscott, Ross. 'An Archaeology of South Africanness: The Conditions and Fantasies of a Post-Apartheid Festival.' PhD thesis, University of Fort Hare, 2012.

Van Coke Kartel. 'Dankie, ek is veilig hier.' *Wie's bang*, Rhythm Records, 2011.

———. 'Dis 'n land.' *Wie's bang*, Rhythm Records, 2011.

Van der Meulen, Lindy. 'From Rock 'n Roll to Hardcore Punk: An Introduction to Rock Music in Durban 1963–1985.' MA thesis, University of Natal, 1995.

Van der Spuy, Jack. 'Here Man, Save Rock and Roll – Van Coke Kartel "Bloed, Sweet en Tranc" CD Review.' *SA Music Scene*, 14 October 2013, samusicscene.co.za/?p=636. Accessed 8 August 2016.

Verwey, Cornel and Michael Quayle. 'Whiteness, Racism, and Afrikaner Identity in Post-Apartheid South Africa.' *African Affairs*, vol. 111, no. 445, 2012, pp. 551–575.

Walker, Murray. 'Van Coke Kartel – "Wie's Bang" Review.' *What's On*, 2013, www.whatson.co.za/blog_read.php?id=319#.UpMpcsTwOAU. Accessed 8 August 2016.

Webster, David. 'Repression and the State of Emergency.' *South African Review*, vol. 4, edited by Glenn Moss and Ingrid Obery, Ravan Press, 1987, pp. 141–172.

Welfare, William. 'Van Coke Kartel: Bloed, Sweet en Trane Album Review.' *Rolling Stone*, 2013, www.rollingstone.co.za/albumsrev/542-van-coke-kartel Accessed 14 November 2013.

Young, Roger. 'Skop, skiet en donner.' *Mahala*, 9 March 2010, www.mahala.co.za/music/skop-skiet-en-donner/. Accessed 8 August 2016.

Zirkie. 'Van Coke Kartel Wie's Bang (Album Review).' *Wat kyk jy?* 3 January 2012, www.watkykjy.co.za/2012/01/van-coke-kartel-wies-bang-album-review/. Accessed 8 August 2016.

INTERVIEW

Lucey, Roger. Personal interview. Cape Town, 13 May 2013.

CHAPTER 8
THE GRAVES OF DIMBAZA: TEMPORAL REMAINS
Gary Minkley and Helena Pohlandt-McCormick

This chapter takes as its starting point a formulation of liberation, read as inaugurating the non-racial as constitutive of the postapartheid social. Or perhaps, stated somewhat differently, liberation (as the 'after' of 1994) is understood as having seemingly prepared the ground for the capacity to move beyond the always already racial individuation of the social (see Van Bever Donker).

Yet liberation also holds within it the folds of a particular materialism and framing discourses of both class and of socialism,[1] as well as how these conceptualisations are sutured to those of race and nation. Materialism and concepts of class also of course function internal to the logic of capitalism, although they are there repressed even as capitalism imagines itself as antithetical to the politics of socialism and the Left. A central proposition to emerge from this is how race and class are stitched together in various formations of disciplinary (history, psychology) and instrumental reasonings (systems of governance), and in a politics of resistance, and are seen to define apartheid (and anticipate the postapartheid), ranging from the Native Republic Thesis and Colonialism of a Special Type (CST), to those of racial capitalism.

In these formulations, often bracketed as the 'race–class debate', three central suppositions for defining the apartheid social can be discerned: (i) race is always already individuated by the imperatives of class; (ii) race is read as irrational and 'false consciousness', and its false irrationalities can be disclosed through class struggle and resistance; and (iii) class will enable the disappearance of race through the modern figure of the worker (and a non-racial modernity). Read from a different vantage point, what remains of the social of apartheid – of race – are fragments, legacies and inheritances that continue to refuse or withhold this non-racial modernity even as the promise of a socialist answer has dissipated.

We wish to add another provocation to this assemblage through a recent engagement seeking to refigure the South African bantustan as constitutive of a South African 'empire', thought simultaneously as a dependent space in which the South African state commanded sovereignty, (despite its 'independence'), and as a theoretical concept to re-examine the unexpected wider, global trajectories of race. This has two components. If, as Jacques Derrida has suggested, apartheid is the 'last word' in the text of racism, the 'most racist of racisms' (291), then, following the logic of South African historiography, it is the bantustan that is its most extreme form of expression. Secondly, how might we interrupt, yet simultaneously extend, these readings through an invocation of an empire of liberation, assembled here through the social itineraries of Dimbaza's remains?

Thinking South Africa as empire brings to mind various imperial histories: British Dominion, Afrikaner nationalism or an increasing conflation of the interests of (British) capital and the (Afrikaner) nationalist and ethnic project of separate development structured around racial capitalism. When thinking about the National Democratic Revolution (NDR), the notion of CST, articulated first by the Communist Party of South Africa (CPSA) in 1962, emerged as a way to explain the peculiarities of the South African colonial situation.[2] Revisiting the early documents of the CPSA and the Communist International, it is evident that they reflect a certain understanding of empire and the colonial subject through which the native and the racial spatial command of the sovereign reverberated. This raises the spectre that the Communist Party and radical positions in South Africa were informed by (and reflective of) uncritical notions of empire that returned to the figure of the backward and tribal subject and reaffirmed this as the racial and racist figure of the native. Stated differently, this means that seemingly antagonistic historical formulations, particularly CST, Africanism and the politics of exile and liberation, which claim anti- and non-racism as their foundations, ironically continue to structure and suture the binary terms of race within their articulations. In tracing the itinerary of CST and the NDR we were prompted to consider that 'time does not pass ... it accumulates' (Baucom 34) and that race, the native subject and empire as the dependent space to command sovereignty may yet continue to inform what we call the 'empire of liberation': a dependent space of anticolonialism and postcolonialism that continues to command sovereignty within the 'native question'.

At the core of this chapter lies a question about the tenacity of racial formations. Given the predicaments of the postapartheid present and the troubling legacies of the past, the concern over the failure or limitations of the transition remains an urgent question. How and why does the 'native' subject continue to be given form through disciplinary categories inherited from the racialised past and through the instrumental reason of a developmental postapartheid state that is concerned with defining and enabling progress and modernity by overturning poverty and creating sustainable livelihoods? How and why does the subject that has been invoked in historical formulations seemingly opposed to apartheid continue to be constituted through concepts and archives that remain racially read?

Our attempt to trace the lines along which the postapartheid fold of time and space, read through Dimbaza, hinges on the concept of race as global apartheid requires that we attend to the various expressions of this fold. Drawing on formulations of montage and imagination, we assemble our arguments through the overdetermined, socially concentrated extreme of Dimbaza to draw on the unstable lines of thought that dominate explanations from different, contradictory angles in order to unsettle, activate and amplify their fissures. In seeking to make apparent the 'materialist undercurrents' of the wager that was apartheid, and in thinking about how this persists into the postapartheid, it is apparent that this rethinking cannot be a return to a reading of race as class.

Rather, we want to think how race might be read through an extended version of global apartheid.

Before we turn to the graves and the ruinous history of Dimbaza, we want to consider a clear cold night on the banks of the Liesbeek River in the Mother City, Cape Town as a possible starting point. The story – one of perhaps many such stories of the socialist Left – begins on Alfred Street in the suburb of Observatory. There, on some nights during the 1980s, young members of a secret cell of the Communist Party produced, on a mimeograph copy machine hidden at the back of the house, thousands of fliers advocating the 'national democratic revolution' (NDR) on behalf of the African National Congress (ANC) and its Alliance partners, which included the Communist Party. The reams of A4 paper fitted perfectly and miraculously into Omo washing-powder boxes emptied of their soapy contents. Resealed, they were in turn, 20 boxes at a time, driven all over the city for distribution at the darkest hour of the night.

But Observatory had eyes, real and imagined, everywhere and even youthful zeal could not dispel mounting anxieties. When it became too much, the young communists dug a large deep hole, again in the small hours of the night, and buried the mimeograph machine on the banks of the Liesbeek River, watched over only by the dark and empty windows of Valkenberg psychiatric hospital.

What we can imagine as a kind of madness, fuelled by the anxiety of discovery, had taken hold of these young communists and abruptly cast the clarity of political conviction and action into doubt. Today, those covert efforts of a minor Communist Party cell on behalf of the ANC and the Alliance might seem clumsy, tenuous and unclear in their distinctions. And yet, in 're: working' the remains of the apartheid social,[3] and in thinking the work that the remainder of race does, we return to the boxes of Omo washing powder and the machine that lies buried on the banks of the Liesbeek River and the thoughts it reproduced.

Walter Benjamin reminds us that 'the historical index of ... images not only says that they belong to a particular time; it says, above all, that they attain to legibility [*Lesbarkeit*] only at a particular time' (*The Arcades Project* 463; Didi-Huberman 89). The scene at the Liesbeek River,

THE GRAVES OF DIMBAZA

covered over by time and thought, becomes legible now in the context of postapartheid anxieties. Returning to that scene, and the memory of those events, made legible a concealed or buried dimension of the question of race: the thought that 'the socialist State, socialism, is marked by racism' and that racism is at work 'in the various forms of socialist analysis, or of the socialist project' (Foucault 261–262) and that this had begun to haunt those who buried the printing press, as it did Michel Foucault.

A further expression of this argument can be attended to by considering global apartheid as an ordering of desire, not only its structuring, and as something that must, yet cannot, be detached from South Africa. An iconic image by Santu Mofokeng, entitled 'Winter in Thembisa, ca. 1991 (Figure 8.1), illuminates the 'non-photographed of apartheid' and the 'invisible of the everyday' (Hayes 42). It features a box-shaped Omo washing-powder billboard tilted precariously towards the figure of a man striding beneath it, head bowed.

Figure 8.1. Winter in Tembisa, ca 1991.
Photographer: Santu Mofokeng.
© Santu Mofokeng Foundation, courtesy of Yale University Art Gallery and Lunetta Bartz, *MAKER*, Johannesburg.

It serves as a reminder of a 1950s advertising slogan, which claimed that Omo 'adds brightness to cleanness and whiteness' and permits us to locate unanticipated racial anxieties within the very small acts of political liberation described above. By the late 1980s, the Omo slogan had changed, but in the context of apartheid South Africa the play on racial anxieties in the original slogan is not exactly subtle and perhaps offers another linking of race and class. Here, an emphasis on the purification of the social body reveals not only the way race was encrypted in class struggle, but also the possibility that this encryption occurred through its container: the text itself and the fliers advocating the NDR on behalf of the ANC. The image or scene that encloses pamphlets of desire hidden in boxes of washing powder, which themselves played on anxieties about cleanliness and racial degeneracy, about the labour of washing and of racial subjectification, locates the subject 'outside itself as a constellation of singularities resistant to its ordering within subjective certainty' (Deleuze and Guattari 448; Van Bever Donker). The disciplinary categories inherited from the racialised colonial past and the instrumental reason of a developmental, postapartheid state are the stolen wheelbarrows of liberation through which race has been smuggled into the postapartheid – here as race's Omo box.[4]

Dimbaza

Dimbaza can be ambiguously evoked as a homeland resettlement village, a betterment rural township, a decentralised industrialisation showcase, a site of political banishment, an international symbol of apartheid difference and as a graveyard of the racially discarded, among other things. Dimbaza was first established as a resettlement village in the Ciskei bantustan, now part of the Eastern Cape, by the apartheid state in 1967. Like other similar settlements, it formed part of the massive social engineering project of apartheid that has come to be called 'forced removals'. It was but one such village in the attempted consolidation of the bantustans as racial ethnic homelands into which apartheid could relocate and separate out African sovereignty and citizenship and consolidate a 'decolonised' white settler nation-state. Conditions in these resettlement villages, including Dimbaza, were dire, a form of what Giorgio Agamben has called 'bare life' (13), marked most tragically by the deaths of hundreds of children from malnutrition and tuberculosis in the first few years of their establishment.

One of the first film critiques of apartheid, released internationally in 1974, chose to title its depiction of the policy of separate development and the accompanying forced removals of people *Last Grave at Dimbaza*, although Dimbaza features only briefly, in the film's conclusion. In direct response to both local and international criticism, both the apartheid government and the soon-to-be 'independent' Ciskei rulers (under the leadership of Lennox Sebe and his Ciskei National Independence Party) implemented a strategy of decentralised industrialisation in the homelands and in particular in Dimbaza. The intention was to make Dimbaza into the showcase industrial centre of the Ciskei, which became 'independent' in 1981. More than 50 largely foreign (particularly Taiwanese) factories were established here on the back of massive power, labour, tax, service, transport and import subsidies offered by the state. As a result Dimbaza was rapidly industrialised and a resident working class emerged in a significant process of rapid forced urbanisation and development. After 1994, with the reincorporation of the bantustans and thus of the Ciskei into South Africa, these subsidised forms of protection for industry located in Dimbaza were withdrawn, and an equally rapid process of de-industrialisation took place. Today, there are only three remaining factories in Dimbaza, all local, small-scale food-processing plants. Alongside this, the 'urban' place and population of Dimbaza remain and continue to expand in the supposedly non-racial liberated space of postapartheid South Africa. Dimbaza is now the object of state-led development, and its problems of poverty, unemployment and need are being addressed by vacant attempts to revitalise its industrial past.

Dimbaza, also thought here as landscape, as place, as an archive, as a concept and a history, provides a particular way of thinking about the historical relationship between the bantustans and the apartheid state, the periphery and the core, that reaches into the global present. It allows us to think about the relationship of historical memory, archives and anti-apartheid nationalist renditions of the past, about the relationship between anticolonial struggle and postcolonial realities, and about the accretions, persistence and compulsion of colonial routines and constituents in the postapartheid present. And it allows us to think about new ways in which to think about 'the native', race, racism and antiracism and the non-racial, and about the recurring relationships between the subject, subjectivity and subject formation, on the one hand, and the socials of apartheid and the postapartheid, on the other.

Through a reading of different 'texts' in and of the archive of Dimbaza, we bring together an assemblage of folds. We draw on several forms of knowledge amenable to being assembled by historical imagination – written documents, letters, contemporary testimonies and visual sources – concentrating primarily on the letter collection in the International Defence and Aid Fund (IDAF)[5] archive and on the film *Last Grave at Dimbaza*. In both there is a literal articulation of apartheid to the global context.

For 35 years, IDAF, an organisation that began in South Africa but was forced to move to England, secretly funded the legal defence of those persecuted by the apartheid state and supported victims' families. IDAF also established a cottage industry of primarily British correspondents, recruited mostly by word of mouth from among anti-apartheid and resistance movement family and friends, trade unions, and school and church organisations (over 700 people were involved by 1991). They exchanged letters in secret every two months or so with thousands of families in South Africa, sending £3 million per year in small postal orders to the dependants of prisoners and ex-prisoners. Across 30 years, over 400 000 letters crossed the globe and tied recipients and senders into lasting relationships. Many of the letters came from and were sent to political prisoners or their families in Dimbaza. They reflect the experience of those who endured Dimbaza primarily as a site of political banishment, hardship and resettled 'bare life' (Agamben 13).

In 1944 the South African liberal Leo Marquard, writing under the pseudonym of John Burger ('John Citizen') in *The Black Man's Burden*, could still argue, 'The ruling class in Britain is thus able to enjoy the financial benefits of association with South Africa *while discarding all responsibility* for the welfare of the mass of the inhabitants' (251, emphasis added). But increasingly, and certainly after 1974 in the aftermath of *Last Grave at Dimbaza*, and with the burgeoning of the international anti-apartheid struggle, this was no longer possible, and – at least for some – Britain could no longer disavow responsibility. This 'responsibility' translated into a system of support and welfare, and appealed to the liberal sensibilities of a certain sector of the British public, who made use of the structures inherited from empire (literacy in English, the art of letter writing and the institution of the post office) to counter some of the worst legacies of British colonial exploitation in South Africa and to turn, as it were, against the South African successor state, now arguably itself an 'empire'. The ANC, which, of all the exiled resistance movements, stood to gain the most from an invigorated anti-apartheid struggle, therefore turned to the British empire and its networks of solidarity, of which IDAF was one, to muster material support.

More or less contemporaneously with IDAF's letter campaign, the film *Last Grave at Dimbaza* was made in 1974. Shot in secret, the documentary was released internationally (being banned in South Africa). It attempted to turn Dimbaza into an international symbol of apartheid difference and mobilised Dimbaza, through its imagery, as a metaphor for the graveyard of the racially discarded. According to one of the producers, Nana Mahomo, the intention was to 'show what it is like for the black people of South Africa to be on the receiving end of the white government's apartheid policy' (in O'Meara 7–8). The film ends in Dimbaza, and in the concluding sequences the camera lingers on the graves marked with baby bottles and small hand-lettered crosses, and on a line of small open graves extending in one shot to the horizon.

The film struck at South Africa's secret heart.[6] Because they were situated in remote rural areas, often unmarked on maps and difficult to access, resettlement villages like Dimbaza were almost unknown to the public at large; being out of sight, they were also out of mind, which was convenient to the apartheid state. But once exposed, the desolation of Dimbaza became the international symbol of apartheid's criminality and enormity, and the prompt for a politics that turned this hidden corner. The film also clearly got under the skin of the authorities. By the late 1970s, the beginning of industrial development in Dimbaza was apparent. The Ciskei homeland administration, in collaboration with the apartheid state, responded to local and international pressure with attempts to make Dimbaza, and the Ciskei bantustan in particular, a showcase of the homeland system. Fuelled by incentives such as cheap financing – subsidised loans, tax concessions and direct subsidies – and the attraction of a cheap and stable captive labour force, Dimbaza was turned into a bizarre model of decentralised industrialisation and the economic viability of 'separate development' and separate sovereignty (attaining putative 'independence' in 1981).[7]

Both IDAF letters and the film, as political discourses of anti-apartheid, mark apartheid Dimbaza's isolated place within the global assemblage. In so doing, they identify not only Dimbaza but apartheid itself as an 'untranslatable idiom' (Derrida 292), set apart from world history. In this frame, these materials (the letters and the film) can be read both as resisting the native subject, and as exemplifying the racial spatial – and, we would argue, the temporal – command of the sovereign, located outside the particular or what is read as the 'unique' of apartheid and within 'the global' of the anti-apartheid moment. Yet we wish to argue that the letters and the film – and the events they inaugurate and conserve – lay the ground from which we might extricate the persistence of the native subject in the postapartheid. What is read as primarily a process of apartheid deterritorialisation was in fact also a reterritorialisation. *Last Grave at Dimbaza*, through the response it provoked on the part of the apartheid government, ironically ended up encouraging industrialisation and super-exploitation. It enabled the discourse of labour to be reterritorialised in the Ciskei homeland – in the very place the film (and radical historiography and liberation politics more broadly) portrayed as its 'graveyard' and where it located its critique of global industrialisation and international capitalism and their complicity in shoring up apartheid capitalist accumulation and force – through its displacement of the 'worthless and the disposable' (Hardt & Negri 167). The IDAF letters also increasingly give expression to a process of 'hierarchical inclusion' (167), as distinct from 'compartmentalisation' (125), as the 'letter subjects' of anti-apartheid aid increasingly began to identify themselves as workers, with wages and prices and the factory as their pressing problems. This narrative formed part of an emerging 'economic body defined by global divisions of labour and power' (167), which not only new South African but also primarily Taiwanese, American and other multinational firms exemplified. In the process, the question of apartheid seems to disappear, or at least to dissolve back into the frames that, as we argued above, marked the race–class debate, which came to define apartheid and resistance. The remainder of this chapter seeks to return to this question through the idea of an 'empire of liberation'.[8]

The empire of liberation

In a parallel essay, we have argued that the archive of Dimbaza authorises a space, one of montage and repetition that simultaneously contains the South African empire and an imaginary of the postapartheid (see Pohlandt-McCormick & Minkley). It is an imaginary of the exteriority of liberation (an elsewhere, a time beyond apartheid) that holds its dominant frame (of class and socialism) in view, but also anticipates its fold into what we have proposed as the 'empire' of this liberation, which is marked by what always already remains there: the conjugated subject of the axiomatic 'native'.

In essence, South African empire can be read into Dimbaza through territory and what we have named as the deterritorialisations and reterritorialisations of the pre-1994 South African state. For this South African nation-state (and its constitution of 'empire'), space was the dimension on which politics and violence were grounded and waged. Space dominated its racial political vision, determining the nature and positioning of the 'other'. In this sense it was about geopolitics (and thus within empire) all along, but it was also caught within the redistributions of territorial sovereignty – between home and homeland. However, once 'countryside industrialisation' and the factories of Dimbaza became deterritorialised objects and marked this homeland territory with a line of flight into class, the political imaginary was opened to the dimension of time over that of space. But – and here is the related fold – the temporality of class (and struggle) is an already overdetermined and dominated terrain whose trajectories are imagined as a particular path to socialist society, with national liberation located as the required advance in time, where historical progress will assure certain victory and where the sovereign body with the legitimacy to wage class struggle is the national liberation party situated in time as the vanguard of history (Buck-Morss). The significant fold of this vanguard is the formulation, by the ANC alliance, of national liberation as liberation from South Africa's form of colonialism – CST.

More generally, in the context of the Soviet Union, Susan Buck-Morss points to the ways that the discourse of time became a field for the exercise of sovereign power. In particular, she points to the ways that the spatial struggle between city and country was translated into the temporal discourse of class struggle, which cast the rural as 'people from the past' (38). The national question was also transposed into a discourse of time, as 'backward cultures and ethnic groups came under attack as vestiges of an earlier era' (39), or were understood to be hostile to revolution and to historical progress, and against revolutionary time, which was equated with industrialisation, modernisation, the urban and the party.

Read from the vantage point of Dimbaza, CST and the form and nature of the articulations of national liberation and class struggle in relation to the spatial and the temporal are significant. In effect, the theory of CST and its antecedents, as well as its determining formulations within ANC and Communist Party politics, prioritised and made class, and the black working class, the 'concrete' determinant of liberation. In so doing, whether through phases, stages, coincidence or a single revolution, achieved through armed struggle and mass struggle, it established the ANC–Communist Party 'alliance' as the sovereign body of the struggle and situated it in time as the vanguard of history. Its legitimacy lay in apparently mobilising this industrial working class on the one hand and,

Figure 8.2. Moses Twebe (fourth from the left) in front of the Moses Twebe Great Hall, 15 March 2007.
Photographer: Gary Minkley

on the other, holding the interest of this working class (where not yet ready or able) in trust for the future through the territory of the nation.

What this entailed in Dimbaza was that those who had been removed to the bantustans as unwanted people, reterritorialised as 'surplus' to the efficient workings of racial capitalism or as threats to the political stability of the state, such as the former political prisoner Moses Twebe (Figure 8.2) and others, were figured as recipients of this trust, beneficiaries of this vanguard, yet still located in this earlier time, essentially in the time of the native. After 1994, bantustan politics is seen to disappear, as much a ghost of the area as the ghostly industrial remains of de-industrialisation that accompanied 'democracy' (see Pohlandt-McCormick & Minkley). The nation-state founded in 1994, which reterritorialised the Ciskei and Dimbaza as part of the new South Africa, holds the promise of a different sovereignty – no longer 'discarded'; its graves no longer in 'foreign' soil. Rather, in the post-1994 era, the politics of race is equally 'seen to disappear' as it 'moves' beyond territory itself, which has been overcome by national liberation. Race then, like apartheid, is stitched to space in these particular ways.

And yet Dimbaza cannot enter the discourse of liberation, and cannot constitute the field for the exercise of sovereign power. The spatial struggle between city and countryside is relocated, or more accurately retemporalised, as the 'not-yet', as a future held in trust. Because, what also always already accumulates here – in this 'empire of liberation' – is the figure of the 'native'. This is not to suggest that what is needed in the postapartheid is a return to the historical role of the vanguard, or a resumption of the revolutionary process, to complete the not-yet. Instead, what is needed is a response to the provocation of what the not-yet holds: the spectre of race and its articulations to global apartheid, which must be, yet cannot be, detached from Dimbaza or from South Africa more broadly.

The social and social acts

Spectres of race continue to haunt the postapartheid present of Dimbaza. Here we turn to photographic and sound archives and their 'outside', brought together through research and projects concerned with 'liberation heritage' and through the encounter with a collection of black and white photographs from Dimbaza – scratched, marked, blurred and haunting – recently located in Bishop David Russell's papers. Our argument can be illuminated by considering two images of Moses Twebe, a communist member of the ANC imprisoned on Robben Island in 1963 for underground activities, released in 1969 and deported to the misery of Dimbaza (see Pohlandt-McCormick & Minkley). In the photographs he becomes the exemplary subject of postapartheid freedom, now invoked as the rights-bearing sovereign citizen subject of the new South Africa, hypothetically beyond race (because of his opposition to racism and its effects), who is celebrated in the naming of Dimbaza's new community centre as the Moses Twebe Great Hall. One is an image of postapartheid subjective certainty: Twebe is seated, alongside other elderly political statesmen, publicly recognised and named in the liberated space of the 'community' (Figure 8.2).

THE GRAVES OF DIMBAZA

Figure 8.3. Moses Twebe, his family and his goat, 15 March 2007.
Photographer: Gary Minkley

But, in the other photograph, where he stands with his family and his goat in front of his house, this subjective certainty slips (Figure 8.3). In part our reading is informed by our conversations with Twebe, his family and other residents of Dimbaza, in part also by the photograph itself: its self-staging at the corner of the house and the presence of the foregrounded goat, tethered to Twebe with rough rope while facing him, but, where the rope tangles the feet of the family, halting movement and progress and tying the family to a former 'homeland' place evoked by the goat. There are other signifiers – the flaking paint, single window and the edge of a zinc roof resonant of bantustan 'surplus' architecture; Twebe's ill-fitting jersey; the bearing of the family; and Twebe's own posture, that of a lonely, isolated, resigned man, set apart from even while alongside his family, literally and physically more attached to his goat than to the ties (here, of the looped rope) that bind him to his family. Narrative and visual knots, they bind Twebe 'into the interstices of bigger or older apparatuses, which then undergo a mutation', and return Twebe, and us, to the 'native' peasant, the 'native' worker, the 'native' former political prisoner – the racial subject (Deleuze xi). Liberation, seen through the coupling of these images, conjures the presence of an always native subject, permanently displaced out of sovereign time. In this way, liberation hinges on the colonial representational repertoires of the 'native' subject, where the spectral lines of race are retraced through a genealogy of the concept of anthropology, as well as of the concept of trusteeship and of postapartheid modernist development.

The goat in this image – tugged into the photograph at the insistence of Moses Twebe – provokes yet another line of flight. From the vantage point of Dimbaza's margins, 'the social' of apartheid and the postapartheid performs, and is performed, in several kinds of space in which different operations take place: what we might call 'other socials'. One such social space is that of regions, in which 'objects are clustered together and *boundaries* drawn around each cluster. Another is the network in which distance is a function of the *relations* between the elements and difference a matter of relational variety' (Mol & Law 643, emphasis added). These are the two topologies with which social theory is familiar and which have come to define the bantustan in the postapartheid. The first is old and secure (less so now because the bantustans have been incorporated into the new South Africa and have been replaced by regional definitions of progress and development), while the second, being newer, is still proud of its abilities to cross boundaries, just as Dimbaza's distance and difference are staged in zones, corridors, nodes and proximities to markets, jobs and services.

However, as Mol and Law argue, there are other kinds of space, too:

> Sometimes neither boundaries nor relations mark the difference between one place and another. Instead, sometimes boundaries come and go, allow leakage or disappear altogether, while relations transform themselves without fracture ... Entities may be similar and dissimilar at different locations, or in the same location and may transform themselves without creating difference. Sometimes then, social space behaves like a fluid (643).

Space enacts a more heterogeneous social; other socials. Thus, in locating 'the social' as a problem – marked by the heterogeneous and venturing into other or many socials – rather than as a given, we are concerned to examine the ways in which the social itself no longer invokes a common set of assumptions about society, culture, representation or methods by which we write and produce history or understanding. Rather, 'the social' and 'other socials' are constituted and, as importantly, *enacted* categories with various itineraries, agencies, actions and actors, modes of performativity and effects of subjectivation that need to be explored.

Following Hannah Arendt's conceptualisation of 'acts' as both 'governing and beginning' (177), we propose that to socially (en)act is to realise a rupture in the givenness of the social and to attend to the unexpected, unpredictable and unknown of the social. Moreover, following Engin Isin, social acts may also be read against habitus, practice, discipline and routine as the ordering qualities of how humans form and conduct the social. Social acts set actualisations in motion, but also a being that acts – within shifting forms of responsibility and answerability to changing affiliations, solidarities or hostilities – to 'begin itself' as subject. Social acts, then, articulate social agents both as object and as subject of history. Read as an act that constitutes the image, Moses Twebe's tugging of the goat into the frame is an act that is not in the image but is rather located there as a trace. Reading this as an act (as opposed to a staging or even crafting) fractures the social through which that image would usually be read. In Roland Barthes's terms, it goes beyond the *studium* (the social), beyond the *punctum* (perhaps recognising the ambiguity of Twebe's status), to the *spectrum* (that which haunts and thereby stays with us – the fracturing and interruption or unsettling of the social through such an act).

Thought in this way, Moses Twebe, in summoning the goat, becomes the 'being that acts', that begins itself as itself, as a subject. To consider such acts is to call into question a dominant cluster of issues in social and political thought that we can define as problems of orders and practices, and how they have become objects of social thought. What does Twebe's act mean? And what does it mean to consider it alongside rupture, disorder and deviation? Following Isin, what might it mean to consider it as 'a rupture in the given' (25)? Moses Twebe's act of summoning the goat, then, as evocative of the stubbornness of the fragments of race that adhere to the postapartheid social, has enabled the rupture in the given of that social, which in turn has enabled our 're: working' of race and our consideration of how race – in the figure of the native, peasant, rural, poor – and racism endure in the developmental postapartheid state.

The Moses Twebe Great Hall is the most visible monumental, indeed reterritorialised, 'object' of the legacy of struggle, liberation and the inheritance of 1994. But more significantly, the hall is a monument to the completed time of the struggle. It is a retemporalisation as well as a detemporalisation, marked between Twebe himself and the Great Hall he becomes. It is the legacy as well as the public history not only of an empire but of a single simple history, that of the inheritance of struggle. At the same time, Twebe is one of those who, despite their proximity to the struggle, were forgotten after 1990; the edifice that is the Moses Twebe Great Hall makes a claim on him in the name of an 'empire of liberation', and in the process once again forgets the real Moses Twebe. In the photograph with the goat (Figure 8.3), what is suddenly emergent, 'what comes together in a flash with the now' (Benjamin, *The Arcades Project* 642), forms a constellation of the subject of freedom, the native subject, the peasant, the worker, and the 'ex prison politicians'.

In this constellation, Dimbaza is always the dumping ground for prisoner politicians; Moses Twebe becomes the hall even as the actual body of Moses Twebe, ragged and with its goat, always remains displaced, the 'before' and, simultaneously, the embodied 'here' and 'after' of this inheritance. He is the figure who accepts what is given – the hall – and returns to what can only remain – the 'rural native'. Here, then, are the two folds that we invoke in the 'empire of liberation': the paradigm of empire, in which the responsibility of the sovereign is given effect in the form of the Great Hall; and the paradigm of the will or testament, in which liberation is bequeathed to the heirs of the hall. The empire seemingly returns liberation in the form of newly built material space yet, ironically and simultaneously, holds Twebe's body and other veteran bodies of Dimbaza – the native 'worker-peasant' family with a goat – at a remove from its very empty, unoccupied and fenced structures, as if awaiting the ritual temporalities of Freedom Day celebrations. It is a fraught act: one of erasure that becomes clear with reference to Twebe's actual life and to a Dimbaza that does not 'hold' or inherit a politics of liberation in the new time of freedom. What this entails in Dimbaza is that Moses Twebe and others, in order to be figured as recipients of this trust and beneficiaries of the new empire, have to be repetitively located in an earlier time, essentially in the time of the native.

Image/archive/testimony

What we have tried to do is to reread the peculiarity of South Africa's history of 'internal colonialism' or CST 'no longer as [only] a matter of territory and the economy', but instead as 'a way of understanding the distinct and yet coinciding folding temporalities lived by South Africa's communities as they have journeyed *together*, belatedly but relatively rapidly, towards modernity' (Pechey 155). What coincides in Dimbaza 'are not two "superstructural" spheres on one "infrastructure" but rather so many "nows" lived alongside each other'. With Graham Pechey, we want to place discourse, language, image, imagination – and the concept of empire – at the centre of this 're: working'. The 'internality' of this form of colonialism can then be understood metaphorically as a redescription of 'South Africa' that bypasses the grand categories of the geopolitical and the world-historical in a new emphasis upon the dialogue that underlies all antagonism, the competing utopias that speak to each other inwardly even as their narrators outwardly turn laws and guns on each other.

While we are wary of Pechey's 'positive tone', we have been intrigued by the concept of 'so many "nows" liv[ing] alongside each other' in Dimbaza and have tried to think through – by way of a kind of interpretative montage – the assemblage, the multiplicity of folds, that can be pieced together out of the always already fragmentary archive of image, text and testimony.

There is another meaning of 'legacy' that explains the multiplicity of the archive of Dimbaza. 'Legacy', as John Mowitt has pointed out, is also associated with the Latin verb *lego* – to choose, select, appoint, collect, gather, bring together, take, steal, traverse, pass through, read (aloud), recite, and, coupled with *lēx* ('a formal motion for a law'), to dispatch, send an ambassador, deputise. It is this choosing, collecting, bringing together, this reading aloud and passing through that constitutes the 'archive' of Dimbaza. But the way in which dispatching and deputising these fragments reveal them as themselves constellations without subjective certainty has also informed our 're: working' of spatial and temporal acts through the concept of empire. Even the small selection of photographs in this chapter evokes the possibilities held within them. Benjamin has alerted us to the force of image and language and to the dialectical relationship between them and the past and present:

> It's not that what is past casts its light on what is present, or what is present its light on what is past; rather, image is that wherein what has been comes together in a flash with now to form a constellation. In other words, image is dialectics at a standstill. For while the relation of the present to the past is a purely temporal, continuous one, the relation of what-has-been to the now is dialectical: is not progression, but image, suddenly emergent. Only dialectical images are genuine images (that is not archaic); and the place where one encounters them is language. [N2a,3] (*The Arcades Project* 462).

> In the dialectical image, what has been within a particular epoch is always, simultaneously, 'what has been from time immemorial'. As such, however, it is manifest, on each occasion, only to a quite specific epoch – namely, the one in which humanity, rubbing its eyes, recognizes just this particular dream image as such. It is at this moment that the historian takes up, with regard to that image, the task of dream interpretation [N4, 1] ... The realization of dream elements in the course of waking up is the canon of dialectics. It is paradigmatic for the thinker and binding for the historian [N4, 4].

If Benjamin's *Arcades Project* 'deals with awakening from the nineteenth century' (464), the images of Dimbaza (in text, film, letters, photographs) urge an awakening from the somnambulant dark dreams of the long twentieth century (Baucom).

In the interviews that form part of the Dimbaza archive, most of them recorded in the early 2000s, the political prisoners (or 'prisoner politicians', as Moses Twebe named them) reinserted and reterritorialised themselves into the liberation movement, as always 'in struggle', always protesting, always marking themselves as political. In this way, these interviews reproduce a postapartheid heroic liberation discourse. But the letters that are part of the IDAF collection call this into question, especially those written at the time of the 'cut', in 1991, the moment when national liberation seemed to have been realised. Their authors, like Moses Twebe, realised that they would remain displaced, would be unable to enter the discourse or the 'real' of liberation time or reconstitute for themselves the field for the exercise of sovereign power. 'What do we do now, now we are left once more desolate and abandoned, with the germ of destruction among us?'[9] That 'germ of destruction' in the form of tuberculosis, as Randall Packard reminded us years ago, originates in the political economy of racial health practices.

For those proximate to the territory of liberation but also reterritorialised, relocated and reinserted in the space of Dimbaza, the limits of historical political change were readily apparent. Ironically, political prisoners released in 1991 would receive more attention than this 'old guard', who had basically been banished to the periphery of South Africa and its politics. For them, the weighty changes of 1990 would mean only further marginalisation and loss, including the loss of a vital lifeline – IDAF – to the outside world.

> It's not that one doesn't want to work, we used not to be employed and now the trouble is when you seek work you are told you are too old for work at the sametime [sic] too young to qualify for old age pension. We are truly going to suffer as we have already started now because we don't know who is really going to be responsible for us i.e. EX PRISON POLITICIANS.[10]

Suffering, responsibility, anticipation, failure, future? Multiple temporalities and so many uncertain nows that are held together in the dream images of the ghost town of Dimbaza. Metaphorically represented as the seeds/germ of destruction in the last letter (in a series of 120) from MMS, and in the context of latter-day ANC/nationalism, there is a certain irony in the fact that the support of IDAF ended right at the time of direst need, when the enduring liberal-radical elements of a colonial empire were being replaced by one of liberation:

> It hurts to think that we won't be hearing from you anymore. Above all when now Khanyiso is becoming an invalid yesterday he was given or rather done T.B. Tests which showed he has a Tuberculosis germ in his blood and is to receive treatment for 6 months.
>
> Oh! Carma you have no idea how we feel to part with you just at the time of difficulties 'cos Khanyiso is on drugs for epilepsy now its T.B.[11]

This letter, like many others, resonates with the possibility that one of the features of the postapartheid is that liberation may no longer be territorialised but is instead retemporalised, in the body of the subject of liberation, in the remaking of dependence within different structures of empire.

If 'liberation' is the absence or ending of subjection, then, in the moment of liberation, of the subject being made free, the externalisation, the-having-been-made-extensive (outside, dependent) of the subject is clear to the knowing returning subject who has experienced the being made external and dependent. As the letters and the postapartheid realities of Dimbaza show, liberation as the ending of subjection does not end externalisation or dependency. In this flash, empire and liberation rub up against each other, are folded into each other – raising the spectre of the continuation of empire relations in the time of liberation, a permanent future in which the subject remains forever native and displaced.

Image and letter, montaged together here, constitute a moment 'wherein what has been comes together in a flash with now to form a constellation' (Benjamin, *The Arcades Project* 642). Something is opened up between the spatiality of the South African colonial 'empire' and the temporal 'empire' of liberation. To return to Pechey one more time, 'in South Africa colony and metropolis are co-extensive – not separated geographically, but (as it were) one on top of the other in the same territory' (154). But, as we have tried to show, 'empire' – thought of as relations of unequal power that involve the imposition and externalisation of the subject (thought also as practice *and* meaning) – is also, at certain points in time, coincident and marked by temporalities that are entangled, enmeshed, folded into each other.

Thinking 'empire' as both spatial and temporal opens up the post- (postapartheid, postcolonial, post-empire), and calls into question the distancing from things past. It demands a contemplation of the complexity of 'empire' (of colonial relations of externality that continue to mark out and seep through the social and its infinite, tenacious, enduring legacies and inheritances). It summons us to the urgent task of understanding, imagining, approaching and rendering intelligible (and the present continuous is chosen deliberately here) the question, the problem and the 'moral and epistemic contours' (Scott 3) 'of racial hate, humiliation [and] cruelty' (Didi-Huberman 154) in Dimbaza's global present.

The film *Last Grave at Dimbaza* resonates not only with the montaged readability of temporal and spatial connections, but also with significant discontinuities in respect of its stated intent. While it is perhaps easy to read the film – in its simple shots, omniscient narration, its articulation of separateness and territoriality – as an exposé, it is also pervaded by an unintended sense of relative apathy and the depiction of its documented subjects as passive victims needing empire (the global anti-apartheid) to save them. In a different sense, though, the film attempts to mark the unique, particular territory of South Africa (as both urban apartheid capitalist state and rural impoverished bantustan) through signposts, maps, journeys, movement and interiors, to signify the central role of black labour in producing white privilege and to open it to global intervention. Read positively, the film globalises apartheid, interpellating the complicity of an 'empire' of capitalist interests with apartheid (through its multiple shots of major international companies 'doing business' in South Africa – globalisation in the 1960s and 1970s) and foreshadowing the overdue stirrings of a global anti-apartheid movement.

But in montaging random, non-indexical film footage and images from all over South Africa (East London, Langa, Durban, Johannesburg, Soweto, Dimbaza, to name but a few), it literally de-deterritorialises its own setting, loses place, loses its place, and unintentionally 'unmarks' the territory of South Africa in order to open it to the global. In effect, the film reterritorialises Dimbaza (effectively through its naming and in its ending) as not just or simply South Africa, but as in and of the global. For there to be the 'last grave', it is this kind of global externalisation, this making extensive of a dependency in sovereign 'liberated' time, that is required. As such, the film marks the prelude to the empire of liberation.

More compelling and occasioning further disturbances is the music. Composed by Philip Tabane and Malombo, the soundtrack is like a lament that marks the graves and desolation, and anticipates something different. It is a requiem, a mass for the deceased. It is also, in its dirge-like soundings and phrasings, a command (to political action), and a guide to direct another possible deterritorialisation. In some senses, it refuses to be contained in either the film's appeal to American or British empire or by South African empire (it was smuggled overseas on a South African Airways flight, a symbol of South African modernity).[12] In its slow sadness, though, the music directs a listening, and a sounding of a premature burial or laying to rest, and anticipates an ongoing soundtrack to the empire of liberation. There is no last grave under the sign of apartheid in Dimbaza, and the funeral is the defining temporality enacted in its postapartheid social.

When *Last Grave at Dimbaza* was rescreened on South African television as part of the so-called *Unbanned* series in 1995, the film was introduced and framed both by one of its producers, Nana Mahomo, and by the cultural commentator Sandile Dikeni, and self-consciously retemporalised, not into the postapartheid discourse of reconciliation, which was the intent of the *Unbanned* series, but as part of 'the search for truth about South Africa, [and] the past [that] isn't dead, it isn't even past'.

Interpretative montage: Imagination and history

In 're: working' 'empire' and 'liberation' through the metaphor and the archive of Dimbaza, we have returned to trying to think that which haunts the 'perilous critical moment' of the postapartheid. No matter how prodigious the archive, in the face of the violence contained in it, what remains of Dimbaza is fragmentary and illusive, flawed and disjunctive, ghostly and brittle. The fragment, or the 'vestige', as Georges Didi-Huberman reminds us, presupposes destruction at the same time as resisting or surviving destruction. Race was always enfolded into the class struggle to which the mimeograph machine was set. What has become legible for us in the postapartheid is not that discovery or capture motivated the burial of the machine, but rather 'the question of race' or, more particularly, the 'spectre of race'. Abiding by Dimbaza allows us to think the meaning of this spectre through the montage of the mimeograph's burial here. The tracings of the act of its burial – read as a performed repression of a reproductive machine – name what the undercurrents of the tropes of race and class were working to guarantee: the reproduction of a particular kind of subject. Read imaginatively back to this performed act, it is not the vanguard, but the rearguard for the reproduction of formations of race within the empire of liberation.

To sift through the debris and the ruins that remain (of history, of the archive) is to create a type of (interpretative) montage that folds into and over each other the haunting memories, the testimony, the letters, the images of Dimbaza. It is a montage that, like Tabane and Malombo's dirge or lament, moves slowly, repeats concepts, accumulates wrongs, accretes meaning, syncopates doubt and redemption, and thereby addresses itself to the 'ethics of the relation created ... between the image [text, concepts] [and imagination] and history' (Didi-Huberman 125).

> Montage is valuable only when it doesn't hasten to conclude or to close: it is valuable when it opens up our apprehension of history and makes it more complex, not when it falsely schematizes; when it gives us access to the singularities of time and hence to its essential multiplicity (121).

Benjamin argued that when an era ends, 'history decays into images, not into stories' (*The Arcades Project* 476). As Buck-Morss has noted, 'Without the narration of continuous progress, the images of the past resemble night dreams, the "first mark" of which, Freud tells us, is their emancipation from "the spatial and temporal order of events"' (68). What might the night dreams of Dimbaza resemble, as its spatial (South African empire) and temporal (empire of liberation) orders break down? The images, burning in the David Russell archive, discarded for their lack of indexicality, become both prophetic and dream images. As such, they refuse the conjugated 'empire' subjects of apartheid and liberation, and show absence from the 'not all there is to see' that they provoke (Didi-Huberman 124). To paraphrase Didi-Huberman, 'Any act of the image that is snatched from the impossible description of a reality becomes a *haunting memory*, a *scourge of imagining*, a proliferation of figures – of resemblances and differences – around the same vortex of time' (125, original emphasis). And to return to Buck-Morss, such images are 'complex webs of memory and desire wherein past experience is rescued, and perhaps, redeemed' (68). However, as she continues,

> Only partial interpretations of these images are possible, and in a critical light. But they may be helpful if they illuminate patches of the past that seem to have a charge of energy about them precisely because the dominant narrative does not connect them seamlessly to the present. The historical particulars might then be free to enter into different constellations of meaning ... To be engaged in the historical task of surprising rather than explaining the present – more avant-garde than vanguard in its temporality – may prove at the end of the century to be politically worth our while (69).

'Where we perceive a chain of events,' Benjamin's angel of history 'sees one single catastrophe which keeps piling wreckage and hurls it in front of his feet' ('Über den Begriff der Geschichte' IX). The storm that we call progress 'has got caught in his wings with such a violence that the angel can no longer close them. The storm irresistibly propels him into the future to which his back is turned, while the pile of debris before him grows skyward'. Is there an angel of history in Dimbaza? If so, she is a very little girl, a child, angel, ghost of the township or bantustan, by montaged implication left alone on a road that fades into the distance, as shown in the concluding images of *Last Grave at Dimbaza*. Unlike Benjamin's angel, this little girl, dressed in a white cardigan, hesitates and turns away – and we with her – from (or is it towards?) the empty graves 'dug in preparation for the next month's toll',[13] from the forgotten printing press buried on the banks of the Liesbeek River – its dreams of a non-racial social withheld – and from the past and present dream world of promises, doubts and betrayals. But the dirt at her (and our) feet is made up of the debris – the rearguard – of race and a future held in trust.

NOTES
1. 'Diagrams' or 'maps' for Gilles Deleuze, 'fragments, regions and levels' for Michel Foucault, that, following Georges Didi-Huberman, invite a resonant montaged readability of temporal discontinuity and of imaginatively putting the multiple and the disintegrated in motion, isolating nothing, showing the hiatuses and the analogies, the indeterminations and the overdeterminations.
2. 'The South African Question' (1928 Resolution adopted by the Executive Committee of the Communist International), Appendix to Lerumo.
3. John Mowitt uses the term 're: working', 're, colon, space, working, ... as a novel way to translate Bertolt Brecht's concept of *umfunktionierung*. More typically, this term is translated either as re-functioning or repurposing, perhaps even reconstructing, all perfectly reasonable choices except for the fact that they fail to capture an important theoretical, even political resonance of the term. Specifically, they drop the reflexivity that mattered to Brecht, a reflexivity that allowed him to suggest that "re: working" radio had to be as much about radio as about work itself. In effect, radio

implicates the labor of our reflection about it in the effort to recast its purpose' (Mowitt 6).

4. We are reminded here of Slavoj Žižek's joke, in *The Plague of Fantasies*, about the man who leaves the work camp each day and has his wheelbarrow checked to make sure he is not stealing anything, but he is in fact stealing wheelbarrows.

5. Since 1992, the IDAF Collection has been part of the University of the Western Cape's Robben Island Mayibuye Archives, at UWC, Bellville, South Africa.

6. As did, similarly, Cosmas Desmond's *The Discarded People*, which drew the world's attention to forced removals and 'separate development resettlement' and inspired the making of the film.

7. After the political transformation of South Africa in 1990, de-industrialisation in turn transformed it into a ghost town; invisible, peripheral and forgotten. What remains visible of Dimbaza, marked by the repetition of the empty rusting skeletons of its factories and warehouses, is the hypocrisy of apartheid and the hollowness of liberation promises.

8. We might think of these new relations and strategies that ensue from the disruption to and within these sites of contestation and the circuits/networks of institutional practices that make up a territory, as a form of 'reterritorialisation' of empire or, read slightly differently, as a positive form of deterritorialisation, a line of flight that leads to 'reterritorialization in an entirely new assemblage' – the 'empire of liberation' (Jacobs 267; Patton 143).

9. Letter, MMS 1991, IDAF/Mayibuye.

10. Letter, MMS 1991, IDAF/Mayibuye.

11. Letter, MMS 1991, IDAF/Mayibuye.

12. 'Mahomo's film statement was clearly not intended for use within South Africa. His intention was to influence foreign decision makers in Britain and the United States, to shift policy from the *National Security Study Memorandum 39* (NSSM 39) mentality, adopted by the Nixon administration in February 1970' (O'Meara 8).

13. Voiceover from *Last Grave at Dimbaza*.

REFERENCES

Agamben, Giorgio. *Homo Sacer: Sovereign Power and Bare Life*. Stanford UP, 1998.

Arendt, Hannah. *The Human Condition*. U of Chicago P, 1958.

Barthes, Roland. *Camera Lucida*. Hill and Wang, 1981.

Baucom, Ian. *Specters of the Atlantic: Finance Capital, Slavery, and the Philosophy of History*. Duke UP, 2005.

Benjamin, Walter. 'Über den Begriff der Geschichte (On the Concept of History/ Theses on the Philosophy of History).' 1940, www.mxks.de/files/phil/ Benjamin.GeschichtsThesen.html. Accessed 8 August 2016.

———. *The Arcades Project*. Translated by Howard Eiland and Kevin McLaughlin, Harvard UP, 1999.

Buck-Morss, Susan. *Dreamworld and Catastrophe: The Passing of Mass Utopia in East and West*. MIT Press, 2002.

Burger, John. *The Black Man's Burden*. Victor Gollancz, 1944.

Deleuze, Gilles. 'Foreword.' *The Policing of Families*, Jacques Donzelot, translated by Robert Hurley, Pantheon Books, 1979, pp. ix–xvii.

Deleuze, Gilles and Guattari, Felix. *A Thousand Plateaus: Capitalism and Schizophrenia*, translated by Brian Massumi, Continuum, 1987.

Derrida, Jacques. 'Racism's Last Word.' *Critical Inquiry*, vol. 12, no. 1, Autumn 1985, pp. 290–299.

Desmond, Cosmas. *The Discarded People: An Account of African Resettlement*. The Christian Institute of South Africa, 1970.

Didi-Huberman, Georges. *Images in Spite of All: Four Photographs from Auschwitz*. Translated by Shane B. Lillis, U of Chicago P, 2008.

Foucault, Michel. *'Society Must Be Defended': Lectures at the Collège de France, 1975–1976*. Picador, 2003.

Hardt, Michael and Antonio Negri. *Multitude: War and Democracy in the Age of Empire*. Penguin Books, 2004.

Hayes, Patricia. 'Santu Mofokeng, Photographs: "The Violence Is in the Knowing".' *History and Theory*, vol. 48, no. 4, 2009, pp. 34–51.

Isin, Engin. 'Theorising Acts of Citizenship.' *Acts of Citizenship*, edited by Engin Isin and Greg Nielsen, Zed Books, 2008, pp. 15–43.

Jacobs, Keith. 'Territorial Modes of Governance and the Discourses of Community Reaction in the State of Tasmania.' *Space and Polity*, vol. 11, no. 3, 2007, pp. 263–277.

Last Grave at Dimbaza. Directed by Chris Curling and Pascoe Macfarlane, Tricontinental Films, 1974.

Lerumo, A. (Michael Harmel). *Fifty Fighting Years: The South African Communist Party 1921–1971*. Inkululeko Publications, 1971.

Mol, Annemarie and John Law. 'Regions, Networks and Fluids: Anaemia and Social Topology.' *Social Studies of Science*, vol. 24, no. 4, 1994, pp. 641–671.

Mowitt, John. 'The Humanities and the University in Ruin.' Dean's Lecture, University of the Western Cape, 13 June 2011.

O'Meara, Patrick. 'Black Man Alive. Last Grave at Dimbaza. Land of Promise. Films on South Africa.' *Jump Cut*, no. 18, August 1978, www.ejumpcut.org/archive/onlinessays/JC18folder/SoAfricFilms.html. Accessed 8 August 2016.

Packard, Randall. *White Plague, Black Labor: Tuberculosis and the Political Economy of Health and Disease in South Africa*. U of California P, 1989.

Patton, Paul. *Deleuzian Concepts: Philosophy, Colonization, Politics*. Stanford UP, 2010.

Pechey, Graham. 'Post-Apartheid Narratives.' *Colonial Discourse/Postcolonial Theory*, edited by Francis Barker, Peter Hulme and Margaret Iversen, Manchester UP, 1994, pp. 151–171.

Pohlandt-McCormick, Helena and Gary Minkley. 'The Graves of Dimbaza and the Empire of Liberation.' *Journal of Southern African Studies*, vol. 41, no. 3, 2015, pp. 617–634.

Scott, David. *Refashioning Futures: Criticism after Postcoloniality*. Princeton UP, 1999.

Van Bever Donker, Maurits. 'The Cut of the Body: The Necessity of Contingency and the Contingency of Necessity'. PhD preliminary exam, University of Minnesota, 2010.

Žižek, Slavoj. *The Plague of Fantasies*. Verso, 1997.

CHAPTER 9
THE PRINCIPLE OF INSUFFICIENCY: ETHICS AND COMMUNITY AT THE EDGE OF THE SOCIAL
Maurits van Bever Donker

> Either ethics makes no sense at all, or this is what it means and has nothing else to say: not to be unworthy of what happens to us (Deleuze 149).

Community works. This is not to suggest that community should be taken as a given or, indeed, as that at which we must arrive, as that whose construction presents a redemptive hope for our present. Rather, it is at play, always, whether as a differential that produces racial formations (such as the invocation of 'the community' at the centre of apartheid legislation)[1] or as a constitutive limit enabling the thinking of what might come after apartheid. In other words, it is already operative, in each instance perhaps, as a function of enclosure for identity or as an unstable edge that flirts with an expression of the new. This is to suggest that limits, markers of the edge of community, in turn function not only as boundaries or curtailments, but also as openings, unfolding on their motile edges towards the new: the opening of a terrain not enclosed within the particularity of the membrane that the limit implies and, I suggest, on which a postapartheid subjectivity might arrive. This subjectivity, this *possible* subjectivity, is the living, mutating ground from which a 'community of the touch', to use a turn of phrase from Jean-Luc Nancy's 'The Inoperative Community', might emerge: this touch does not penetrate; it knows nothing of being enclosed in a common skin but rather plays on the surface, abiding in a proximity that touches, always. It is this question of the subject, a sense of subjectivity at its own edge as the constitutive limit for community, which this chapter explores.

It is, however, not simply an abstract question. The question of community and the social is threaded with the persistence of what can be understood as apartheid's remainders as these cut into the potentialities of life in our present. Indeed, it seems that an urgent demand of the present moment in South Africa is for life to be practised, or at least for such a practice to be learned, in the wake of apartheid.[2] These remainders, the persistence of the limit *qua* limit and its enclosure of subjectivities within reified expressions of race, ask of us that we think the social in a more conceptual and yet rigorously lived sense. More particularly, I contend that it is through an attempt at thinking the social in this way that it becomes possible to make sense of the demand that life in the postapartheid remains to be learned.

In this chapter I examine this problem in three stages. In the first, I construct a sense of community as a concept that hinges on what Maurice Blanchot names, reading Georges Bataille, as 'the principle of insufficiency' (5). Through reading Blanchot's *The Unavowable Community*, I suggest that the productive edge of community is operative precisely at that point where the subject is not enclosed within subjective certainty. Locating this edge as a gift, in the second stage of this chapter I bring this into relation with Claude Levi-Strauss's reading of community as it functions in the Oedipus myth. In particular, it is in the character of Antigone that I begin to texture the principle of insufficiency in relation to the weight of everyday life: the constitutive struggle between autochthony and copulation. It is through positing a principle of insufficiency as an organising concept for the self and the social that I suggest a productive and ethical edge is opened for thinking. In the final stage I press this edge further through reading Phaswane Mpe's intervention on the formation of this concept in his novel, *Welcome to Our Hillbrow*. As such, my reading presses Mpe's intervention beyond that of a work of mourning, or elegy, or indeed of a reinscription of humanism from an African perspective, as important as all of these are.[3] Rather, I suggest that *Welcome to Our Hillbrow* elicits a particular reading from its reader, a reading that sets to work on the very terrain that structures the terms for a work of mourning or an expression of humanism.

While Blanchot is brilliant in his reading of the lines of community and its relation to the self, and Levi-Strauss's reading of the role of emergence in the Oedipus myth is instrumental for a refiguring of the problem of indigeneity as this comes to bear on the social, it is, I argue, in Mpe's intervention that a sense of the ethical adequate to the concept of community and to 'lived experience' is formulated. This is not to suggest a simple progression between these texts, or that Mpe's novel should be reduced to the interpretative framework of the former. Rather, in bringing these into relation with each other I construct a particular weave that enables a sense of the ethical, in line with the epigraph to this chapter, as being 'adequate to that which happens to us', an ethical and philosophical point of view that Mpe's intervention produces in relation to the problem of lived experience in postapartheid South Africa. In short, his novel 're-works', in a Benjaminian sense, the social and ethics so as to offer itself as a practice for the learning of life, of learning to learn, on the terrain of the motile edge of community.[4]

On the edge of community

In *The Unavowable Community*, Blanchot produces a sense of the concept of community that can be read as resistant to the disciplinary strictures of the state or religion – in other words, as resistant to its figuring in the light of a redemptive notion. As Blanchot phrases it, community is always painted, in the narratives of history, on the background of disaster and is, as such, always turned towards the possibility of a new humanity. Stated differently, political community is always offered as a means through which to overcome, or at least to come to terms with, a particular trauma; a coming to terms that requires, ultimately, a new sense of the human to be effective. This formulation clearly resonates across many attempts to think the transition into the postapartheid, and indeed into what is now understood as the problematic of global apartheid, particularly through a consideration of the connections between ethics, politics and community.[5] What is striking in this formulation is the insistence on the creation of the new, a refusal to deliver the concept of community into such a straightforwardly redemptive narrative, where community is that which either redeems us or is redeemed through our return to it. Rather, Blanchot wants to preserve the concept of community from the tendency for it to be folded into 'the state', and the expressions of the subject and its attendant communities that constitute its terrain. As he argues in his later discussion of Marguerite Duras's *The Malady of Death*, community and, by extension, the indefinable category of 'the people ... are not the State, not any more than they are the society in person, with its functions, its laws, its determinations, its exigencies which constitute its most proper finality' (33). The productivity of the concept of community needs to be pressed beyond the confines of a political programme. The key, for Blanchot, is located in the task of thinking what he calls 'the absence of community' (3), to think how the unworking of community might, ultimately, be integral to how it works. This, it seems, extends beyond community as such, touching rather on the sense of the subject.

For Blanchot, thinking this absence requires more than an understanding of absence as lack, as though community is that which must be produced so as to make the social whole. Instead, resisting this quasi-Freudian sense through which the subject and community come to be constituted through a lack, Blanchot orients his development of the concept through Bataille's insistence that there is 'the principle of insufficiency at the root of all being' (4). Insufficiency, in this instance, does not imply that being can be understood as an attempt to attain sufficiency. Rather than a principle that seeks to bring itself to completion (that is, to satisfy itself), Blanchot argues that for Bataille insufficiency 'cannot be derived from a model of sufficiency [as it searches for] the excess of a lack that grows ever deeper even as it fills itself up' (8). This can perhaps be most easily grasped through the example of the face-to-face encounter. Blanchot argues, in a formulation that discloses his proximity to Emmanuel Levinas, that the individual can only ever know itself as an individual in the moment of an encounter with an other.[6] This is to say that an 'I' only ever recognises itself as an 'I' in the recognition of an other's recognition of this. In short, we are only ourselves among other selves. This, it seems, immediately voids the claim to subjective certainty, as the recognition of this is only ever located in a contest between others. Although Hegel produces a similar conundrum in the assertion of subjective certainty, for him the struggle is to assert the 'I' as *mine*, and thereby to silence the disquieting effect of the insufficiency that echoes at the root of all being.[7] It is in that contest that being takes place, which is to say that the 'I' can never assert its individuality as an individuality as such. In Blanchot's formulation, 'a being is either alone or knows itself to be alone only when it is not' (5).

While the principle of insufficiency names the condition whereby, for the subject, being can only take place in the contest with others, this is not equivalent to the assertion of a fusional multiplicity, as though being is simply a holding in common.[8] What distinguishes it from a fusional multiplicity, which Blanchot likens to an existence as a herd, is that insufficiency actually does result in individuation, even if it is only an individuation that is already impossible even as it takes place. As he says of Bataille's sense of insufficiency: 'It is however not as easy as all that to understand' (8).

If this development of the principle of insufficiency is correct, then its most clear instance can be located in the moment in which an 'I' witnesses the death of an other who is, for it, the principle of its own recognition as an 'I'. To state this plainly: it is in the death of the other that my awareness of myself as individual also dies. Only an 'I' can witness the other's death, but this 'I', which has been brought into consciousness through that other, precisely in that moment of that other's death, can no longer witness that death in relation to *this I*. This is, perhaps, the starkest example of insufficiency, where being takes place, and, in a dramatic shift away from the political uses of community that Blanchot tries to unsettle, it constitutes the disaster on which the concept of community is painted. This concept, in order to be adequate to the principle of insufficiency, needs to acquire a sense of absence.

Produced in the limit-experience of the encounter with an other that is the most adequate expression of being (it is its principle), absence is precisely that to which the concept of community must become adequate.

Community, however, as its name implies, is worked out in collections of persons or groups. Holding onto this difficulty whereby absence would seem to directly contradict community, and recalling the tendency for absence similarly to be located in the production of a master signifier through lack, Blanchot offers a reading of a society associated with Bataille named 'Acéphale' – literally, 'headless'. In it, Blanchot reads the possibility of an offer of the impossible 'gift' of community (13). To be clear, the principle of insufficiency, as that to which community must be adequate, implies both that community must be resistant to the production of a sense of subjective certainty and, consequently, that it must resist its production through a programme, as this latter assumes the former as its condition of possibility. Acéphale was to be established as a community through the willing sacrifice of a victim, who was to be sacrificed in the simultaneous suicide of the performer of the ritual. This ritual – which never occurred – would have refused the possibility of either figure in the community being established with the subjective certainty of the agent, or as sovereign, as a figure whose absence unifies the community into One. It is this unity through the sacrifice of the figure which becomes sovereign that structures the quasi-Freudian sense of community which finds its repetition in the centrality of the Oedipus myth in psychoanalysis. While this ritual, as a principle, would be adequate to the sense of insufficiency through its refusal of the subjective certainty of the self, it would fail precisely through its role as a ritual: it would be a work, a programme, designed to produce community and, as such, would violate the very conditions necessary for a successful expression of community.

Blanchot, however, reads this failure as a gift, as the condition of possibility of the new. Rather than producing a community structured around the death of the father, what is produced in the failure of Acéphale is the gift of 'infinite abandonment' to insufficiency, the unworking work of community (16). This is not, however, a gift that can be grasped through its retention in some form of 'intimate' 'inner experience' that could potentially accommodate the absence of the other (16). Rather, what most clearly emerges from Bataille's sense of insufficiency is that

THE PRINCIPLE OF INSUFFICIENCY

the self emerges as such only in the movement to the outside that is produced in the moment of encounter with an other. This is to say that that which is most intimate, namely the knowledge of the insufficiency that is primarily one's own but that one can never adequately know except in the death of the other, which both reveals it and makes it impossible, is always located in the site where being takes place. While it is clear that this 'ecstasy' always 'runs the risk' of being marked as 'the individual' – a risk that is most often realised – Blanchot suggests that it is precisely this movement to the outside that enables a different thinking of community, one offered in 'the paradoxical form of the book' (17).[9] Paradoxical, precisely, as it always works in multiple directions.

Writing, as a form of communication rather than an act of communion, not only mimics the movement towards the outside that is co-constitutive with the principle of being, but in fact operates as precisely such a movement. It is in reading, understood as a form of literary community, a community produced through what Nancy names as 'touch', that the communication of writing is grasped, as Blanchot phrases it: 'Reading – *the unworking labour of the work* – is not absent from [the friendship of the encounter with the other], though it belongs at times to the vertigo of drunkenness' (22, emphasis added). What this metaphor of drunken vertigo offers is the sense in which the friend, in its moment of enunciation (the friend reads the text), 'absents itself' much like a drunk friend who passes out, ensuring that communication does not slide into communion (25). The touch that occurs in the moment of reading (which is an entirely passive work in the sense that it does not produce a text) holds out the potential through which an adequate sense of the subject and of community might emerge: a touch of the absent and yet destined-to-be-repeated communication of the writer and the reader. It is in this realisation that Blanchot locates a sense of community as 'unavowable' – it cannot be declared, or claimed, in advance (46). In contrast with a sense of community that comes to be associated with the language of autochthony, with 'earth', 'blood' and 'race', in other words with homogeneity, Blanchot offers a sense of community 'gathered around a choice', which both makes it possible and immediately denies

231

its possibility (46), a choice not unlike Antigone's affirmation of the right to bury her brother. In the absence of the potential to build community through a sovereign act of the will, what such an elective community might offer is the capacity to think new concepts in relation to the always present and yet already absent community of the touch.

Between autochthony and copulation

Perhaps one of the clearest articulations of the potentialities of such an 'elective community' can be found in *Antigone*, the first play by the Greek playwright Sophocles that deals with questions surrounding the myth of Oedipus. As is well known, the character of Antigone constitutes the central node through which the problematic of justice is expressed in relation to the state, the law, gender and deity. Stated differently, Antigone presents the very sense of community that Blanchot resists as a problem for thought and that I intimated above as a limit for the thinking of the postapartheid. It is for this reason, especially Antigone's explicit foregrounding of the tension between these two different concepts of community, as well as the centrality of the Oedipus myth in Western thought and the manner in which its terms haunt *Welcome to Our Hillbrow*, that I seek to both abide by and trouble a reading of this myth offered by Lévi-Strauss.

Inasmuch as Antigone's role in the myth as a monster (of a peculiar type due to incest) enables her to function in the manner that she does, it is worth elucidating the role of the monster with some care, especially as this figure repeats, persistently, in Mpe's troubling of community. There are two conventional monsters in the myth: the Dragon and the Sphinx. The Dragon is the first to appear and is that which would prevent the founding of Thebes (the slaughtering of Cadmus' men) and, consequently, is killed by Cadmus. It is, however, from the cultivation of the Dragon's teeth that the Spartoi emerge from the ground and assist in the city's founding. Quite clearly, as Lévi-Strauss argues, the Dragon symbolises an autochthonous sense of becoming: the founders of the city emerge from the earth, a sense of becoming that is similarly signalled by the Sphinx as a chthonic creature. However, both these creatures are killed by men.

THE PRINCIPLE OF INSUFFICIENCY

As such, Lévi-Strauss argues that their structural role in the myth is to signal the 'denial of the autochthonous origin of man' (215). It is in the names of *men* that Lévi-Strauss suggests the opposite function to these creatures is to be located, as the names of Oedipus (swollen foot), his father Laios (left-sided) and his grandfather Labdacos (lame), all indicate difficulty with walking or lameness. Their names, he suggests, indicate a persistence of the 'autochthonous origin of man', to the extent that this difficulty in walking marks them as 'born from the earth' (216). Walking, quite literally, is a function of standing upright, of becoming bipedal and extending oneself away from the earth. These characters slaughter the most evident expressions of autochthonous origin, and yet carry in their names the very unravelling of that act of separation.

The tension between these two functions is reinforced, according to Lévi-Strauss, through a resonant pair of functions, namely the 'overvaluing of blood relations' (that is, community as constituted through family) and the 'undervaluing' of the same that is evidenced, on the one hand, in the search for Europa, Oedipus' marriage to Jacosta and the burial of Polynices and, on the other, by the killing of Laios and the mutual killing of the brothers Polynices and Eteocles (214–215). As such, Lévi-Strauss contends that it is the scaffolding of this tension (a tension that he suggests similarly structures the Freudian iteration of the myth) that forms the function of myth more generally. Myth, it would seem, operates as a stage on which the tension between these two understandings of community and the social can be held. To support the claim that it is the question of emergence, particularly as it pertains to emergence from the one (autochthony) or the two (copulation; that is, being as emerging from community and enclosed within its skin), that is held in the structure of myth, Lévi-Strauss turns to a series of myths from the Americas to highlight, through a discussion of cultivation and its relation to autochthony, how the same structure can be located in them.

That this question of emergence has to do with the question of the subjective certainty of Man becomes apparent through the Sphinx's riddle. It is not simply due to the fact that the answer to the riddle is 'man', but rather to a sketching of a trajectory in relation to the earth. The Sphinx asks, 'What has four legs in the morning, two legs in the afternoon, and three legs in the evening?' On this trajectory, one that Oedipus affirms through his answer, Man emerges in close proximity to earth, distances itself from earth and then, ultimately, enlists the assistance of a prosthetic so as to resist the return to earth through the failure of its body. Myth, as a narrative form, might be read as fulfilling such a role of prosthetic to the extent that it resists a resolution of the problem. The struggle that defines Man, it seems, is a struggle to stand and remain standing, to enforce some form of separation from autochthony. It is interesting how this question comes to be troubled in the character of Antigone.[10]

While Lévi-Strauss argues that Antigone is an integral element in the myth only when it comes to the question of the 'overvaluation' of blood (which he reads as resonant with the question of autochthony), I suggest that, in reading, Antigone – particularly through her name, which can be read as signifying opposition to birth – becomes available as a singularity that exceeds the demands of the Symbolic Order of the Law, the demand of institutionalised difference.[11] To make this argument, it is necessary to read Antigone, to grapple with her character, at the level of the name, action and existence. Antigone's name, which Lévi-Strauss chooses not to read, situates her as being against her blood, opposed to the marker of her birth. However, in a reading that can be taken as contesting this, Paul Allen Miller argues through his detailed analysis of the opening lines of the play, which he describes as 'a text that constantly escapes itself' (5), that it is Antigone's desire for the singularity of 'same-wombedness [the term with which she addresses her sister Ismene in the opening line] that is at the heart of the Oedipal family romance' (4). This desire, which he reads as an affirmation of birth as it is an invocation of the mother, comes to be expressed in Antigone's desire to be united with her brother in death through flouting the law of the tyrant. In this formulation Antigone's actions work against her name in a very similar manner to how the action of Oedipus with regard to the Sphinx works against the operation of his name. However, Antigone's claim to same-wombedness, a claim that positions her as a monster due to the implicit affirmation of incest, also enables her to respond to the attempt to resolve the

THE PRINCIPLE OF INSUFFICIENCY

dislocation inherent in the myth (the dislocation brought about by the tension between autochthony and copulation). In this reading Creon (the tyrant who is also her uncle, the brother of Jacosta) signifies the realm of the Symbolic Order of the Third, of the institutionalisation of difference, while Antigone signifies a desire for sameness, of immanence, that resists the injunction of this Third.

Antigone emerges in this moment as a potential mediator in the struggle that lies at the heart of the myth.[12] However, Antigone is significantly unlike Creon, who first attempts to secure the return of Oedipus and, failing this, following the battle between Polynices and Eteocles, issues a decree that was designed to situate the sovereign as the source of right in Thebes (that is, to resolve the problem of emergence through subsuming it within societal structure, a reduction of the social to One). Instead, Antigone responds to the event of her brother's death through maintaining the disjuncture that structures the myth. To phrase this a little more pointedly so as to draw it in line with the understanding of ethics that emerges in my reading of Blanchot, Antigone's freedom is articulated in her attempt at communication, which would entrench a particular understanding of the condition of Man as universal as it is materialised through the lived experience of her actions. What is entrenched, I suggest, is the principle of insufficiency as the root of being: the irresolvable tension between autochthony and copulation. The resistance to the Symbolic Order of the Law that is signified by Antigone enables a glimpse of the 'embrace of Being' (Miller 12), perceived in a flash as she articulates the impossibility of not choosing death so as to bury her brother. This choice is not simply one of blood over society, understood as the State; rather, Antigone accepts the authority of Creon to put her to death for flouting his decree even as she declares it to be unjust in relation to the law of the gods. As such, Antigone affirms both senses of right, obeying both as sources of authority even as she rejects the expression of Creon's own affirmation of his authority (which would resolve the tension between these two laws). Critically, her 'action' in this moment is articulated as a double passivity: she fulfils her responsibility to the death of her

235

brother as well as to Creon. Her capacity to produce such a statement of justice as an expression of the ethical – I think particularly of her refusal of Creon's edict in lines 391–409, and the subsequent perception of its consequences in lines 730–736 and 788–796 (see Sophocles) – is, however, dependent on her particular monstrosity: Antigone's desire for her brother, expressed in the metaphor of same-wombedness and her consequent actions and statements, recalls precisely that which Creon's decree sought to repress, namely the disjuncture that is held in the structure of the myth, the problem of Man as it comes to be worked out in the actions of Oedipus and his sons. Antigone, then, can be read as a nodal point, one produced through her action, which is revealed immediately also as a passivity, an unworking work, at which the myth of Oedipus – and any resolution of it through repression or the law and the attendant *socius* brought into existence through this – begins to unravel itself, to shift towards a potential understanding of the social through its remains: the unavowable community, realised here in death.

Of scripts and insufficiency

If abiding by Blanchot's reading of Bataille and Duras enables a sense of community that might be adequate to a notion of the subject indelibly marked by insufficiency rather than certainty or lack, it is in the brief reading of the Oedipus myth that the ethical potential of this sense of community is produced for thinking. At stake here is not simply an attempt to dismiss a quasi-Freudian concept of community as carrying a redemptive potential for the postapartheid. Rather, as will become clear in my reading of Mpe's *Welcome to Our Hillbrow*, the refiguring of community and subjectivity that I am unfolding here is reworked in Mpe's novel so as to take account of the weight of lived experience. As I begin to show in the remainder of this chapter, such a practice of reading hinges on a sense of the ethical as an attempt to adequately respond to the principle of being as insufficiency. I suggest in my reading of the concept of community in *Welcome to Our Hillbrow* that it might enable us to posit an adequate sense of the ethical, one that asks us 'not to be unworthy of that which happens to us'; in other words, to posit a sense of the ethical that is capable of abiding by insufficiency into the midst of the dominant concerns that mark the postapartheid.

It has, however, become commonplace to read Mpe's novel as a 'work of mourning', as a literary instance in which community might be redeemed through attending to the loss of being African in the world (whether this is understood through the lens of slavery, colonialism or apartheid) and, in the case of Neville Hoad's reading, for example, maintaining this as a constitutive lost object into our present: melancholia, in this case, as an ethical relation.[13] While this figuring of Mpe's novel enables Hoad to read it as producing an 'insurgent and rooted, yet open, cosmopolitanism' (113), his reading does not take account of what, precisely, is mourned (neither does it bother to theorise cosmopolitanism, treating this rather as a simple good). It is not death, nor is it an African sense of cosmopolitanism, but rather the hoped-for potential of what could have been if the community of writing, one adequate to 'not owning life', adequate, in other words, to insufficiency as the principle of being, had been constitutive of lived experience. It is, I will argue below, this failure of exiting the script of autochthony that is worked out throughout the pages of Mpe's novel.

Welcome to Our Hillbrow is striking both for its use of narrative voice and for the manner in which it works through indigeneity (the question of autochthony and copulation) as a problematic that must be reckoned with. The majority of the novel, what we might call its first part – which circles the character of Refentše and his suicide through narrating the different strands that intertwine around this event – unfolds through an omniscient narrator that is not easily locatable within the contours of the narrative. The narrator is not, however, disinterested in the unfolding of the novel, occupying rather the place of a companion to Refentše (the main character in the novel), who is himself also removed from the story that is told. While it is tempting to locate the narrator as a voice emerging from the television set that, in its own way, narrates elements of the story from its vantage point in heaven, it is perhaps most accurate to speculate, given the centrality of writing in the novel, that the narrator emerges from the stories that the characters propose to write now that they are dead. While the narrator is rigorously maintained as a voice from nowhere in the first part of the novel, there are three moments in which the narrative voice slips from one that is almost extradiegetic to one that is explicitly placed inside the narrative. In these instances, which all have to do with the insufficiency of existence and a particular monstrosity (through being marked as foreign, as impoverished or as unfaithful to an ideal), the narrator joins with Refentše through the use of the plural pronoun 'we' (8, 67) and the possessive 'our' (23). The effect of this slippage is to render the narrator as omniscient but not pure – it loses its sovereignty in the realisation that the narrator is itself complicit with the story that is told. In the final two chapters of the novel, where the reader discovers Refilwe's impending death from Aids, the narrative voice again shifts, this time towards that of a straightforward third-person narrator that addresses, for the most part, the reader directly. The force of this shift is to place the reader suddenly in the position of a character in the novel, as spoken to, and has to do with the ethical potential of the concept of community that is developed in it.

So as to adequately address the ethical potential of the novel, it is necessary to first offer a reading of two themes that thread it, namely, that of autochthony and that of writing. After the epigraph, which prepares the reader for a battle that will take place through words, a battle that carries weight for our present, the novel immediately offers what it calls 'Hillbrow: the Map'. This map, which is presented in relation to the particularities of Hillbrow but which can be read as a map for the entire novel, is constituted through tracking Refentše's first movements through Hillbrow on his way to register for a degree at the University of the Witwatersrand. What emerges in this chapter is a sense of life as constituted through a question of 'routes' and 'roots' (2). In other words, it has to do with the way life is negotiated as well as from where it is negotiated, or, to phrase it in the terms of my reading of the Oedipus myth, it has to do with a distinction between autochthony and copulation. This distinction will come to structure the entire novel, and is expressed in the disagreements Refentše has with his cousin over xenophobia, crime, disease and the responsibility of those who name themselves as South Africans, and is perhaps most

THE PRINCIPLE OF INSUFFICIENCY

starkly articulated in a relationship that Refentše develops with a local 'beggar'. While Refentše's cousin simply ignores the elderly man as 'a beggar', Refentše decides to return his greeting, a decision that will be repeated continuously for five years as he walks past the old man on his way to and from the university. This interaction between Refentše and the beggar is read by Hoad as an exemplary instance, particularly in the moment of that character's death, of the 'shared vulnerability' (121) that marks all humans in the novel. It is this that Hoad reads as carrying the potential of an African universalism, a humanism that enables a sense of a rooted cosmopolitanism as the ethical weight of Mpe's novel.[14] I suggest, however, that what is at stake in this decision to greet is an orientation in existence away from the sufficiency of the self (which almost everyone in the novel fights for) and towards a responsibility to the other, an orientation that leads Refentše to the desire to write on the problems of 'our Hillbrow' (Hoad 30). Critically, as the reader rapidly realises through the unfolding of the novel, Refentše is not capable of simply walking, or writing, his way out of the script that produces him. This lack of the capacity to simply walk away is reinforced through the becoming absent of punctuation in the final passages of all the chapters – an absence that can be read as a textual performance of the inescapable flux in which all the narratives and characters in the novel are, to some extent, lodged.

This script from which it is not easy to escape is that of autochthony or, rather, indigeneity and its concomitant claims to a moral order of purity, and it is marked through a disjuncture between not knowing and the certainty of knowing too well. While the narrator consistently troubles the certainty of knowledge in which the characters of the novel act – instructing them in how they would have acted if they had known more – the voices of 'the community', initially that of Refentše's home village of Tiragalong but, as the novel progresses, also Hillbrow, Alexandra, South Africa and London, always speak from a perspective of absolute certainty. However, given the broader perspective that the narrator brings to the events on which these voices speak, the often repeated phrases of 'everyone knows' (44), 'it is known' (82), 'as [the local people] well knew' (54), come to take on a measure of irony in that they mark precisely the limit at which this emplotment of events should fail. Yet, as the narration of Refilwe's response to Refentše's death makes clear, these emplotments are what persist in the social precisely because they conform, as 'valid testimony', to the scripts along which the social is produced. This is not a scripting that is unique either to the postapartheid or to the encounters between the rural and the urban. Rather, as the narrator explicitly points out, these are held in common with apartheid rationality, where people were fixed in place through land (bantustans) and 'any criticism of Apartheid thinking became a threat to public morals; where love across racial boundaries became mental instability …' (57). The manner in which the narrator does not finish the comparison but rather trails off into an ellipsis draws attention to the resonance that these formulations have with the emplotments that affirm autochthony as the basis of morality – it is not necessary to specify the remainder of the list; it functions here as an echo. This scripting is also, through the movements of Refilwe, expanded into a global phenomenon, what we today refer to perhaps as 'global apartheid', which is premised both on race and, as Refilwe discovers upon her entry to the United Kingdom, on a perceived rootedness to a political perspective or agenda, a perspective described as 'white civilisation', a civilisation that includes South Africa as an emblem of liberalism.

It is precisely because it is not possible simply to walk out of a script, not even through hard work, that Refentše decides to begin to write. However, what emerges in this moment is not a revolutionary, or even an adequate, text in relation to that which constitutes the contours of community in postapartheid South Africa, but, rather, insufficiency, since 'to have these answers would be to know the secrets of life itself' (61). This knowledge, which the narrator suggests would amount to 'owning life', reducing it to a calculable One, is precisely what Refentše is unable to achieve:

> I do not own life, you often said when you tried to laugh your difficulties away.
>
> Many people could not see that you were not merely throwing jokes around. You did not own life when you were alive. Now that you are

alive in a different realm, you know for sure that you do not own life. You have watched God and Devil, gods and Ancestors, wondering whether *they* owned it, this thing called life (67).

This question of owning life, with the implication that such ownership would grant a semblance of control over life, to specify its outcomes (the passage occurs in the midst of Refentše being told that he is not able to intervene in the world of the living), is not necessarily posed as an instance of regret. Whereas ownership, the transformation of life into an object that is yours, enables a programmatic relation to life, the lack of ownership requires that the subject, in this case Refentše, must respond adequately to the life that takes place. In other words, the lack of ownership asks for an ethical relationship defined by not being unworthy of what happens to us: a demand to resist the reduction of life to an object, to something defined through autochthony.

As a gesture towards the ethical, then, the short story that Refentše writes in the novel, a story that mimics the novel into which it is laid, actually fails: Refentše commits suicide. His suicide, the reader learns by (in a sense) listening in on the narrator's speech to Refentše, has more to do with his own sense of shame and guilt than with the act of infidelity performed by Lerato and Sammy (Refentše comes home one afternoon to find his girlfriend, Lerato, and his best friend, Sammy, in the midst of an intimate sexual encounter). In the months after his death, the facts of his act have, through the careful work of Refilwe, become produced along the lines of a morality tale: if you have sexual relations with a 'makwerekwere' (a derogatory term for a foreigner), then you too will plummet to your death. This tale is not limited to sexual relations, as through it Refentše's mother is accused of witchcraft and subsequently murdered, and Lerato also takes her own life, as a result of the emplotments that seek to apportion blame anywhere outside Tiragalong, outside the zone of autochthonous belonging. The reader, of course, knows that this emplotment of events is entirely specious, as Lerato is, as a matter of empirical reality in the novel, a descendant of a man from Tiragalong, Tshepo's father, and thus an element of the exact expression of the social that considers her an outsider. In addition to this empirical objection is the sense of life that Refentše tries to produce through his short story – a sense of life not reducible to its stamping into a reified sense of the self as sovereign. Even with such an intention, the narrator is clear that failing in the demand of the ethical has real effects for which the subject is always responsible: the narrator names Refentše as 'a killer', not because of his suicide, but because that event provided the kernel around which the other stories were spun, stories that resulted in the death of his mother and Lerato, as well as the madness of Sammy.

Despite her role in manufacturing the stories about Refentše's death, it is the character of Refilwe that undergoes the most dramatic shift in the novel. Hers is a movement away from the subjective certainty ordered on a sense of autochthony (that is, the sovereign self, what Creon tries to protect as a possibility in the Oedipus myth) and towards an understanding of the self as rooted in insufficiency – an insufficiency that is made real to her through the death of Refentše and the continued effect of his writing. Through reading Refentše's fiction, Refilwe comes to realise the severely limited and unethical expression of existence that marks her life; she comes to understand the ethical weight of her actions:

> It was because of these frustrations, because she had come to value so greatly the importance of literary honesty and risk-taking, that Refilwe appreciated Refentše's story so much… She had read the story many times, and each time it made her weep anew. Partly because of the memories it brought of Refentše. And partly because it made her see herself and her own prejudices in a different light (95–96).

The transition that is marked in this passage, from an identity premised on place (autochthony) to a sense of the self derivative from a series of encounters with the other, is not sufficient to enable Refilwe to walk out of the script that has produced her. Although Refilwe does leave South Africa to study at Oxford Brookes University and, while studying abroad, meets and falls in love with a Nigerian man, her existence in the United Kingdom is an ambiguous one, for her South African identity as a marker of liberalism guarantees her the treatment of a 'white' person as she moves through passport control and, later, through society, while all other Africans are made to wait and are examined for markers of disease. This ambiguity is accentuated when Refilwe is diagnosed, along with her lover, as having contracted Aids.

The disease did not come, as Tiragalong would expect, from her Nigerian lover, just as it also, in his case, did not originate with Refilwe. In both cases they had been living with the disease for over ten years, which, for Refilwe, means that she contracted the disease while she was still a student in her home village of Tiragalong. This medical fact does not, however, result in Refilwe escaping the emplotment that works to reify the autochthonous claims to morality that structure the social in Tiragalong, Johannesburg and the world: these 'gods and devils of Tiragalong', the narrator informs the reader, relentlessly transform Refilwe's lived experience, where she wastes away into 'the scarecrow figure of Refentše's fiction', into a morality tale (112, 120). This emplotment is presented, in these final pages of the novel, as an expression of welcoming that seeks to affirm that to which the one being welcomed arrives, rather than as openness to the other's arrival. As the returnee, Refilwe recognises and understands the emplotments that take place even as she grasps through the instruction of the narrator that she too is 'a Hillbrowan. An Alexandran. A Johannesburger. An Oxfordian. A *Lekwerekwere*, just like those you once held in such contempt' (123). Refilwe attains this status as an expansion of the grounds for her ethical existence, an existence premised on the insufficiency of being structured on the contingency of encounter, while from the perspective of Tiragalong she attains this status as she is now marked by the disease of the other. It is owing to the extent of this disjuncture that Refilwe realises that she, too, will die within the emplotments of Tiragalong, and that no amount of reasoned argumentation in itself will order her escape from these scripts.

In the wake of this narrative of emplotment through a reduction to homogeneity, to the claim to autochthony that structures the world, the reader is brought to the final page of the novel where its ethical injunction becomes plain. The narrator, who is both in the story and separate from it, and who is instrumental in the development of a sense of the self marked by insufficiency and the ethical expressions that this might give rise to in contradiction with the social order of homogeneity and its attendant morality, speaks from a non-place in the novel. On the final page, as Refilwe dies, the narrator reflects on 'our continuing existence' in the zone that it names as 'heaven', which it argues is

> located in the memory and consciousness [which, throughout the novel, is synonymous with 'script'] who live with us and after us. It is the archive that those we left behind keep visiting and revisiting; digging this out, suppressing or burying that. Continually reconfiguring the stories of our lives, as if they alone held the real and true version. Just as you, Refilwe, tried to reconfigure the story of Refentše; just as Tiragalong now is going to do the same to you. Heaven can also be Hell, depending on the nature of our continuing existence in the memory and consciousness of the living (124).

The novel ends by welcoming Refilwe to 'our heaven', to the site of continued existence in the modes through which those who persist beyond the novel (that is, its readers) respond to the emplotments encountered through the characters. As such, the reader is placed in the position of Refilwe after she read Refentše's fiction. Confronted with the modes through which our consciousness, as an expression of the postapartheid as a condition is produced along the lines of its scripts, and confronted with the possibility of an ethics that could perhaps be adequate to a sense of the self premised on insufficiency, the narrator poses a question for the reader: in what way will the reader respond to the remains of the social, to this heaven? However, the overall force of *Welcome to Our Hillbrow* does not carry a utopic resolution of this question: every instance of the realisation of an ethics falls short precisely on the script that it attempts to evade. The edge of community, it would seem, falls back on its limit, enclosing a terrain rather than opening it up to its outside. However, its offer functions in a similar mode to that of the impossible ritual that establishes Acéphale as a potential community adequate to insufficiency, or of the passive obedience that leads Antigone to her death: in its failure it maintains an openness to a future. It is this openness, coupled with an insistence on the weightiness of lived experience, which is offered for thinking in Mpe's novel. Indeed, in his consideration of this problematic, it is in the decidedly unstable configuration of writing that an expression of community adequate to this weight and structured on the principle of insufficiency might be realised. However, the expression of community as always enclosed within its own limit – in its own skin, so to speak – consistently resurfaces as a claim that seeks to undo the potentiality of this community of the touch found in writing. Regardless of whether the difficulty is resolved materially or ideally, through bodily flesh or through philosophical thought, the attending concept stumbles on the tension of this claim. This limit, however, is also an abiding by the openness of the touch, a duration in which *a* difference might yet still be produced. As Mpe's *Welcome to Our Hillbrow* makes clear in its re-working of the principle of insufficiency as this slices through the script of autochthony, the weight of lived experience demands that such an opening be consistently produced, even in its failure, as a possible opening onto the future.

Acknowledgements

I acknowledge the Centre for Humanities Research (CHR) at the University of the Western Cape for providing the funding that made this research possible. Opinions expressed and conclusions arrived at are those of the author and are not necessarily to be attributed to the CHR.

NOTES

1. See the central role that community plays in the *recognition* of racial categories in Section 2 of the Group Areas Act (No. 41 of 1950).
2. On the question of a practice of life that remains to be learned, see Jacques Derrida and Gayatri C. Spivak.

3. For influential readings of Mpe's novel along these lines, see Neville Hoad and Rob Gaylard.
4. For Walter Benjamin's understanding of the work of re-working, see his 'Theory of Distraction'.
5. I think particularly of Sam Durrant's *Postcolonial Narrative and the Work of Mourning* and Mark Sanders's *Ambiguities of Witnessing*. For a reading of the Truth and Reconciliation Commission (TRC) that 'troubles' Sanders's rendering of it through drawing attention to the weight of the TRCs genealogical precursors in both colonialism and apartheid, see Adam Sitze.
6. This sense of insufficiency is very similar to that of 'need' in the thinking of Levinas, especially in his early essay *On Escape*.
7. For a thorough discussion of Hegel's recognition of this problem and his attempts to work around it through a consideration of *Aesthetics*, see Paul de Man and Jacques Derrida.
8. As Frantz Fanon phrases it in his introduction to *Black Skin, White Masks*, investment in a sense of 'fusional multiplicity' deserves the diagnosis of 'idiocy' as it maintains the very structure from which it is necessary to escape (xi).
9. For a discussion of how this risk generally comes to be resolved through an assertion of particular individuality, see Jacques Lacan.
10. *The Theban Plays* have received an immense amount of attention, which I do not have the space to replicate here. Perhaps one of the most sustained discussions of the problem of ethics as it pertains to the relation between two rights is offered by Hegel through his reading of 'Antigone' in his *Phenomenology of Spirit*, particularly in his discussion of the unity of self-consciousness and the self in its relation to 'the ethical order' and the realisation of morality.
11. See 'Antigone' in Patrick Hanks, Kate Hardcastle and Flavia Hodges, where it is argued that the two terms that constitute her name, namely *'anti'* (meaning 'opposed') and *'gen'* or *'gon'* (meaning 'birth'), signify opposition or contrariness to birth.
12. Although the figure of the mediator forms a central component in the structure of myths originating in the Americas, it is not mentioned by Lévi-Strauss in relation to Oedipus.
13. On *Welcome to Our Hillbrow* as a work of mourning, see Sam Durrant's 'The Invention of Mourning', as well as Hoad, especially pp. 114, 123 and 125. Hoad's

intervention is useful both in terms of how it figures *Welcome to Our Hillbrow* in relation to a potential queer politics and its situating of the novel within the broader contours of South African literature. For the former, however, I would suggest that its potentiality can be pressed further through attending to the disembodiment that structures many of the descriptions of sex acts, not as a marker of alienation but rather as a refusal of the markers of autochthony. For the latter, it is still the case that the intricacies of this intertextuality remain to be read.

14. For a reading of Mpe as producing a plea for a reconstituted African sense of humanism in the midst of a dystopian postapartheid, see Rob Gaylard.

REFERENCES

Benjamin, Walter. 'Theory of Distraction.' *The Work of Art in the Age of Its Technological Reproducibility, and Other Writings on Media*, translated by Edmund Jephcott, Rodney Livingstone and Howard Eiland, edited by Michael W. Jennings, Brigit Doherty and Thomas Y. Levin, The Belknap Press of Harvard UP, 2008, pp. 57–58.

Blanchot, Maurice. *The Unavowable Community*. Translated by Pierre Joris, Station Hill Press, 1998.

Deleuze, Gilles. *The Logic of Sense*. Translated by Mark Lester with Charles Stivale, The Athlone Press, 1990 [1969].

De Man, Paul. 'Sign and Symbol in Hegel's *Aesthetics*.' *Aesthetic Ideology*. Edited by Andrzey Warminski, U of Minnesota P, 1996, pp. 91–104.

Derrida, Jacques. 'The Pit and the Pyramid: Introduction to Hegel's Semiology.' *Margins of Philosophy*. Translated by Alan Bass, U of Chicago Press, 1982, pp. 69–108.

Duras, Marguerite. *The Malady of Death*. Translated by Barbara Bray, Grove Press, 1986.

Durrant, Sam. *Postcolonial Narrative and the Work of Mourning: J.M. Coetzee, Wilson Harris, and Toni Morrison*. State U of New York P, 2004.

———. 'The Invention of Mourning in Post-Apartheid Literature.' *Third World Quarterly*, vol. 26, no. 3, 2005, pp. 441–450.

Fanon, Frantz. *Black Skin, White Masks*. Translated by Richard Philcox, Grove Press, 2008 [1952].

Gaylard, Rob. '"Welcome to the World of Our Humanity": (African) Humanism, *Ubuntu* and Black South African Writing.' *Journal of Literary Studies*, vol. 20, no. 3/4, 2004, pp. 265–282.

Hanks, Patrick, Kate Hardcastle and Flavia Hodges. *Dictionary of First Names* (2nd edition). Oxford UP, 2006.

Hegel, Georg Wilhelm Friedrich. *Phenomenology of Spirit*. Translated by Arnold V. Miller, Oxford UP, 1977 [1807].

Hoad, Neville. *African Intimacies: Race, Homosexuality and Globalization*. U of Minnesota P, 2006.

Lacan, Jacques. 'Logical Time and the Assertion of Anticipated Certainty.' *Écrits*. Translated by Bruce Fink, W.W. Norton, 2006, pp. 162–175.

Levinas, Emmanuel. *On Escape/De l'évasion*. Translated by Bettina Bergo, Stanford UP, 1935.

Lévi-Strauss, Claude. 'The Structural Study of Myth.' *Structural Anthropology*. Translated by Claire Jacobson and Brooke Grundfest Schoepf, Basic Books, 1963, pp. 206–231.

Miller, Paul Allen. 'Lacan's Antigone: The Sublime Object and the Ethics of Interpretation.' *Phoenix*, vol. 61, no. 1/2, Spring–Summer 2007, pp. 1–14.

Mpe, Phaswane. *Welcome to Our Hillbrow*. U of Natal P, 2001.

Nancy, Jean-Luc. 'The Inoperative Community.' *The Inoperative Community*. Edited by Peter Connor, translated by Peter Connor, Lisa Garbus, Michael Holland and Simona Sawhney, U of Minnesota P, 1991, pp. 1–42.

Sanders, Mark. *Ambiguities of Witnessing: Law and Literature in the Time of a Truth Commission*. Stanford UP, 2007.

Sitze, Adam. *The Impossible Machine: A Genealogy of South Africa's Truth and Reconciliation Commission*. U of Michigan P, 2013.

Sophocles. *The Theban Plays: King Oedipus, Oedipus at Colonus, Antigone*. Translated by Edward F. Watling, Penguin Books, 1996.

Spivak, Gayatri Chakravorty. 'From Haverstock Hill Flat to U.S. Classroom, What's Left of Theory?' *What's Left of Theory? New Work on the Politics of Literary Theory*, edited by Judith Butler, John Guillory and Kendall Thomas, Routledge, 2000, pp. 1–39.

CHAPTER 10
THE TROJAN HORSE AND THE 'BECOMING TECHNICAL OF THE HUMAN'

Premesh Lalu

The pursuit of learning is to increase day after day
The pursuit of Tao is to decrease day after day
It is to decrease and further decrease
Until one reaches the point of taking no action
No action is undertaken,
And yet nothing is left undone (Little, *The Warrior Within* 117).

Given all that has been written and done in memory of the student movements in South Africa, it is surprising that we have not had an adequate account of the drives and desires that animated an unprecedented movement of school students over a period of six months in 1985. In an effort to address the omission, the historian Colin Bundy argues that the students were driven by a sense of 'immediatism' expressed in what he charmingly calls a combination of street sociology and pavement politics. The resort to charm, however, encounters its limit in the political calculation surrounding what came to be known as the Trojan Horse Massacre in which three students were killed in Athlone, Cape Town, on 15 October 1985, and in a similar event staged by the state the following day in nearby Crossroads where two young people died.

In several scholarly works and documentary films, not to mention memorials, poems and works of art, the Trojan Horse incident has lent itself to ideological prescription rather than attentiveness to what was at work in the student movement that triggered the state killings in 1985. As a result, we have an event that is returned again and again to the realms of ideology or is memorialised in a way that re-enacts a habituated memory of attachment to war and violence – as if these were the only games in town to play.

The scene of the Trojan Horse incident, and the prehistory of that tragic occurrence, are what preoccupied the Cape Town writer Richard Rive in his novel *Emergency Continued* (1990). The intensity of Rive's novel has recently been recalled by Adam Sitze in his essay titled 'Between Study and Revolt: Further Notes on *Emergency Continued*'. Sitze nudges the reader to ask what we are to do with the idea of 'school' – and *scholē* – which seems to have been a specific site of both indecision and intensification under the conditions of the permanent emergency of apartheid. This question is of particular significance in an age when deschooling had increasingly become the modality of neoliberalism with the availability of the internet, distance learning and MOOCs (Massive Open Online Courses). If 'nothing was left undone' in the process of six months of protest and street fighting in 1985, might the lessons of that struggle be drawn on today to harness a modality of schooling that offers us a way of life and not a means of subjection?

In what follows, I locate the notion of the school along the contours of technogenesis, as that which is made rather than received as a means to an end. Placed in a field of technogenesis, the school under apartheid functioned both as a prohibition on learning and an apparatus that lent itself to a memory of the future – by which I mean a tertiary memory, following Bernard Stiegler, something akin to the industrialisation of memory. More precisely, tertiary memory advances Edmund Husserl's concept of retention and protention through a shift in the history of the exteriorisation of technics:

> The twentieth century is the century of the industrialisation, the conservation and the transmission – that is, the selection – of memory. This industrialisation becomes concretised in the generalisation of the production of industrial temporal objects (phonograms, films, radio and television programmes, etc.), with the consequences to be drawn

concerning the fact that millions, hundreds of millions of consciousnesses are every day the consciousnesses, at the same time, of the same temporal objects (see Stiegler, *Technics and Time, 1: The Fault of Epimetheus* 106).

For Stiegler, the industrialisation of memory lends itself to a problem of de-individuation at one level, and the becoming technical of the human at another.[1] The question is one of how we might retrieve *spirit* from the inevitable surrender of memory to technology. In asking for a reconsideration of the cinematic qualities of consciousness, Stiegler invites an inquiry into another version of the becoming technical of the human, one that supplements the loss of memory with the re-enchantment of the world. Here, in the double bind of de-individuation resulting from the surrender of memory and the becoming technical of the human, we may discover a possibility of renewing our understanding of a technology of the school and the renewal of the understanding of schooling that was revealed most powerfully in the student movement of 1985.[2]

Several recorded accounts provide us with the outline of the event. In mid-1985, students of the schools of Athlone, together with several other schools spread over the Cape Peninsula, decided to suspend their studies in protest against the declaration of a state of emergency by the apartheid government on 21 July in 36 magisterial districts in the Eastern Cape and present-day Gauteng. This 'schools boycott', as it came to be known, would spread across the length and breadth of the Cape Flats, resulting in militant uprisings against the state and pitched battles against the army and police force. On the surface, the name given to this uprising has seldom been subjected to scrutiny. Variously referred to as a schools boycott or as a mass movement, the student generation of 1985 soon realised that their lives were being overtaken by history at an incalculable speed. What generated this movement among students was perhaps less their enthusiasm for a specific ideological position and more a sense of freedom in which memory was redirected towards a desire to think ahead, to generate something new and different from the wretched script of apartheid, rather than glance backwards over the shoulder, in the direction of the threat of the police (see Figure 10.1). In the friction

REMAINS OF THE SOCIAL

Figure 10.1. Juliette Franciscus (glancing over her shoulder), Karen Britten, Sean Stockenstroom, Belgravia High students on the corner of Thornton and Kromboom roads, Athlone, 1985.
Photographer: David Hartman

between these two competing emphases, the evaluation of whether nothing indeed was left undone remains.

During the state of emergency, the school effectively became a zone of suspension. It resembled an interval, not too dissimilar to the interval associated with the language of cinematography, which Trinh T. Minh-ha develops in her study *Cinema Interval*. Minh-ha argues that the Russian film-maker Dziga Vertov, especially through his elaboration of the idea of cine-seeing, saved cinematography from the 'frightful venom of habit' (vii). Vertov's technique failed in the context of Soviet society, where it first made itself known, perhaps because he ultimately ceded ground to the more romantic vision of Sergei Eisenstein. (Neither would have their films shown in the commercial cinemas of Athlone, although Eisenstein was a favourite of those frequenting Leftist film societies on the Cape Flats.) What matters for my reading are two aspects of Vertov's theorisation of cinematography that help us make sense of the performance of students and the script of apartheid in Athlone in 1985. Something in Vertov's vision may allow us a different way of conceiving the student movement and, with it, the work of schooling (or, as he might have preferred to call it, retooling).

Minh-ha's reading of Vertov's manifesto *Kinoks: A Revolution* presses home the point that 'intervals are what cine-images, cine-documents or cine-poems are built upon, that is: "upon a movement between the pieces, the frames, upon the proportions of these pieces between themselves, upon the transitions from one visual impulse to the one following it"' (iv). The first point of interest is how Vertov rearranges relations through the device of the camera, producing the interval as the most productive instance of cinema. As Minh-ha notes, 'in his "hall of intervals" where "frames of truth" are minutely edited, all is a matter of relations: temporal, spatial, rhythmic relations; relations, as he specified, of planes, of recording speed, of light or shade, or of movement within the frame ... cinematography is in itself a multiplicity of cinema intervals' (iv). In his determination to retheorise cinematography, Vertov may well have revealed a process of the technical becoming of the human. Here the fabric of the everyday is woven into the visual machine, so that film's uniqueness lies in its immediacy and proximity to the present.

What is crucial is not that Vertov sought to approximate journalism or history or reality TV to produce what Paul Virilio might call a post-Bergsonian sense of 'virtual reality'. As Carloss James Chamberlin notes in his punningly titled essay 'Dziga Vertov: The Idiot', Vertov may have given us not only a theory of cinematography, but also an education about aesthetic education, or *bios* and *techné*:

> How does a nation of backward hick farmers become the industrialized fulfilment of Marxist prophecy? What dynamic element can make this transformation happen: Factories, Tractors, Machines?

> It is thus with the people – the hot fiery blast of socialism and the wind of a thousand slogans hurls away their tsarist trinkets and entertainments, their religion, their selfishness, and their vodka – and re-tools them into supermen, Shock Workers, Machine-Men and Machine-Women of Steel. That is the real object of the word Stalinism and the Five Year Plan. The steelification – the Stalinization – of the human being.

The interval, I suggest, is a space for redirecting this seemingly fateful destiny, not only by dislodging technology as a means, but finding in it the very circumstance for an education about aesthetic education. If cinema had the kind of consequence that I attribute to it and its development in Athlone, it should be read not as a means to an end, but as a phase – an interval – in the technogenesis that gave us the memory of the student movement and the meaning of schooling. To return to the scene of Athlone with Vertov is to ask for a fresh attentiveness to both the human and the technology that awakened the students in 1985.

While many would attribute the upsurge of student protests in the 1980s to the economic plight that awaited black youth under apartheid, in which they faced a future of being transformed into 'hewers of wood and drawers of water', a biblical phrase that recurred in a range of propagandist pamphlets of the time (see SADET 880), there was something else that was latent in their agency. We may speak of this latency as thought, but that would not be helpful, simply because it dialectically pits thought against action, in which thought is eventually negated. Neither was it the repressive atmosphere of corporal punishment and authoritarianism omnipresent in local schools that explains the upsurge in Athlone. Nor was it a simple act of solidarity with the despair facing students elsewhere in South Africa, subject to a state of emergency. What drove the students to action was precisely that upon which they acted, namely, schooling.

Perhaps a better way to think about the generative force unleashed by students is through the notion of a memory of the future, a formulation with which I hope to rename the activity upon which thousands of students embarked in 1985. To this end, I ask for a shift in the

THE TROJAN HORSE AND THE 'BECOMING TECHNICAL OF THE HUMAN'

designation of the upsurge of 1985, from terms such as 'schools boycott' and 'mass movement', towards something that disaggregates the relation between student and movement in the co-constituting couplet 'student movement'. Such a move seeks to place the commonplace understanding of the students as violent and militant against an agency that may be read as seemingly more passive, as thoughtful, one which lay at the very erosion of the interval in the speed at which the events unfolded.

What we now call an event is symptomatically described by a name that Athlone shares with the Greeks. In 1985, a large 'horse and trailer' belonging to the South African Railways carried death to the streets of Athlone. Policemen and soldiers hidden in wooden crates on the back of an enormous railway truck enacted what notoriously became known as the Trojan Horse Massacre. The name 'Trojan Horse' resounded through the streets of Athlone, as if the burden for an explanation for the massacre was lifted by the name given to the atrocity. But that cannot be.

How did this event come to be named in terms of a memory of war between the Trojans and Greeks, handed down to us by Homer through his wonderfully long and meandering *Iliad*? What if we discover that this is the name that the South African state had in mind all along? What if the Trojans, the students who faced the hail of bullets, had through no fault of their own not yet arrived at the lesson dealing with Homer's *Iliad*, and the scene of war that gave rise to the name given to their own massacre? To anticipate my argument briefly, I suggest that these questions belong neither to history nor to art. Rather, the questions need to be entrusted to a blind and illiterate poet, Homer perhaps, to offer us a name for the memory of the future that will endure into the future.

To begin the journey of renaming, I want to turn to the scene of the bioscope (the popular local name for the cinema) – which teemed with life, long before the physical structures which housed worlds hitherto unseen were turned into a grammar of despair and consumption housing bottlestores, banks and supermarkets in the wake of apartheid. I suggest that the bioscope may offer us a point of entry into the scene I wish to assign to the memory of the future. Films such as *Spartacus* (1960), *The Trojan Horse* (1961), *The Good, the Bad and the Ugly* (1966) and *Enter the*

Dragon (1973)[3] helped to filter the world of apartheid by placing tactics of battle in a field of slave rebellion, ancient warfare, fortune-hunting and martial arts, respectively. *The Trojan Horse* may have been invented by the Greeks through epic poetry, and Rome may have put down the rebellion of the slave army of Spartacus; *Enter the Dragon* may have uncannily affirmed subalternity, and *The Good, the Bad and the Ugly* may have called into question the limits of binary thinking. We cannot know for sure. What we can say is that in Athlone, the mythic, the legendary and the heroic – or the good, the bad and the ugly – were initially threaded through the moving image of the bioscope.

The institution of the bioscope was internally segmented at the levels of competition between bioscopes, film genres and the censor board. More than a history of experience, the bioscopes of Athlone reveal the mode of technogenesis offsetting the technologies of population control instituted in the name of apartheid. In Athlone alone, within the space of a kilometre, there were four cinemas – the Empire (700 seats, established by Basil Rubin), the Athlone (500 seats, established by the Moosa family), the Regent (700 seats, established by a Mr Stark) and the Kismet (1 323 seats, established by S.J. Patel, but, because of Group Areas legislation, placed under the nomineeship of a manager from the designated 'coloured' group). Of these, the Kismet was announced at the time of its opening in 1958 as a luxury cinema complex and was supplied, as were cinemas on the Cape Flats more generally, with films by the major distribution networks of African Consolidated Films in Cape Town and Hollywood Films in Johannesburg.

The first level of segmentation could be tracked in the competition between cinemas in Athlone, often spurred on by film distributors and their mechanisms of costing films. The second involved segmentation at the level of genre, often driving interest and taste. In the 1960s, the films that attracted audiences were those belonging to the genre known as 'spectacles'. These films – about *Hercules* (Italy, 1958, with Steve Reeves), *Samson and Delilah* (USA, 1949), the *Maciste* series (Italy, 1960s), *Spartacus* (USA, 1960, directed by Stanley Kubrick and starring Kirk Douglas and Jean Simmons) and *The Trojan Horse* (Italy, 1961, with

THE TROJAN HORSE AND THE 'BECOMING TECHNICAL OF THE HUMAN'

Figure 10.2. Trojan Horse Massacre memorial, Thornton Road, Athlone.
Photographer: Paul Grendon

Steve Reeves and Juliette Mayniel; see Figure 10.2) – 'glorified Greek and Roman heroes' and starred mostly 'bodybuilders', who became the poster boys of Athlone. By the mid-1960s, the spaghetti westerns had emerged as the most watched films, alongside the 'tearjerker' genre – for which cinema owners supplied free tissues to audiences. The latter included films such as *All Mine to Give* (1957), *The Bread Seller* (1960) and *Madame X* (1966). *Tarzan's Greatest Adventure* (1959) with Gordon Scott as the eponymous hero and *From Russia with Love* (1963) with Sean Connery in the lead role also had considerable appeal for audiences. This was followed in the early 1970s by kung-fu films from China, representing the high point of cinema viewing in Cape Town. The introduction of Chinese cinema was also the point at which a third level of segmentation occurred.

From the perspective of the censor board, Chinese films were deemed to be 'aspiring to communism' (Patel interview), and as a result the bioscopes were increasingly subjected to police raids and harassment. H. Ming, a distributor who was allowed to import a batch of 'films solely designated for the local Chinese community' (Patel interview), cleverly subtitled about 15 films for circulation on the Cape Flats. The first Chinese films, *The Hero* (1972) and *King of the Boxers* (1973), with Jimmy Wang Yu, proved to be highly successful (that is, lucrative and popular). Jimmy Wang Yu paved the way for the arrival of *The Big Boss* (1971), *Way of the Dragon* (1972), *Enter the Dragon* (1973) and *The Game of Death* (1978), which brought Bruce Lee to the life and times of Athlone.

Film showings were organised around the 'double feature', a screening consisting of two films. These ran daily and were mostly sold out on Saturdays and Fridays – which included a midnight show. The Saturday five o'clock performance proved most popular, with 'young lovers dressed to the nines' and 'tucked away in the corner seats' (Patel interview). At the Kismet, as with other cinemas, there were up to 100 permanent advanced seat reservations at any given time. On any Saturday, some 8 000 people circulated through the cinemas of Athlone – mostly residents from Langa, Gugulethu, Manenberg, Belgravia, Kewtown, Silvertown, Bridgetown, Hazendal, Crawford and Athlone – often defying censor board regulations and racial restrictions then governing cinemas in South Africa.

Apartheid had the final say in the segmentation of the institution of the bioscope. Audiences were demarcated and restricted through three categories of censorship – A: films deemed fit for everybody; B: restricted to ages 4–12 (films deemed fit for whites); C: restricted to ages 4–12 (films not deemed fit for 'Bantu'). To abide by the censorship laws effectively meant that a film categorised as 'B' could be seen by a 'coloured' youth of 13 but not by an adult classified under apartheid as 'Bantu'. The regulations were more regularly enforced by cinema owners in Athlone after 1968, following the showing of *I Want to Live!* (1958, with Susan Hayward and directed by Robert Wise). This film centred on the story of Barbara Graham – said to be the 'wildest of the jazzed up generation' and 'driven by a thousand desires' – who had been sentenced to death in the USA for murder. The film, which carried a 'C' censor board rating, was due to be shown after *A Train for Durango* (1968). Just prior to the interval, the police raided the cinema and expelled half of the audience – those who were perceived to be 'Bantu', for whom the film carried a prohibition.

What these levels of segmentation reveal is the extent to which the duration of the bioscope was marked by interruptions and intervals. Read alongside Vertov's theory of cinematography in which the human is folded into a technical apparatus – much like Charlie Chaplin in *Modern Times* – we may discern the way the bioscope constituted a 'fabric of relationships woven in the vision machine' (iv), where it functioned as an emotional prosthesis for the memory of street fighting for years to come.

The bioscope screen was a surface that conveyed an expansive globality. Across the Cape Flats, the image thus enlarged helped to counter the limits that Stephen Spender conveyed in his 1964 poem titled 'An Elementary School Classroom in a Slum' – a poem which was widely taught to a generation of students on the Cape Flats.

> Far far from gusty waves, these children's faces.
> Like rootless weeds, the hair torn round their pallor.
> The tall girl with her weighed-down head. The paper-
> seeming boy with rat's eyes. The stunted unlucky heir
> Of twisted bones, reciting a father's gnarled disease,
> His lesson from his desk. At back of the dim class
> One unnoted, mild and young: his eyes live in a dream,
> Of squirrels' game, in tree room, other than this.

> On sour cream walls, donations. Shakespeare's head
> Cloudless at dawn, civilized dome riding all cities.
> Belled, flowery, Tyrolese valley. Open-handed map
> Awarding the world its world. And yet, for these
> Children, these windows, not this world, are world,
> Where all their future's painted with a fog,
> A narrow street sealed in with a lead sky,
> Far far from rivers, capes, and stars of words.

Surely, Shakespeare is wicked, and the map a bad example
With ships and sun and love tempting them to steal—
For lives that slyly turn in their cramped holes
From fog to endless night? On their slag heap, these children
Wear skins peeped through by bones, and spectacles of steel
With mended glass, like bottle bits on stones.
Tyrol is wicked; map's promising a fable:
All of their time and space are foggy slum,
So blot their maps with slums as big as doom.

Unless, governor, teacher, inspector, visitor,
This map becomes their window and these windows
That open on their lives like catacombs,
Break, O break open, till they break the town
And show the children to green fields, and make their world
Run azure on gold sands, and let their tongues
Run naked into books, the white and green leaves open
The history theirs whose language is the sun.

A direct comment, with avowedly socialist sympathies, on the temporality of the slum in a world mediated through the demands of high culture, Spender's poem exceeds a politics of identification or even representation of those who 'wear skins peeped through by bones'. Its object is discernibly schooling. Like Jorge Luis Borges's map of the world that is the size of the world (in his short story 'On Exactitude in Science'), Spender derides a schooling that destroys dreams and kills desire. As the map awards 'the world its world', Spender invites us to consider conflicting durations of memory, between that which opens onto a world already unavailable, and a world where attention and play are commanded by books, in a language crafted to create something other than habituated spaces of bourgeois civility.

The poem was taught at many schools in Athlone as a form of protest against an increasingly regimented schooling system. A generation of intellectual teachers formed in the Teachers' League of South Africa and the United Democratic Front, railed courageously against apartheid schooling (see Rassool). Art teachers would frequently bemoan the inspectorate from the Department of Education, warning against their scurrilous attempts to stifle all creativity. Music teachers might rehash the lyrics of a Woodie Guthrie song, replacing the names of American landmarks with a South African landscape rendered barren by the desertification of apartheid:

This land is your land, this land is my land,
From the Great Limpopo, to Robben Island.

In other classrooms, the teaching of George Orwell's *Animal Farm* as a text of radical history was pitted against surreptitious intent on the part of educational authorities to educate students about the perils of communism. And elsewhere there were further cautionary tales about the dangers of a society of control. In a context where the world was normatively raced, sexed and classed, such instances of discernment produced an interval in which there was a change of direction.

Yet despite these attempts, the infrastructure of the school persisted, with intercoms placed to listen into classrooms and deliver sermons and daily prayers from on high, and lines drawn across schoolyards to marshal students into a general discipline of the cane. In this milieu, the bioscope functioned as an antidote to a geography that was all but uninhabitable. To borrow liberally from Paul Virilio, in Athlone the bioscope offered a substitute horizon to the geographies of apartheid. One consequence of this was a massive alteration of the visual field – to one that could accommodate Bernardo Bertolucci and Stanley Kubrick as well as Clint Eastwood, Bruce Lee and James Coburn. More importantly, the bioscope provided an interval that disturbed the binaries of global and local, inside and outside, home and the world.

Globality was also conveyed through a technological mechanism of the bioscope that introduced a measure of speed to the everyday, giving rise to a field of potential attraction, collision and orbit, of potential centripetal and centrifugal movements. Languages, accents, race and ethnicity, identification and misidentification, all lent themselves to a feeling of 'walking as controlled falling' (Massumi 14). The motion picture presented itself as a form of rhythm in which movement produced the very assemblages and gestures that exceeded apartheid's technology of subjection. In a place where private transport was a middle-class luxury, the bioscope offered a ride.

Whatever the conditions of precarity, Athlone was at the very least marked by a series of intervals. In this sense, neither popular culture nor the dyad of space and time is adequate for understanding its texture. Mostly, Athlone was a constellation of varying speeds in which the logic of apartheid's regimes of time could no longer be contained by a culture industry.

If anything, the bioscope in Athlone was a space where intervals mattered, functioning even as a model for apprehending the distributions of the sensible of the everyday. Mostly organised around the double feature, the showings themselves were interrupted by a brief interlude between the two films. The double feature often pitted film genres against each other, so it was not unlikely that viewers might see a spaghetti western hinged by the interval with a kung-fu film. The bioscope was not all about time: it was also about the interval, the enduring possibility of a second take after the first had run its credits. In all the ways that the interval was orchestrated, in the space of the 'everything else', lay a complex interlude in the subsuming of life into the drudgery of apartheid. The bioscope lived inside memory, as a prosthesis of memory of spaces not yet inhabited.

Following Stiegler and Vertov, let us think about the interval of the bioscope as a particular mode of grammatisation, one that placed a resource and rhythm at the very heart of the constitution of the political subject of apartheid. As a process of grammatisation, Athlone offers us a familiar regime of labour, that of 'hewers of wood and drawers of water'. Rather than pursuing the bioscope as instrument of effect, or a scene of leisure or even popular culture, it may be more useful to think of its composition in terms of a certain relation of time and technics into which the subject of apartheid was folded. In this configuration, the figure of the human – otherwise raced, classed and gendered – was

THE TROJAN HORSE AND THE 'BECOMING TECHNICAL OF THE HUMAN'

a script of excess in which movement was crafted synchronously with the speed mobilised by light falling upon moving images. Twenty-four frames per second initially to be exact, cast through 35mm projectors, accomplished greater foresight than the memories contained in fading photographs of the forced removals which had brought people to the Cape Flats. Besides offering a ride, the bioscope offered a memory of the future. Rather than functioning in a hierarchy of the senses, film and photograph complemented each other in recreating form and style as constitutive elements of a life in the shadows.

But movement, as we know all too well, also produces collisions and accidents. If the Soweto Uprising of 1976 marks such a collision, it is to the extent that this major student revolt converged with the collision between the time of the bioscope and the technics of television in South Africa. Television arrived in this country in May 1976, with 25 frames per second as opposed to the familiar 24 frames per second, on the eve of the Soweto student protests. Some of the earliest images broadcast on public national television were of the confrontations between students and police in Soweto. What gradually disappeared in the process of the displacement of the bioscope by the televisual was precisely the interval. We should consider here specifically how the bioscope gave us the interval as an opportunity to change directions. By contrast, the televisual, with its programmed format, abolished the time interval in the visual field, only to dilate the image of space.

This is a conception that follows in the tracks of Virilio's *Information Bomb*, which worries at the question of the hyperconcentration of telecommunications that gave us globalisation. For Virilio, the extreme reduction of distances ensues from a temporal compression of transport and transmission and the spread of telesurveillance. In short, late apartheid, unlike late colonialism with its administrative apparatus and indirect rule, could be said to resemble a techno-scientific development with a hyperconcentration of telecommunications, at the expense of the travel afforded in the interval in which the bioscope functioned. For the youth of the Cape Flats, this amounted to a double displacement: both home and, in its second iteration, a space lost to the compression of time. A history of transport on the Cape

Flats soon reveals the anxiety that this sense of entrapment produced. This was a drive with the sense of desire entirely eroded.

To be more precise, what the shift from bioscope to television symbolised was an inability to change direction. Suddenly, Bruce Lee was replaced by the *Brady Bunch*. And, with it, all the passions that charged the interval, from animated flying kicks to the projection of antiracial solidarities, seem to have waned. Nostalgia for the bioscope would return only to mark the memorials of apartheid's atrocities. But in that brief moment, a shift was imaginable in the movement of the body, in its rhythms, flows and change of direction.

Nothing could epitomise this more than the sheer excitement that filled the air when in *Way of the Dragon* (1972) Bruce Lee met Chuck Norris in the Colosseum in Rome. This specific scene is as crucial in terms of discerning the filmic qualities of Athlone as it is for a general study of the field of *techne* in the age of globalisation. Paul Bowman writes about the scene in a way that rephrases what I am hoping to suggest by the productivity of the interval that bioscope occasioned:

> The most famous illustration of Lee's ideal of broken rhythm is reputedly seen in *Way of the Dragon*. In this fight, Lee is at first formal and predictable; hence his equally formal opponent is able to fare well against him. Upon realizing this limitation, Lee's character switches to a more anarchic, fluid and unpredictable style, one which Miller argues was heavily indebted to Lee's attempts to emulate the movements of boxer Muhammad Ali. Lee's new style then breaks through his opponent's formal movements and rhythms. This scene is widely held to constitute a Jeet Kune Do lesson which illustrates the need to 'be like water' and to use 'broken rhythm' (21).

The scene would recall a pervasive mythology surrounding Lee's untimely death, as it also marked a racial identification that was increasingly taking hold under apartheid. He was, it was repeatedly and disdainfully claimed, killed by Chuck Norris in the end, a foreboding prophecy of what awaited Athlone. If the televisual field put the drive into overdrive, it would do

THE TROJAN HORSE AND THE 'BECOMING TECHNICAL OF THE HUMAN'

so by clipping a desire that extended well beyond the law that called it into being in the first place. And, with it, the technical becoming of the human was rescripted by the design of apartheid, in the form of a mode of transport laden with armed security and railway police hidden in crates on its carriage.

In their bid to redirect education from the dangerous course of its death drive, the students of Athlone undertook to reintroduce a mode of education intended to disable the authoritarian impulse, cynical reason and punitive function of apartheid education. It also sought to reorient the meaning of education.

All of this came to a head as the very movement unleashed by the students in July 1985 resulted in a tussle over the political imprint of the movement, and in the decision by the House of Representatives (the separate chamber for 'coloureds' in the apartheid Parliament) and the Department of Education and Training to close schools. In response to a spirited call for the reopening of schools by a group calling themselves the Concerned Teachers Association, which in all probability was issued jointly by teachers and students, thousands of parents, teachers and students across the Cape Flats heeded the call to defy the closure of schools.[4] In the resultant siege, it became clear that the students faced a state that had mobilised the army and not only the police.[5] The redirection of education attempted by the students of 1985 encountered its limit in the shift from police to military power. The closure of schools by Carter Ebrahim, education minister in the House of Representatives, was an attempt to draw students into the streets, into open confrontation.[6] The ambush that was laid for 15 October 1985, and that became known as the Trojan Horse Massacre, had a long gestation.

What now marks the massacre as an event relates to the speed of the circulation of the image, one that immediately dissolved the interval in which the student movement could be thought of as primarily a question of schooling. In its aftermath, violence coded the Athlone movement, not only that of the state but also of the students. The speed that accelerated the drive for a standoff with the state was idiomatically expressed in terms of journalism. The struggle was no longer focused on the school in a discourse of revolt and study that Sitze has concisely identified in his reading of Rive's *Emergency Continued*. Caught in the impasse between study and revolt, the struggles of 1985 petered out into a stasis that signalled not only an impasse, but civil war. Stasis was a condition, to borrow from Stiegler, of the proletarianisation of politics, in which the very question of the subject and of knowledge was short-circuited. In the catastrophe of the senses, something of the order of the police was reinforced as the condition of politics.

In this way, the state undercut a shift from schooling as ideological function to schooling as a desire to learn, putting to an end the connection of individuation to the process of transindividuation that had been struck up in the student movement. School was a technology of power from which one could only free oneself through a technogenesis of school, not through a counter-hegemonic or countercultural standpoint. In this, the relation between individuation and transindividuation would prove crucial. Transindividuation owes its emergence to the philosophy of Gilbert Simondon and, more recently, to Stiegler. By transindividuation, Simondon and Stiegler mean the process of co-constitution of individual and group psyches, in which the individual is always also a phase inserted into a longer process. Drawing on Freud, Stiegler combines this understanding of transindividuation with concepts of desire and technics, in which both function not only at the level of individual sexuality, but also as collective psyche. In an environment of schooling where Orwell's *Animal Farm* was meant to be read as a warning against the perils of communism, and where Chinua Achebe's *Arrow of God* was withdrawn by an overzealous education department for containing a sexually explicit scene, the interval for re-exploring the seam that bound individuation and transindividuation was short-circuited by the Trojan Horse Massacre. More succinctly, the Trojan Horse Massacre short-circuited the technogenesis of schooling that was under way in the student movement. Schooling as a site of struggle was returned to the problem of its function as an ideological state apparatus, leaving behind a memory with no future.

A CBS film crew happened to be filming in Thornton Road on the day of the shootings. Chris Everson, Greg Shaw and John Rubython filmed the unfolding events in Athlone (Weaver interview). Describing the

THE TROJAN HORSE AND THE 'BECOMING TECHNICAL OF THE HUMAN'

footage as explosive, they called the journalist Tony Weaver, who set to work on selecting three frames from the footage for an article on what he called the Trojan Horse Massacre for the *Cape Times* the following day. In the meantime, the CBS journalists chartered a plane to Nairobi and transmitted the footage to New York. Broadcast on television around the world, the Trojan Horse Massacre became a placeholder for a movement, the potential of which was lost to the immediacy and urgency demanded by the act of state violence. The entire story of the Trojan Horse had been given over to the question of communication, through boxes, in which the televisual was synchronised by the death carried in a railway truck turned into a war machine, not unlike the gift of the Greeks.

Much has been said and written about the Trojan Horse Massacre and its memorialisation (see Marschall).[7] Perhaps, not enough has been said and written to release us from the trappings of the speed of the operation that would change the course of history on which the students had embarked. But in all the ways the Trojan Horse has been memorialised, what is not clear is the extent to which the killings resulted in a process of disindividuation – a process where the very psychic apparatus fell upon a scene of drives disconnected from desire. The idea of schooling that had been problematised in the student movement had resulted in a fetishisation of school as ideological state apparatus, leaving no language for a memory of the future that the desire for schooling kindled among students in 1985.

The memorial that marks the site of the Trojan Horse killings, erected by an African National Congress-led City of Cape Town and replacing the more modest artistic marker by Tyrone Appollis (see Kros; see also Rassool & Van Bever Donker), recalls something of the compunction to mark time that was lost to compression. It has been roundly criticised for overemphasising the role of the perpetrators of state violence – a claim now supported by the loss of the plates depicting the stories of the mothers of three youth who were killed, told in their own handwriting. In the lukewarm reception of the memorial, perhaps there lurks a reason: the way in which it repeats the story of a drive without a hint of desire, of nostalgia for a dilated space, but not the interval that may have offered a different direction for the idea of schooling. The image, notwithstanding the criticism, is a familiar one for Athlone. It replays the motif of the war-film posters that once adorned the edifice of the bioscopes of Athlone. If this appears as an interpretative leap at first, it is only because the Trojan Horse memorial returns us to the stasis that once dominated the compression of time we have come to know as Athlone, and that is recalled not only as a memory of the past, but a memory of that which must be repeated – namely, war.

This is a mode of technogenesis of which we may need to remain fearful. For the human thus folded into the machine is only ever a technical becoming of the human who is a compression of movement, of uncontrollable speed and undulating sadness. This at least is how we may read Willie Bester's unsettling sculpture, *Trojan Horse III* (Figure 10.3), as a cautionary tale of precisely that operation which folds the human into technology, making technics a part of the figuring of the

Figure 10.3. Willie Bester (b.1956), *Trojan Horse III*, 2007.
Courtesy of the artist and Julian Jans/Bowman Sculpture
© Willie Bester

THE TROJAN HORSE AND THE 'BECOMING TECHNICAL OF THE HUMAN'

industrialisation of memory. Like the Greeks who folded the human into a war machine, Bester's work warns against the practice of a memory of the past that is the condition of teletechnics, with surveillance, threat, control, mobility and death rolled into an indistinguishable scene of unending battle.

Returning to the interval, consider an event four years after the Trojan Horse killings, in which student activists Coline Williams and Robert (Robbie) Waterwitch were killed in an ambush orchestrated by the state security apparatus. As the record indicates, they were killed in July 1989 while attempting to plant explosives at the magistrate's court in the central business district of Athlone. The story of their deaths has become legendary on the Cape Flats, not least because death was brought about by the same means of dirty tricks and surreptitious ambush that had delivered the Trojan Horse to the streets of Athlone and Crossroads. As the Truth and Reconciliation Commission was to suggest in one interpretation, the deaths of Robbie Waterwitch and Coline Williams resulted from a zero-timed explosive device, issued by the covert state apparatus through the agency of a security police informer who had infiltrated an underground resistance cell. The aim of this act of infiltration was to ensure that the two operatives were killed.

In their memory, the space outside the magistrate's court today carries a statue of Robbie and Coline as they have been popularly inscribed into a public imaginary. Coline glances suspiciously over her shoulder, as if to recognise the scene of interpellation. Robbie walks confidently abreast of her (Figure 10.4).

In descriptions of their fateful deaths, the magistrate's court has notoriously become the target of their attention, like a scene from Franz Kafka's 'Vor dem Gesetz' (Before the Law), where the law reveals itself as the very condition for violence. It may be read as a cautionary tale about never being complacent before the law. Yet, in a broader optic, the space of the memorial brings into view the bioscope that was once immediately ahead, across the street from where the sculpture is placed today. The building now houses the government department of communication and information. Once it was home to the Kismet

Figures 10.4 and 10.5. Sculpture in memory of Coline Williams and Robert Waterwitch, Athlone.
Photographer: Paul Grendon

bioscope, a name that, when translated, gives us recourse to that which remains to be said about the spectre of death in Athlone. It is a word that has its beginnings in Arabic (root *qasama*, meaning 'to divide'), that developed into *qisma* (meaning 'division', 'portion' or 'lot') and, with the rise of the Ottoman Empire, entered Turkish as *kismet* (meaning 'fate' or 'destiny'). From here it was deposited into Hindi and Urdu, retaining its Turkish inflection, before travelling to Athlone where it simply came to mean 'the bioscope'.

That at least is what is left of the memory of the future, a scene of desire that shares in the fate of reschooling and, in the process, retooling. The student movement of 1985 was nothing of the order of a schools' boycott. It was a desire for a return to an interval, in a space of intensity in which compression of time diluted and dilated space, giving students a mode of communication with little prospect of advance, let alone retreat. What the bioscope shared with the school was a different conception of the interval: one that promised a non-sectarian future in place of the difference marked out by the interval of apartheid.

NOTES

1. This is a greatly truncated rendering of a systematic elaboration that deserves to be read at length (see Stiegler, *Technics and Time, 1: The Fault of Epimetheus* 106).
2. Heidi Grunebaum addresses precisely this problem in her consideration of how the memory of Robert Waterwitch and Coline Williams often erodes lives beyond the event of their untimely deaths at the hands of the apartheid security forces.
3. Black audiences were initially barred from viewing Sergio Leone's 'Man with No Name' series, which includes *The Good, the Bad and the Ugly*. It was only after resubmission to the censor boards in the 1970s that viewing was permitted (Patel interview).
4. Pamphlet by Concerned Teachers Association, Robert van Niekerk, private collection.
5. Basil Swart, submission to the Truth and Reconciliation Commission, 2 June 1997, www.justice.gov.za/trc/special%5Ctrojan/swart.htm. Accessed 23 August 2016.
6. The most outlandish report on this comes from the *New York Times* – see Alan Cowell.
7. With the recent removal of the bronze plaques containing the narratives of the mothers of those killed, we may have to reconsider the idea of vernacular expressions that Sabine Marschall identifies in her suggestive essay. See also the paper by Gary Minkley and Phindi Mnyaka.

REFERENCES

Achebe, Chinua. *Arrow of God*. Heinemann, 1964.
Bowman, Paul. *Beyond Bruce Lee: Chasing the Dragon through Film, Philosophy and Popular Culture*. Columbia UP, 2013.
Bundy, Colin. 'Action Comrades, Action! Street Sociology and Pavement Politics in Cape Town in 1985.' *The Angry Divide: Social and Economic*

History of the Western Cape, edited by Mary Simons and Wilmot James, David Philip, 1989, pp. 206–217.

Chamberlin, Carloss James. 'Dziga Vertov: The Idiot.' *Senses of Cinema*, Issue 41, November 2006, sensesofcinema.com/2006/feature-articles/dziga-vertov-enthusiasm/. Accessed 10 August 2016.

Cowell, Alan. '454 Schools Shut for Mixed Races in Cape Town Area.' *New York Times*, 2 September 1985, www.nytimes.com/1985/09/07/world/454-schools-shut-for-mixed-races-in-cape-town-area.html. Accessed 23 August 2016.

Grunebaum, Heidi. *Memorialising the Past: Everyday Life in South Africa after the Truth and Reconciliation Commission*. Transaction Publishers, 2011.

Kafka, Franz. 'Before the Law.' *The Trial*, translated by Breon Mitchell, Schocken Books, 1998 [1915].

Kros, Cynthia. 'Prompting Reflections: An Account of the *Sunday Times* Heritage Project from the Perspective of an Insider Historian.' *Kronos: Southern African Histories*, vol. 34, no. 1, 2008, www.scielo.org.za/scielo.php?pid=S0259-019020080001 00007&script=sci_arttext. Accessed 10 August 2016.

Little, John. *The Warrior Within: The Philosophies of Bruce Lee*. Contemporary Books, 1996.

Marschall, Sabine. 'Commemorating the "Trojan Horse" Massacre in Cape Town: The Tension between Vernacular and Official Expressions of Memory.' *Visual Studies*, vol. 25, no. 2, September 2010, pp. 135–148.

Massumi, Brian. 'Navigating Movements.' www.brianmassumi.com/interviews/NAVIGATING%20MOVEMENTS.pdf. Accessed 22 August 2016.

Minh-ha, Trinh T. *Cinema Interval*. Routledge, 1999.

Minkley, Gary and Phindi Mnyaka. 'Spears, Warriors and a Victorious Past: Visuality and the Post Anti-Apartheid Heritage Complex.' Paper presented at the conference 'The Politics of Heritage', Museum Africa, Johannesburg, 8–9 July 2011.

Orwell, George. *Animal Farm*. Secker & Warburg, 1945.

Rassool, Ciraj. 'Taking the Nation to School: IB Tabata and the Politics of Knowledge.' Paper presented at the South African History and Contemporary

Society Seminar, Department of History and Institute for Historical Research, University of the Western Cape, 2001.

Rassool, Ciraj and Maurits van Bever Donker. 'South African Apartheid: The White Man Must Govern.' *Apartheid: The South African Mirror*, curated by P Subirós, catalogue of the exhibition 'Centre de Cultura Contemporània de Barcelona and the Centro Cultural Bancaja of Valencia, 2007–2008', Barcelona, 2007.

Rive, Richard. *Emergency Continued*. Readers International, 1990.

SADET (South African Democracy Education Trust). *The Road to Democracy in South Africa: Volume 2 (1970–1980)*. Unisa Press, 1990.

Sitze, Adam. 'Between Study and Revolt: Further Notes on *Emergency Continued*.' Paper presented to the South African Contemporary History and Humanities Seminar, Centre for Humanities Research, University of the Western Cape, August 2014.

Spender, Stephen. 'An Elementary School Classroom in a Slum.' *Selected Poems*, Random House, 1964.

Stiegler, Bernard. *Technics and Time, 1: The Fault of Epimetheus*. Translated by Richard Beardsworth and George Collins, Stanford UP, 1998.

———. *Technics and Time, 2: Disorientation*. Translated by Stephen Barker, Stanford UP, 2009.

———. *Technics and Time, 3: Cinematic Time and the Question of Malaise*. Translated by Stephen Barker, Stanford UP, 2011.

Virilio, Paul. *The Information Bomb*. Verso, 2000.

INTERVIEWS

Patel, Kantilal. Personal interview. 15 August 2014.

Weaver, Tony. Personal interview. 20 August 2014.

ABOUT THE CONTRIBUTORS

 Please consult the ORCiD registry for further information on our authors www.orcid.org

Jaco Barnard-Naudé is Professor of Jurisprudence in the Department of Private Law in the Faculty of Law at the University of Cape Town. He is an NRF-rated researcher and a recipient of the UCT Fellows Award. His wide range of research interests includes postmodern and poststructural legal theory, law and sexuality, postapartheid jurisprudence and law and literature. Of late, his work has increasingly moved into a psychoanalytic mode of inquiry. He holds the degrees BCom (Law), LLB and LLD from the University of Pretoria and an MA in Creative Writing from the University of Cape Town. He is an honorary research fellow in the Birkbeck Institute for the Humanities, University of London, and has been a visiting professor at the University of Westminster and at Birkbeck College, University of London.

Aidan Erasmus is currently a doctoral candidate in the Department of History and an Early Career Fellow at the DST-NRF Flagship for Critical Thought in African Humanities at the Centre for Humanities Research, University of the Western Cape. His dissertation, titled 'A Phonography of War', is invested in constituting sound as a modality through which to think the resonant contours of imperial war, through the examination of aesthetic production in music, radio and cinema under apartheid and in the postapartheid.

Derek Hook is Associate Professor of Psychology at Duquesne University. He is a scholar and a practitioner of psychoanalysis, with expertise in the area of critical psychology and psychosocial studies. Before moving to Duquesne, he was in Psychosocial Studies at Birkbeck College, University of London. He is the author of *Foucault, Psychology and the Analytics of Power* (2007), *A Critical Psychology of the Postcolonial* (2011) and more recently *(Post)apartheid Conditions: Psychoanalysis and Social Formations* (2013). He is a research fellow of the Independent Social Research Foundation and a lead researcher in the Apartheid Archive Project.

Premesh Lalu is Professor of History and the Director of the Centre for Humanities Research at the University of the Western Cape. He has published widely in academic journals on historical discourse and the humanities in Africa and is a regular contributor of public opinion pieces to local and international newspapers. His book, *The Deaths of Hintsa: Postapartheid South Africa and the Shape of Recurring Pasts* (2009), argues that in order to forge a concept of apartheid that allows us to properly formulate a deeper meaning of the postapartheid, what is necessary is a postcolonial critique of apartheid. Lalu is a board member of the international Consortium of Humanities Centers and Institutes and Chairperson of the Handspring Trust for Puppetry in Education.

Annemarie Lawless earned degrees from Trinity College, Dublin (BA), Durham University (MA), and the University of Minnesota (PhD). Her doctoral research explores the idea of love, as a mode of knowledge and a form of ethics, in the work of Walter Benjamin and Gilles Deleuze, in particular Benjamin's understanding of redemption and Deleuze's concept of immanence; the relation between knowledge and the aesthetic image; and the function of the image in texts by Shelley, Kierkegaard and Beckett, among others. Her current research is focused on the connection between being and the image in the work of Deleuze, Heidegger and Blanchot. She currently teaches courses in critical theory in the English Department at the University of Minnesota.

ABOUT THE CONTRIBUTORS

Gary Minkley currently holds the NRF SARChI Chair in Social Change at the University of Fort Hare in East London. He has a PhD from the University of Cape Town. He worked in the History Department at the University of the Western Cape until 2003, and then at the University of Fort Hare as a Senior Researcher, a Professor of History and as the Director of Post-Graduate Studies. His research interests are in South African and Eastern Cape history and the dynamics of social change, public and visual history, and public space, and he has an extensive publication record that reflects these interests.

Helena Pohlandt-McCormick is Associate Professor of African History at the University of Minnesota and has served as the ICGC/UWC Mellon Research Chair at the University of the Western Cape. She received an MA in Communications from the Ludwig Maximilian University in Munich in 1984, an MA in Journalism from the University of Michigan in 1986, and a PhD from the University of Minnesota in 1999. Her research focuses on postcolonial and postapartheid history and theory, archival studies and gender/sexuality studies. Her book, *'I Saw a Nightmare ...' – Doing Violence to Memory: The Soweto Uprising, June 16, 1976*, examined competing historical memories and representations of the Soweto Uprising and was published by Columbia University Press and the American Historical Association in 2005.

Mari Ruti is Professor of Critical Theory at the University of Toronto, where she teaches contemporary theory, continental philosophy, psychoanalysis, and feminist and queer theory. She is the author of ten books, including *The Singularity of Being: Lacan and the Immortal Within* (2012); *The Call of Character: Living a Life Worth Living* (2013); *Between Levinas and Lacan: Self, Other, Ethics* (2015).

Ross Truscott is currently a Next Generation Scholar at the DST-NRF Flagship for Critical Thought in African Humanities at the Centre for Humanities Research, University of the Western Cape. He has a PhD from the University of Fort Hare, where he studied at the NRF SARChI Chair in Social Change. He has held fellowships at Duke University, the University of Minnesota, and the London School of Economics. He has published on psychoanalysis, history, and postcolonial theory, post-apartheid empathy and its discontents, nationalism, popular culture, race, gender and sexuality.

Maurits van Bever Donker is currently Academic Coordinator and a Next Generation Scholar at the DST-NRF Flagship for Critical Thought in African Humanities at the Centre for Humanities Research, University of the Western Cape. His research interests are in postcolonial theory and literature, critical theory, African literature and history, Black Consciousness philosophy, transnational articulations and intersections of race and gender, and desire in the postcolonial.

LIST OF FIGURES

Figure 3.1. 'Emabutfo'
© Nandipha Mntambo, courtesy of STEVENSON Cape Town and Johannesburg

Figure 3.2. 'The Rape of Europa'
© Nandipha Mntambo, courtesy of STEVENSON Cape Town and Johannesburg

Figure 3.3. 'Narcissus'
© Nandipha Mntambo, courtesy of STEVENSON Cape Town and Johannesburg

Figure 8.1. Winter in Tembisa (ca 1991).
Photographer: Santu Mofokeng
Medium Gelatin silver print
Yale University Art Gallery
Gift of Mary Jo and Ted P. Shen, B.A. 1966, M.A. (HON) 2001.
© Santu Mofokeng Foundation, courtesy Lunetta Bartz, *MAKER*, Johannesburg

Figure 8.2. Moses Twebe (fourth from the left) in front of the Moses Twebe Great Hall, 15 March 2007.
Photographer: Gary Minkley

Figure 8.3. Moses Twebe, his family and his goat, 15 March 2007.
Photographer: Gary Minkley

Figure 10.1. Juliette Franciscus (glancing over her shoulder), Karen Britten, Sean Stockenstroom, Belgravia High students on the corner of Thornton and Kromboom roads, 1985.
Photographer: David Hartman

Figure 10.2. Trojan Horse Massacre memorial, Thornton Road, Athlone.
Photographer: Paul Grendon

Figure 10.3. Willie Bester (b.1956), *Trojan Horse III*, 2007.
Mixed media sculpture
Courtesy of the artist and Julian Jans/Bowman Sculpture.
© Willie Bester

Figure 10.4 and 10.5. Sculpture in memory of Coline Williams and Robert Waterwitch, Athlone.
Photographer: Paul Grendon

INDEX

9/11 catastrophe 103

A
'Abduction of Europa' 85
Abraham, Nicolas 126–127, 131
absolute/Absolute 159–161, 165, 166 (n 4), 169 (n 17)
Absolutism 150
Abu Ghraib (prison) 97
Abuses 166 (n 1)
accountability 24, 94, 100, 104
'Acéphale' 230
Achebe, Chinua 266
Adieu to Emmanuel Levinas 128
Adler, Alfred 75, 88 (n 7)
Adorno, Theodor 30 (n 2)
Aesthetics 246 (n 7)
Afghans 98
Africa Is a Country 31 (n 10)
African Art as Philosophy 35 (n 26)
African Consolidated Films, Cape Town 256
African National Congress (ANC) 48–49, 57, 60, 198, 200, 203, 206, 208, 216, 267
Africanism 197
Afrikaans 173, 186
   balladry 176
   ballads 187 (n 15)
   language 173
   light music artists 187 (n 13)
   music scene 173
   musicians 173
   pop 175
   popular music 174, 187 (n 13)
   punk-rock 172
   rock 172–194
   rock band 172
   rock junkies 174
Afrikaans-speaking
   communities 172 188 (n 18)
   protest movement 188 (n 21)
   resistance 189 (n 28)
   the term 189 (n 23)
   white youth 173
Afrikaansness 173
Afrikaner(s)
   identity 180, 189 (n 25)
   middle-class 180
   nationalism 173, 187 (n 15), 196
   patriarchal society 177
   society 177
   the term 188–189 (n 23)
   women 188 (n 18)
Agamben, Giorgio 118, 201
Ahmed, Sarah 88 (n 11)
Aids 61 (n 3), 148, 238, 243
Alexander 168 (n 12)
Ali, Muhammad 264
allegory 146, 149–154
Allen, Amy 108–109
Althusser, Louis 27
Ambiguities of Witnessing 246 (n 5)
American/Americans 58, 96–98, 205, 218
American Historical Association 277
ANC *see* African National Congress
Animal Farm 261, 266
anthropological
   empathy 26
   knowledge 79
   knowledge production 81
anthropologist(s) 79–80
anthropology 78–79, 210
Anthropology (Kant's) 3
Anthropology (Tylor's) 79
anti-apartheid 188 (n 21), 204–205, 217
   activities 176
   movement 204, 218
   renditions of the past 202
   resistance 202
   struggle 203
anti-Enlightenment predilections 104

anti-racism 197, 202
Antibiotika 186
anticolonial
　revolution 31 (n 11)
　struggle(s) 107, 202
anticolonialism 197
Antigone 28–29, 226, 232, 234–236, 245, 246 (n 11)
Antigony 232
apartheid 1–3, 6–11, 14–27, 32 (n 14), 35 (n 29, 30), 65–66, 78, 81, 95–96, 113, 119, 137, 140–141, 173, 175–181, 183–186, 187 (n 10), 195–205, 208, 217–218, 220, 222 (n 7), 225–226, 237, 240, 246 (n 5), 250–258, 261–265, 271, 271 (n 2)
　culture of hate and separatism 61
　difference 13–14, 175, 200, 203
　discourse 8
　dismantled 44
　end of 7, 36 (n 31), 181
　ends of 117–145
　genealogy 18
　global 7, 14–22, 24, 27–28, 35 (n 29), 41, 44, 95, 112–115, 118–119, 137, 197–199, 208, 227, 240
　government 189 (n 28), 204, 251
　memorials of atrocities 264
　relations 86
　resistance 107
　schooling 261
　separate development policy 3
　social 196, 198, 210
　socials 202
　South Africa(n) 112–113, 118, 200
　state 201–204
　structural divisions 56
　transition 56
　wake of 8–13, 24, 137, 175, 255
apartheid's children 177–181
Aporias 128
Appollis, Tyrone 267
The Arcades Project 153–154, 214
Arendt, Hannah 24–25, 27, 107, 117–145, 211
Arrow of God 266

Art contre/against Apartheid 35 (n 27)
As jy met vuur speel sal jy brand 172, 186
Association of Artists of the World Against Apartheid 35 (n 27)
Athlone cinema 252, 256, 258
Athlone movement 265
autochthony 28, 226, 231–243, 245, 247 (n 13)
autoeroticism 82

B
Bailly, Lionel 52
bantustans 27, 200–201, 217, 221, 240
　Ciskei 204
　consolidation 200
　defining 210
　politics 207
　refiguring 27, 196
　reincorporation 201, 210
　removal to 207
Barnard-Naudé, Jaco 24–25, 117, 275
Baroque 160
Barthes, Roland 26, 149–152, 155–156, 166 (n 3, 6), 168 (n 11, 14), 211
Basson, Lauren 190 (n 29)
Bataille, Georges 226, 228–230, 236
Batman 58–59
Baudelaire, Charles 155
Bauer, Ida 87 (n 4)
Bauer, Phillip 69
'becoming-with-others' 12, 31 (n 12)
being 30 (n 1), 33 (n 19), 94, 99–100, 106, 169 (n 18), 228–229
　emerging from community 233
　obstinacy of 92
　principle of 231, 236–237
　root of 235
Benjamin, Jessica 106
Benjamin, Walter 26, 149–156, 162–165, 166–168 (n 2, 6, 7, 9, 11, 13), 198, 214, 220–221, 227, 246 (n 4), 276
Bergson, Henri 169 (n 17)
Bergsonian
　dilation 29
　post-Bergsonian sense of 'virtual reality' 253

INDEX

Bertolucci, Bernardo 261
Bester, Willie 268, 268 (fig), 269
Between Levinas and Lacan: Self, Other, Ethics 277
Biko, Steve 3–5
biopolitical forces 95
biopolitics 118, 141 (n 3)
bios politikos 130
bioscope(s) 29, 255–264, 268–270 *see also* cinema
The Black Man's Burden 202
Black Skin, White Masks 4, 13, 20, 31 (n 7), 32 (n 15), 246 (n 8)
'Black Souls in White Skins?' 3
blackness 4–5
　affirmation 10
　mechanism of blackness/whiteness 5
　metaphysics 4
Blanchot, Maurice 28–29, 226–232, 235–236, 276
Bloed, sweet en trane 172, 174
Body Transformations 166 (n 1)
Bond, Patrick 141 (n 1)
Borges, Jorge Luis 260
Botha, PW 176, 185
Bouazizi, Mohammed 142 (n 5)
Bourdieu, Pierre 147
Bowman, Paul 264
Brady Bunch 264
Brand Suid-Afrika 186
Brecht, Bertolt 221 (n 3)
Breytenbach, Breyten 187 (n 11)
British Dominion (history) 196
Britten, Karen 252 (fig)
Brothers and Sisters 60
Brown, Tony 3
Brown, Wendy 101
Buck-Morss, Susan 167–168 (n 9, 12), 206, 220
Bundy, Colin 249
bureaucracy 27, 122–123
Burger, John (pseud of Leo Marquard) 202
Butler, Judith 23–24, 92–112, 115
Butlerian theory 106
Byzantine, 160

C

Cadava, Eduardo 151, 167 (n 9), 168 (n 14)
The Call of Character: Living a Life Worth Living 277
Camera Lucida 151, 155
Cape Times 267
capitalism
　demand for efficiency 103
　global 57, 113, 138
　global liberal 2
　international 204
　logic 195
　neoliberal order 113
　racial 195–196, 207
　white monopoly 13
Cartesian
　itinerary 19
　subject 18
Casarino, Cesare 169 (n 16)
Cavarero, Adriana 105
CBS 266–267
censor board(s) 256–258, 271 (n 3)
censorship 258
Centre for Humanities Research (CHR) 245, 275–277
Césaire, Aimé 21
Chamayou, Grégoire 79–80, 88 (n 10)
Chamberlin, Carloss James 253
Chinese
　cinema 257
　community 258
　films 257–258
Chipkin, Ivor 62 (n 4)
CHR *see* Centre for Humanities Research
Christodoulidis, Emilios 120, 135–138, 142 (n 6)
cinema 253–255 *see also* bioscope
Cinema Interval 252
cinemas 256
cinematography 253
　retheorise 253
　theorisation 253
　theory of 253

283

Ciskei 201
  bantustan/homeland 200, 204
  reincorporation 201
  reterritorialised 207
Ciskei National Independence Party 201
Clarke, James 133
Clegg, Johnny 190 (n 28)
Clewell, Tammy 126
'Coast Scene with the Rape of Europa' 85
colonial
  and apartheid relations 86
  Commission of Inquiry 6, 30 (n 4), 78
  concept 86
  domination 65
  empire (South African) 216–217
  exploitation (British) 203
  governmentality 76
  past 11, 102, 200
  representational repertoires 210
  rule 23, 66, 78
  situation (South Africa) 196
  state 77
  subject 196
  suppression of revolt 78
  temporality 26
  thinking 66
  visual codes 66, 87 (n 1)
  world 16
colonialism
  European 15–16, 85, 113
  internal 213
  late 263
  lens of 237
  logic 16
  modern
  South Africa's form of 206
  thingification 13
  thinking 23
  violence 33
Colonialism of a Special Type (CST)
  195–197, 206, 213
colonisation 16
colonised people 76–77
Commission of Inquiry *see* colonial
  Commission of Inquiry
Communist International 196, 221 (n 2)

Communist Party *see* South African
  Communist Party
Communist Party of South Africa
  (CPSA) 196
community 225
  Acéphale 230, 245
  angst 26, 181
  becoming expressive of 28
  being emerging from 233
  black 50
  centre (Dimbaza) 208
  collections of persons or groups 230
  concept of 28, 226–229, 232,
    236–237
  contours of 240
  edge of 225–232, 244
  elective 232
  ethics and community 225–248
  expression of 230, 245
  'gift of' 230
  global human 107
  identity 53
  lines of 227
  literary 231
  of writing 237
  political 102, 227, 229
  refiguring 236
  role in recognition of racial categories
    245 (n 1)
  scientific 77
  sense of 230–232, 236
  separate development of 35 (n 30)
  tensions 28, 233
  thinking of 231
  troubling of 232
  unavowable 236
  white liberal 50
The Community 166 (n 1)
conceptions
  and perceptions 156
  conventional 136
  of thought 157
Concerned Teachers Association 265,
  271 (n 4)
conformity *see* sameness
Connery, Sean 257

INDEX

constitution
 of a social to come 19
 of new senses 17
 of the political subject 262
 of the social 22
 political 20
 socioeconomic rights 138
Constitution (South African) 139, 180
constitutional
 obligations 139
 settlement (South Africa) 137
Constitutional Court 138
constitutionalism 138
copulation 28, 226, 232–238
Cortés-Rocca, Paola 151, 168 (n 14)
Cowell, Alan 272 (n 6)
The Creative Mind 169 (n 17)
Creon 235–236, 242
Crises of the Republic 129
Critchley, Simon 128
A Critical Psychology of the Postcolonial 276
A Critique of Postcolonial Reason 3
CST *see* Colonialism of a Special Type
Curran, Leo 72–83, 87 (n 5)

D

DA *see* Democratic Alliance
Dallas 60
Dangerous Emotions 166 (n 1)
The Dark Knight Returns 58
das Ding 99
David Russell archive 220
Dawes, Nic 42, 56
De Kock, Eugene 65, 81
De Man, Paul 246 (n 7)
The Deaths of Hintsa: Postapartheid South Africa and the Shape of Recurring Pasts 276
decolonisation 10–12, 14, 30 (n 6)
'A Defence of Poetry' 74
Deleuze, Gilles 13–14, 17, 20, 26, 32 (n 15), 36 (n 32), 147, 150–151, 156–165, 169 (n 18), 221 (n 1), 276
democratic
 experimentalism 137
 government 133

 processes and institutions 43
 state 42
 transition of 1994 173
Democratic Alliance 61 (n 2)
democratisation (Tunisia) 142 (n 5)
Department of Education 261, 265
Derrida, Jacques 1, 15, 21, 25, 35 (n 28–30), 107–108, 115, 119–121, 125–129, 132, 136, 196, 245 (n 2), 246 (n 7)
Derridean
 mode of reading Freud 31 (n 8)
 mourning 120, 128–136
 mourning and melancholia 24
Desargues, Girard 160
Descartes, René 18, 26, 31 (n 13), 33 (n 21), 113, 160, 169 (n 15)
Desmond, Cosmas 222 (n 6)
deterritorialisation 204–206, 218, 222 (n 8)
Diagne, Souleymane Bachir 35 (n 26)
Dialectic of Enlightenment 30 (n 2)
Dialectical Images 167 (n 9)
Dialectics of Seeing 167 (n9)
A Diary in the Strict Sense of the Term 67
Didi-Huberman, Georges 219–220, 221 (n 1)
difference 9, 17, 20–21, 66, 123, 151, 164, 169 (n 18), 183, 185–186
 apartheid's 9, 14, 20, 175, 200, 203
 as a marker of life 7
 between Empire and colonialism 16
 category of 7
 empathy's 82
 extrinsic 6, 13, 17, 20
 institutionalised 234–235
 of reason 79
 racial 181
 sense(s) of 3, 17, 20
Difference and Repetition 13, 163, 169 (n 18)
Dikeni, Sandile 218
Dimbaza 195–224)
 archive 27, 205
 de-industrialisation 201, 207
 graves 195–224
 history 198
 industrial development 204
 industrialisation 200–201, 204, 206

285

'Dis 'n land' 175–179, 181, 186, 187–188 (n 14, 15, 18)
The Discarded People 222 (n 6)
discourse of
  class struggle 206
  decolonisation 11
  empathy 66
  generalisability 110
  labour 204
  liberation 27, 208
  mourning 98
  psychoanalysis 69
  race war 27
  reconciliation 218
  revolt 265
  the colonial state 77
  the saviour 44
  time 206
Discourse on Metaphysics 162
Dlamini, Jacob 43–44
'The Doctrine of the Similar' 155
Dora 23, 67, 69–74, 79, 86, 87 (n 3, 4)
Dostoyevsky, Fyodor 104
'double interval' 159–160, 169 (n 18)
Du Plessis, Koos 186
Duncombe, Stephen 182–184, 189 (n 27)
Duras, Marguerite 228, 236
Dürer, Albrecht 85
Durrant, Sam 246 (n 5, 13)
'Dziga Vertov: The Idiot' 253

E

Eastwood, Clint 261
Ebrahim, Carter 265
'Echo' 83, 88 (n 8)
Echo/echoic 23, 83–86
Edelman, Lee 176
Eendag op 'n slag 172, 174
'Einde van die wêreld' 181
Einfühlung 68–69, 74
Eisenstein, Sergei 252
Ek sing 175, 187 (n14)
Elective Affinities 149
'An Elementary School Classroom in a Slum' 259
'Emabutfo' 67 (fig)

Emergency Continued 250, 266
empathy 23, 25, 36 (n 31), 65–91, 148
  anthropological 26
  capacity for 65
  echoic 84
  ontogenetic 82
  phylogenetic 82
  postapartheid 72
  temporality 82
Empire 7, 16
Empire 15–17, 27, 32 (n 18), 113
empire 212, 216
  British 203, 218
  building 102
  colonial 216–217
  complexity 217
  concept 213–214
  global 15–16, 113
  notions 196
  of liberation 27, 196–197, 205–208, 212, 216–220, 222 (n 8)
  Ottoman 270
  reterritorialisation of 222 (n 8)
  South African 27, 196, 205, 218, 220
  structures of 216
Empire cinema 256
The Encounter 66–67, 69, 81, 83, 85
Energie 188 (n 21)
Enlightenment 2, 6, 30 (n 1, 3), 107–109
  blackmail of 3
  concept 3
  dialectic (n 2)
  morality 117
  norms 24
  productivity 34 (n 22)
  rationality 105, 109
  thinking 30 (n 2)
  transcendental 111
  values 3, 30 (n 2)
Enter the Dragon 256, 258
epistemic project/structure of apartheid 26
epistemophilic pleasure 31 (n 8)
'equality among peers' 122
Erasmus, Aidan 26, 172, 275
Eteocles 233, 235

INDEX

ethical
   accountability 24, 100, 104
   attitude (Levinasian) 104
   caution 147
   imperative of mourning 128
   injunction (Levinasian) 104
   order 246 (n 10)
   potential of the concept of community 238
   responsibility 94, 104
   sense of the 227, 236
   transgression 148
ethic(s) 109, 112, 227, 235, 244, 246 (n 10)
   and community 225–248
   and justice distinction 24, 104
   connections with politics and community 227
   of becoming-with-others 12
   of empathy (postapartheid) 86
   of equality 94
   of mourning 101
   of precarity 24, 92–116
   Levinasian 24, 104–105
   Protestant 99, 103
   without norms 106
Ethics 156–157
'The Ethics of Precarity: Judith Butler's Reluctant Universalism' 23
ethnology 78
Eurocentrism 2, 4, 15
Europa 72–73, 81, 85, 233
European
   colonialism 15, 85, 113
   colonisation 16
European Commission 119
'Evening' 191 (n 30)
Everson, Chris 266

F

facies totius naturae 151, 157–159, 161, 165
Fanon, Frantz 4–6, 11, 13–14, 20, 31 (n 7), 32 (n 15), 35 (n 25), 105, 246 (n 8)
Fanonian language 13, 31 (n 11)
fantasies/fantasy 53, 55, 113, 177
   age of fantasy and hysteria 10
   bonds of 53–55
   end of 54
   functioning as protective shell 55
   Mandela as 62 (n 4)
   of being inviolable 103
   of sovereignty 99, 106
   shared social (Mandela) 22, 53
   traversing 62 (n 5)
Fascism 8, 27
First Person Singular 166 (n 1)
Fokofpolisiekar 172–175, 178, 180, 183–186, 189 (n 25)
Fokofpolisiekar: Forgive Them 173
The Fold 161–162
forced removals 200–201, 222 (n 6), 263
Foreign Bodies 166 (n 1)
Foucault, Michel 3, 23, 27, 141 (n 3), 199 221 (n 1)
Foucault, Psychology and the Analytics of Power 276
'Fragment of an Analysis of a Case of Hysteria' 67
Franciscus, Juliette 252 (fig)
Frau K 69–71
Frederickson, George 48
freedom 18, 24, 30 (n 2), 49, 107, 132–134, 213
   Antigone's 235
   as an absence 124
   conception of 124
   experience of 134, 139–141
   in the modern age 132
   loss of 124
   notion of 124
   political/politics as freedom 25, 136, 138
   postapartheid 208
   power of 141
   properties of 19
   South Africa's 2
   subject of 212
Freedom Day celebrations 212
French Revolution 117, 122, 124
Freud, Sigmund 6, 8, 13, 23, 30–32 (n 3, 8, 9, 15), 45, 61 (n 1), 67–79, 82, 87 (n 3, 4, 6), 88 (n 7), 100, 120, 125–131, 220, 228, 266

Freudian
  concept of community 236
  incorporation 128
  melancholia 121, 125–126
  melancholic or 'nostalgic'
    yearning 131
  mourning 121, 125, 127
  primal father 62 (n 7)
  sense of community 230
'From the Native's Point of View' 67
futurity 22, 26
  devotion to 175
  investment in 178
  reproductive 86, 177

G
Gaddafi, Muammar 60
Galois, Evariste 160
Garb, Tamar 66
Gastrow, Vanya 134–135
Gaus, Günter 135
Gaylard, Rob 246 (n 3), 247 (n 14)
gaze 11, 32–33 (n 19), 73, 167 (n 6, 9), 180
  empathic 66, 73–74, 84, 86
  psychoanalytic 34 (n 23)
  Sartrean 34 (n 23)
  viewer's 73
Gearhart, Suzanne 70
Geertz, Clifford 67
geopolitics 26, 205
Ginzburg, Carlo 76
global
  anti-apartheid 217
  anti-apartheid movement 218
  apartheid 7, 14–28, 35 (n 29), 44,
    113–115, 118–119, 137, 197–199,
    208, 227, 240
    concept of 95, 112
    forms of 41, 44
  capitalism 57, 113, 138
  divisions of labour 15, 205
  Empire 15–16, 113
  externalisation 218
  financial meltdown (2008) 141 (n 1)
  geopolitics 26
  human community 107
  industrialisation 204

inequalities 113
justice 24, 104
neoliberal capitalism 2, 113
neoliberal realpolitik 57
North 14
oppressions 112
order 16, 102
political economy 141 (n 1)
power imbalances 98
present 17, 201, 217
society 118
solidarities 115
structures of power 97
trajectories of race 196
West 14, 113
whiteness 12
global (the) 218
  of the anti-apartheid movement 204
globalisation 1, 33 (n 20), 119, 218, 263
  age 264
  capitalist 119
  of apartheid 113
  segregationist dimension 119
globalising apartheid 95
globality 261
Gobodo-Madikizela, Pumla 65, 81
Goethe *see* Von Goethe, Johann Wolfgang
The Good, the Bad and the Ugly 255–256,
  271 (n 3)
Gordian knot 168 (n 12)
Grendon, Paul (photographer) 257 (fig),
  270 (fig)
Grossberg, Lawrence 184–185
Group Areas Act 245 (n 1)
Group Areas legislation 256
group psychology 9–10
'Group Psychology and the Analysis of the
  Ego' 8
Grunebaum, Heidi 271 (n 2)
Guattari, Félix 17, 147, 156
Güntert, Hermann 168 (n 13)
Guthrie, Woodie 261

H
hagiographic memorialisation 22
hagiography 40–43
Half Price 190 (n 29)

INDEX

Handspring Trust for Puppetry in
   Education 276
Hanks, Patrick 246 (n 11)
Hardcastle, Kate 246 (n 11)
Hardt, Michael 7, 15–21, 24–27, 32 (n 8),
   33 (n 20), 113–114
Harris, Verne 41
Hartman, David 252 (fig)
Haverkamp, Anselm 154, 162, 167 (n 9)
Hegel, Wilhelm Friedrich 31 (n 13), 119,
   229, 246 (n 7, 10)
Hegelian
   dialectic 20
   subject 19
Herr K 69–72
Hertz, Neil 70
Hill, Samantha 128
Hitler's National Socialism 110
HIV and Aids pandemic 61 (n 3)
HIV-positive pregnant women 139
Heidegger, Martin 31 (n 13), 276
'Hemel op die platteland' 172
Herder, Johann Gottfried 81–82
Hoad, Neville 237, 239, 246 (n 3, 13)
Hobbes, Thomas 33–34 (n 21, 22)
Hodges, Flavia 246 (n 11)
Hog Hoggidy Hog interviews
   190 (n 29)
Hollywood Films, Johannesburg 256
Holmes, Sherlock 76
Holocaust memoirs 105
homogeneity 231
   of opinion 122
   reduction to 243
   social order of 244
homogenising 112
   imperatives of the social 122
   logic 25, 140
   the social 22
homogenous
   society (behaving masses) 139
   unity (people as) 140
Hook, Derek 22, 30 (n 5), 40, 275
Horkheimer, Max 30 (n 2)
House of Representatives 265
household 122, 139
housekeeping 122

A Human Being Died That Night 65, 81
human condition 25, 96, 139–140
The Human Condition 120, 129–130, 132
human rights 98, 107–108
Husserl, Edmund 250
Huygens, Christiaan 160

I

'I' 12, 18–19, 31–33 (n 13, 19), 34, 93,
   228–229
'I Saw a Nightmare …' – Doing Violence
   to Memory: The Soweto Uprising,
   June 16, 1976 277
IDAF *see* International Defence and Aid
   Fund
Idea(s) 155, 162, 164, 168–169 (n 13, 15)
identity 225, 242
   Afrikaner 180, 189 (n 25)
   awareness 139
   categories 95
   concealment 76
   groupnigs 114
   imagined 53
   loss of 32
   politics 10, 102
Image-repertoire 151–152
The Imperative 166 (n 1)
imperial histories 196
imperialism 32 (n 18), 109
The Impossible Machine 78
'The Inoperative Community' 225
insufficiency 225–248
   Bataille's sense of 229–230
   of existence 238
   principle 28, 225–230, 235–236, 245
   sense of 230, 246 (n 6)
interiorisation 125–127
   of action 132
   of loss 127
   of the dead Other 127
   of the loss of politics 129
Internal Security Act of 1982 175
International Defence and Aid Fund
   (IDAF) 202–205, 215–216
   archive 202
   Collection 222 (n 5)
   letter campaign 203

International Monetary Fund 119
Introduction to Kant's Anthropology 3
introjection 9, 126–128, 131
Iraq War 60
Iraqis 98
Isin, Engin 211
Ismail, Qadri 79–80
Ismene 234
Israel policies 110, 112
Israeli state violence 107, 110

J
Jacklin, Heather 2–3, 30 (n 2), 33–34 (n 20, 22)
Jacosta 233, 235
Jeet Kune Do 264
Jennings, Michael W 167 (n 9)
Jewish history 110
Johannes Kerkorrel 188 (n 21)
Jones, Ernest 75
Juluka 190 (n 28)
Jung, Carl 75, 88 (n 7)
Juno 83
Jupiter 72–73, 81, 83, 85–86
Jury, Brendan 187 (n 13)

K
Kafka, Franz 269
Kahane, Clare 70
Kant, Immanuel 2–3, 30 (n 1, 3), 33 (n 21), 107
Kantian critique/problematic 6
Kennedy, Hunter 189 (n 25)
Kennedy, John F 58
Keuzenkamp, Carike 26, 175–179, 181, 187–188 (n 14, 15, 18, 21)
Khanna, Ranjana 141 (n 4)
Kinoks: A Revolution 253
Kirkby, Joan 128
Kismet cinema 256, 258, 269
Klopper, Annie 183
knowledge
  anthropological 79
  forms of 157–159
  production 81
Köhler, Gernot 14, 32 (n 16, 17), 118

Kristeva, Julia 130, 135, 141
Kubrick, Stanley 256, 261
Kuhn, Thomas 32 (n 18)

L
Labdacos 233
Lacan, Jacques 10, 34 (n 23), 58, 71, 87 (n 3)
Lacanian 22, 45, 99
  discourse theory 48
  psychoanalysis 45, 62 (n 4), 176
LaCapra, Dominick 108
Laclau, Ernesto 51
Lacoue-Labarthe, Philippe 118
Laios 233
Lalu, Premesh 1, 29, 249, 276
language(s) 19, 21, 34–35 (n 23, 24), 92, 151, 214, 261
  Afrikaans 173
  Fanonian 13, 31 (n 11)
  of Adam 151
  of autochtony 231
  of cinematography 252
  of masks 13
  of photography 167 (n 9)
  of Thomas Kuhn 32 (n 18)
  psychoanalytic/psychoanalysis 6, 23, 65
  realm of 35 (n 24)
  Spinoza's 161
  utopia of 151
Lanzer, Ernst 61 (n 1)
Laplanche, Jean 93
Last Grave at Dimbaza 203–204, 222 (n 13)
Lavigne, Avril 191 (n 31)
Law, John 210
Lawless, Annemarie 25–26, 36 (n 32), 146, 276
Lee, Bruce 258, 261, 264
Leibniz, Gottfried Wilhelm 160–162
Lekwerekwere 243
Leone, Sergio 271 (n 3)
Lermolieff, Ivan (pseud of Giovanni Morelli) 76
Lévi-Strauss, Claude 226–227, 232–234, 246 (n 12)
Leviathan 33 (n 21)

INDEX

Levinas, Emmanuel 12, 23–24, 31 (n 13), 35 (n 24), 92, 94, 103–105, 228, 246 (n 6)
Levinasian
   ethical attitude 104
   ethics 24, 105
   insights 92
   psychoanalytic model of relational ontology 93
   vision 107
liberation 124, 210
   discourse 27, 208
   empire *see* empire of liberation
   feeling of 186
   formulation 105
   heritage 208
   history 44
   legacy 212
   movement 215
   national 206, 208, 215
   political 200
   politics 197, 204, 213
   promises 222 (n 7)
   subject 216
   territory 215
libidinal
   dynamism 58
   economy 10, 13, 40–64, 67, 79
   investiture 130
   investment(s) 22, 86, 125–126
Lingis, Alphonso 26, 146–150, 166 (n 1, 3)
Lipschitz, Ruth 87 (n 1)
Liriope 83
'A Little History of Photography' 166–167 (n 6, 9)
'The Lived Experience of the Black Man' 32 (n 15)
Locke, John 34 (n 21)
Lodge, Tom 42–43, 48, 52
'logic of essence' 159
'logic of the concept' 159
'logic of the sign' 159
Long Walk to Freedom 42
Lorrain, Claude 85
loss 8–9, 12, 14, 93, 97–103, 124–129
   genealogy of 121

   of action 130
   of being African 237
   of equality 140
   of freedom 124
   of identity 32 (n 13)
   of metaphysical foundations 109
   of plurality 124, 140
   of political concept of power 124
   of politics 24–25, 118, 120, 122–125, 129–132, 135, 139, 141
   of respect 134
   of speech 130
   politics of *see* politics of loss
The Lover's Discourse 151, 168
Lugsteuring 186
Lyotard, Jean-François 40

M

'Madiba magic' 47
Mahomo, Nana 203, 218, 222 (n 12)
'makwerekwere' 241
The Malady of Death 228
Malema, Julius 40
Malinowski, Bronisław 67, 79
Malombo (musical group) 218–219
Man 4–5, 32 (n 15), 132, 233–236
   concept 4, 14, 21
   worldliness 124
'Man with No Name' series 271 (n 3)
Mandela Imaginary 40–64
Mandela, Nelson 22, 40–61, 61–62 (n 2, 4, 6)
   as transcendent signifier 48–53
   metonymy and enchantment 46
Manhunts: A Philosophical History 79
Marcus, Stephen 70
Marquard, Leo 202
Marschall, Sabine 271 (n 7)
'Marx before Spinoza' 169 (n 16)
mass
   administration 122
   movement 251, 255
   rise of mass society 123
   struggle 206
   uniformly behaving 139

masses
  behaving 139
  uniformly behaving 132
Massive Open Online Courses (MOOCs) 250
Mayibuye Archives 222 (n 5)
Mbeki, Thabo 59
Mbembe, Achille 5–6, 10–13, 16, 19, 23, 31–32 (n 10, 11, 16), 54, 112
McCarthy, Mary 133
McClintock, Anne 35 (n 29, 30)
Meditations on First Philosophy 33 (n 21)
megalomania 77
melancholia 8–9, 24, 31 (n 9), 99–101, 120–121, 125–127, 129, 131, 237
melancholic trace 135
melancholy 151
Merleau-Ponty, Maurice 17–19, 32–35 (n 19, 23, 24)
Messianic
  Kingdom 149–150
  time 151
Metamorphoses 72–73, 83–85
Mill, John Stuart 34 (n 21)
Miller, Paul Allen 234, 264
Ming, H 257
Minh-ha, Trinh T 252–253
Minkley, Gary 1, 27, 195, 207 (fig), 209 (fig), 271 (n 7), 276
Minos 85
Minotaur 73, 81, 85–86
'Minotaur Caressing the Hand of a Sleeping Girl with His Face' 72–73
Mntambo, Nandipha 23, 66–69, 67–68 (fig), 72–74, 79, 81–86, 83 (fig), 87 (n 1)
Mnyaka, Phindi 27 (n 7)
modalities of love 55
modernity 16, 197, 213
  crisis 18
  dawn of 15, 88 (n 10), 113
  emergence 32 (n 18)
  itinerary 18, 26
  non-racial 196
  postmodernity 140
Mofokeng, Santu 199

Mol, Annemarie 210
MOOCs 250
Moosa family 256
Morelli, Giovanni 75–76
'The Moses of Michelangelo' 23, 68–69, 74–78, 82
Moses Twebe Great Hall 207 (fig), 208, 212
Mouffe, Chantal 51
mourning 7, 9, 13–14, 22, 24–25, 31 (n 9), 32 (n 14), 97–98, 100–101, 103, 117–145, 226–227, 237
Mowitt, John 213, 221–222 (n 3)
Mpe, Phaswane 28, 226–227, 232, 236–237, 239, 245, 246 (n 3), 247 (n 14)
Muholi, Zanele 66, 87 (n 1)
'Multitude' 16, 17, 19–20, 24–25
multitude theory 114
Multitude: War and Democracy in the Age of Empire 7, 15, 20, 113
Myburgh, Wynand 184, 188 (n 18)

N
Nancy, Jean-Luc 118, 129, 225, 231
narcissism 12, 23, 31 (n 9), 62 (n 6), 69, 82, 84
  moral 148
narcissistic 25, 58, 84
  empathy 86
  identification 23
  investments 12
  love 55
  mutually 77
'Narcissus' 83 (fig), 84
'Narcissus and Echo' 83
National Democratic Revolution (NDR) 196–198, 200
National Security Study Memorandum 222 (n 12)
National Socialism 110
Native Republic Thesis 195
Nazi
  genocide 110
  regalia 189 (n 27)
  symbolism 183

INDEX

Nazism 110
NDR *see* National Democratic Revolution
necropolitical forces 95
Negri, Antonio 7, 15–21, 24–27, 32–33 (n 18, 20), 113–114
negritude 20, 35 (n 26)
Nelson Mandela Foundation 41
neoliberal
  age 12
  market consumerism 119
  order of global apartheid 15
  order of global capitalism 113
  politics 14
  realpolitik 57
  structural adjustment programme 136
  university 13
neoliberalism 113
  deschooling 250
neurosis
  obsessional 22, 45–46, 61 (n 1)
  sexuality as source of 88 (n 7)
Nevirapine 139
New York Times 271 (n 6)
Nixon 58
Nixon administration 222
Nixon, Richard 58
Nixon, Rob 35 (n 29, 30)
non-racism 197
Norris, Chuck 264
Norval, Aletta 140
nostalgia 126
  for a dilated space 267
  for a still intact past 140
  for the bioscope 264
nostalgic 120
  anxiety of place and belonging 177
  conservatism of the past 141
  yearning 120, 131
Nussbaum, Martha 30 (n 1)
Nxumalo, Manqoba 50

O

obsessional neurosis 61 (n 1)
Oedipal 70, 234
  defiance 77

Oedipus 233–236, 246 (n 12)
  complex 30 (n 3)
  myth 28, 226–227, 230, 232, 236, 238, 242
On Creaturely Life 166 (n 2)
On Escape 246 (n 6)
'On Exactitude in Science' 260
'On Language as Such and the Language of Man' 166 (n 5)
On Liberty 34 (n 21)
On Revolution 129, 133, 142 (n 6)
'On the Power of the Intellect, or, On Human Freedom' 157
The Order of Things 23
The Origin of German Tragic Drama 152, 155, 162, 164, 167 (n 9)
The Origins of Totalitarianism 132, 140
Orwell, George 261, 266
Osborne, John 167 (n 10)
Otherwise than Being 35 (n 24)
Ovid/Ovidian 72–73 82, 84–85

P

Packard, Randall 215
Palestinians 107, 110, 112
'Paranoia' 189 (n 25)
Parkinson, George HR 168 (n 15)
Parow, Jack 173
Parting Ways 95, 105, 109–110, 112
Pasiphae 85
Patel, SJ 256
Pechey, Graham 213, 217
perception(s) 18, 32 (n 19), 34 (n 23), 161
  external 114
  frames of 98
  human 156
  of similarity 155
  ordered 162
Perpetual Peace 33 (n 21)
perversion 3, 77
The Pervert's Guide to Ideology 58
Phenomenology of Spirit 246 (n 10)
'A Phonography of War' 275
Picasso, Pablo 72–73
Pigman, George 68
Pistorius, Oscar 40

The Plague of Fantasies 222 (n 4)
pluralisation 109
plurality 24, 120, 122–123, 134, 136,
    139–142
  as politics 25
  loss of 124
  of a nation/people/society 120
  of the human condition 25
  political 137
Pohlandt-McCormick, Helena 27, 195, 277
polis 132, 141 (n 2)
political
  action 25, 99, 132–134, 136, 138
  acts 25
  agency of the people 43
  aspect of mourning 128
  community 102
  concept of power 124
  conditions 119
  conflict 78
  democratic processes 43
  economy 141 (n 1), 215
  equality among peers 122
  hagiography 43
  liberation 200
  oppression 134
  order 41
  organisation 20
  paralysis 115
  participation 137
  philosophy 17, 120
  practices 20
  praxis 20
  process(es) 132, 138
  project 3, 10, 180
  responsibilities/responsibility 54, 110
  revolutions 42
  solutions 101
  South African sphere 57
  speech 132
  system of rule 119
  theorists 51
  transformation (1990) 222 (n 7)
  transition (South Africa) 137
political (the)
  retreat of 118

politics 24, 30 (n 1), 120–121, 123–124,
    128, 134–138, 204–205, 227
  acknowledged 176
  affective 87 (n 1)
  ANC and Communist Party 206
  as freedom 25, 136
  bantustan 207
  biopolitics *see* biopolitics
  community 227, 229
  condition of 266
  decline of 121
  demise of 117
  emancipatory 43, 48
  failure of 130
  fate of 135
  geopolitics *see* geopolitics
  identity 10, 102
  institutionalised 138
  Keuzenkamp's 179
  liberation *see* liberation politics
  loss of *see* loss of politics
  memory of 131
  modern 132
  mourning for 131–132
  neoliberal 14
  of Afrikaner society 177
  of anger 11
  of apartheid 137, 140
  of enchantment 47
  of exile and liberation 197
  of identification 260
  of impatience 10–11
  of liberation *see* liberation politics
  of lionisation 42
  of loss 117–145
  of mourning 128–129
  of pain 11–12
  of postapartheid 140
  of race 207
  of resistance 195
  of socialism 195
  of the failure of politics 129
  of the social 25, 117–118, 129, 133, 138,
    140–141
  of youth 185
  oppositional 184

INDEX

pavement 249
post-1994 179
principles and practices of 135
progressive or left 95
proletarianisation of 266
proper 120
queer 247 (n 13)
totalitarian 27
waiting 10
Polynices 233, 235
Poseidon 85
Posel, Deborah 47, 62 (n 4)
post-Enlightenment ethics 92
post-Fall 151
post-postapartheid era 2, 52
postapartheid 1–3, 12, 14, 28–29, 32 (n 16), 36 (n 32), 56, 181, 185, 187–188 (n 10, 23), 195, 197, 217, 219, 240
   adjective 7
   anxieties 199
   articulation of whiteness 26
   concerns 237
   condition 47, 56, 65, 244
   condition of life 7
   consensus 61
   context 53
   developmental state 197, 200, 212
   discourse of reconciliation 218
   dystopian 247 (n 14)
   empathy 72, 86
   era(s) 46, 56, 140, 188 (n 23)
   experience 53
   fellow feeling 65–91
   forms 52
   framing 4
   freedom 208
   global discourse 27
   imaginary 61, 205
   legacies 197
   liberation discourse 215, 216
   life 226
   modernist development 210
   nation 10, 46
   native subject 204
   notion 180
   objects and aspirations 51
   predicaments 197
   present 16, 202, 208
   psychosocial condition 65
   psychosocial transformation 23
   redemptive potential 236
   social 5, 7–8, 11, 14, 22, 25, 28, 35 (n 26), 175, 195, 210, 212, 218
   socials 202
   society 54
   South Africa 2, 10, 136–139, 140–141, 141 (n 1), 173, 201, 227, 240
   subjectivity 225
   thinking of 232
   transformation 65, 67, 81, 121
   transition 137, 227
(Post)apartheid Conditions: Psychoanalysis and Social Formations 276
postcolonial 33 (n 20), 278
   constitution 138
   critique of apartheid 276
   history 277
   process of nation-building 140
   psychoanalysis 23, 79
   rape 85
   realities 202
   state 178
   theory 278
Postcolonial Narrative and the Work of Mourning 246 (n 5, 13)
postcolonialism 197
postmodernity 140
postpolitical
   age 118
   biopolitics 118
   condition 138
system of rule 119
poverty 15, 24, 102, 112–113, 118, 201
   depoliticising 136, 138
   existence of 117–118, 121, 124, 128–129, 134, 139–140
   distribution of 137
   liberation from 120, 135–136, 142 (n 6)
   material 118, 129, 137
   overturning 197
   question of 118, 120

poverty (*continued*)
  relief 135
  violence of 10, 113
pre-Fall state 151
Precarious Life 96, 104, 111
precariousness 92–93, 96, 98, 100, 112
  condition of human life 109
  generisability 94
  human 108–109
  of some individuals/populations 95
  unequal/uneven distribution 95, 97
  universal condition 94
precarity 22, 24, 107
  conditions of 262
  critque expressed in 24
  ethics of 23–24, 92–116
  shared 101
  unequal allocation of 95
  uneven distributions of 23–24
predation 72
  empathic 80
  sexual 73
  technologies 79
The Primitive, the Aesthetic, and the Savage 3
Prokosch, Frederic 191 (n 30)
Protestant
  ethic 99
  work ethic 103
Proust, Marcel 155
psychoanalysis 6–7, 23, 31 (n 8), 34 (n 23), 55, 61 (n 1), 67, 69, 76, 78–79, 92, 275, 277–278
  centrality of Oedipus myth 230
  history 61 (n 1), 78
  Lacanian 45, 62 (n 4), 176
  language 23, 65
  postcolonial 79
psychoanalytic 23, 45, 57, 86
  circle (Freud's) 88 (n 7)
  classical model of obsessional neurosis 45
  concept *Einfühlung* 69
  discourse 23, 69
  experience 87 (n 3)
  frame 31 (n 8)
  gaze 34
  ideas deployment 78

insights 92
interventions 87 (n 2)
language 6
mode of inquiry 275
model of relational ontology 93
perspective 47–48, 54
practice 69
relationship between melancholia and mourning 125
theory 10, 71
transference 23
traversal 6, 30 (n 5)
treatment 62 (n 5)
view 42
psychological
  antidotes 78
  configurations of white South Africans 180
psychology 69, 78, 195, 275
  "empathy" 69
  group 9–10
  human 41
  of Fascism 8
psychosocial
  condition (postapartheid) 65
  studies 275
  transformation 23, 65, 86
psychotherapeutic discourse 30 (n 4)
Pure Immanence 163

Q

Quayle, Michael 180–181, 188 (n 23)
Queer Phenomenology 88 (n 11)

R

race 3, 5, 14, 17, 28, 182, 184, 195, 197, 199–200, 208, 221, 231, 261–262
  and class 195, 200, 202, 219
  and nation 195
  as class 197
  as global apartheid 197–198
  boundaries 61
  categorisation 114
  disappearance 196
  discourse 182
  divisions 47

INDEX

expressions of 226
formations 219
fragments 211
global trajectories 196
new ways to think about 202
permeation 182
politics of 207
're: working' of 212
social of 196
spectral lines of 210
struggle 27
war 27
racial purity 27
racism 27, 31 (n 7), 35 (n 29), 112, 196, 199, 202, 208, 212
   modern 27
   white 4
   worldly 21
'Racism's Last Word' 21, 35 (n 27), 119
Ramones 189 (n 27)
'The Rape of Europa' 67, 68 (fig), 72–74, 81–85
Re-Imagining the Social in South Africa: Critique, Theory and Post-Apartheid Society 2, 6
Real (the) 34 (n 23)
reconciliation 10, 48, 50, 218
'Red October' 180, 189 (n 24)
Refentše 237–244
Refilwe 238–244
Regent cinema 256
remainder(s) 7, 9, 20, 22, 115, 226
remains
   concept 13, 25
   function of 9
   of a loss of politics 25
   of apartheid 7
   of the apartheid social 198
   of the social 6, 8, 244
   temporal 195–224
Rembrandt, Harmenszoon van Rijn 85
Reni, Guido 85
reterritorialisation 204–205, 207, 212, 215, 218, 222 (n 8)
Richlin, Amy 87 (n 5)
Rieff, Philip 87 (n 6)

Ritter, Johann Wilhelm 154
Rive, Richard 250, 266
Robben Island 208, 261
   Mayibuye Archives 222 (n 5)
Roland Barthes by Roland Barthes 168–169 (n 14)
Rose, Jacqueline 87 (n 4)
Rubens, Peter Paul 85
Rubin, Basil 256
Rubython, John 266
Russell, David 208
Ruti, Mari 23–24, 92, 277

S

Sachs, Wulf 88 (n 9)
sameness 139
   core of 96
   indivisible 169 (n 18)
   kernel of 112
   of labour 139
Sanders, Mark 5–6, 8–10, 13, 25, 31–32 (n 7, 9, 14), 246 (n 5)
Santner, Eric L
Savuka 190 (n 28)
Schaap, Andrew 120, 133
'schools boycott' 251, 255
Sebe, Lennox 201
Second Treatise on Government 34 (n 21)
segregation 96, 113, 119
The Seminar of Jacques Lacan 10
semiotics 76
separate development 3, 35 (n 30), 196, 201, 204
resettlement 222 (n 6)
service delivery protests 61 (n 3)
Shaw, Greg 266
Shelley, Percy Bysshe 74
signifier 230
   apartheid 119 141
   evil 5
   Mandela 22, 48–53, 61
   postapartheid 7
Simondon, Gilbert 29, 266
singular 17, 112, 163
   and the universal 94–95
   essence 164, 169
   life 164

singularities/singularity 19, 114, 147, 234
   and universality 109
   constellation of 200
   dynamics 17
   field of 33
   multiple 23
   of time 219
The Singularity of Being: Lacan and the Immortal Within 277
Sionizm 110
Sitze, Adam 30 (n 4), 78, 246 (n 5), 250, 265
Six Feet Under 60
'Skadu's teen die muur' 186
Skop, skiet en donner 186
Sloterdijk, Peter 119
Smit, Sonja 173
social
   equality 137
   justice 103
social (the) 13
   as necessity 138
   formulation of 9
   of apartheid 196
   rise of 117–145
   traversal of 30 (n 6)
social-political divide 137–138
society 50–51, 55, 61, 132
   emergence/rise of 122–123
   global 118
   of behaving masses 139
   of control 261
   of labour and consumption 139
   patriarchal Afrikaner 177
   plurality 120, 122
   postapartheid 54
   production and reproduction 17
   socialist 206
   Soviet 252
   white 50
   world 118
Society Must Be Defended 27
solidarity 133–135, 254
   British Empire's networks of 203
   of suffering 100
   principle of 133

solipsism 12, 15
Sophocles 232
South African Communist Party 49, 60, 196, 198, 206
'The South African Question' 221 (n 2)
souvenir 146, 149, 167 (n 11)
Soweto
   student protests 263
   Uprising of 1976 176, 263, 277
spaghetti westerns 257, 262
Spender, Stephen 259–260
Sphinx 232–234
'Spinoza and the Three "Ethics"' 157
Spinoza, Baruch 18, 26, 36 (n 32), 150–151, 156–161, 169 (n 15, 16, 18)
spirit 251
Spirit 19
Spivak, Gayatri Chakravorty 3, 83–85, 88 (n 8), 245 (n 2)
Stage (magazine) 190 (n 29)
Standard Edition (of the Complete Psychological Works of Sigmund Freud) 68, 77
Stark, Mr 256
state of emergency 175, 180–181, 251–252, 254
'The State of South African Political Life' 10
Steingo, Gavin 180
Stiegler, Bernard 29, 250–251, 262, 266, 271 (n 1)
Stockenstroom, Sean 252 (fig)
Stone, Oliver 58
Strachey, James and Alix 68
sub species aeternitatis 151
subaltern 20
   inclusion 114
   necessity 20
subalternity 256
subject 8, 18, 28, 126, 202, 211, 219, 226, 266
   autonomous 105
   Cartesian 18
   characterise the 34 (n 2)
   citizen 208

colonial 196
concept of 33(n 21)
construction of 32 (n 15)
empathic 82
expression(s) of the 29, 228
externalisation 217
formation 202
Hegelian 19
human 79
identity of 53
made free 216
marked by insufficiency 236
maturity of the modern 80
native 27, 197, 204–205, 210, 212, 216
of apartheid 220, 262
of freedom 212
of history 211
of liberation 216
positioning 183
preconstituted 31 (n 8)
produce the 34 (n 21)
psychic space of 82
racial 210
recentering of 106
sense of the 28, 228, 231
tribal 196
viewing 155
Western 101–102
white 180
subjection 103, 216, 250, 262
   of body to mind 18, 114
subjective certainty 19, 33 (n 21), 214, 200, 226, 229–230, 233, 242
subjectivities/subjectivity 9, 17, 164, 202
   enclosure of 226
   equated with subjection 103
   individuated 19
   itineraries of 67
   metaphysical model of 93
   open to learning from the other 19
   postapartheid 225
refiguring 236
   sense of 226
   South African 56

supra-sovereign institutions 119
Swart, Basil 271 (n 5)
Symbolic Order of the Law 234–235
Symbolic Order of the Third 235
symptomatology 76, 255

T

Tabane, Philip 218–219
Teachers' League of South Africa 261
The Theban Plays 246 (n 10)
Thebes 232, 235
'Theologico-Political Fragment' 149
Theseus 81
The Third Reich (group) 183
Timaeus 169 (n 18)
Tiresias 84
Titian 85
Torok, Maria 126–127, 131
'Totem and Taboo' 8, 31 (n 9), 77
transference 14, 23, 58–59, 71–72
Trauerspiel 166 (n 5)
TRC *see* Truth and Reconciliation Commission
Treatment Action Campaign 138, 142 (n 7)
The Trojan Horse 255–256
Trojan Horse III 268, 268 (fig)
Trojan Horse incident/killings/massacre 29, 249–250, 255, 265–267, 269
Trojan Horse Massacre memorial 257 (fig), 268
Truscott, Ross 1, 23, 25, 30, 65, 180, 277
Trust 146, 148, 166 (n 1)
Truth and Reconciliation Commission (TRC) 6–8, 26, 30 (n 4), 42, 65, 78, 81, 246 (n 5), 269, 271 (n 5)
'Tumult Commission' 78, 81
Twebe, Moses 207 (fig), 207–213, 209 (fig), 215
Tylor, Edward 79

U

UDF *see* United Democratic Front
Umkhonto we Sizwe 48–49

The Unavowable Community 28, 226–227
Unbanned series 218
uniformity 122–123
uniformly behaving masses 132, 139
United Democratic Front (UDF) 261
United States (US/USA) 113, 183, 258
   army 96
   military 98
   revolutionary student movement
      129–130
   soap operas 60
universal 119, 182
   and the particular 112
   and the singular 94–95
   condition of man 235
   emancipatory politics 48
   end of justice 49
   ethics of equality 94
   human condition 96
universals 24, 157
universalising 111, 114
universalisation 96, 109, 111–112, 115
universalism 92–116, 239
universalist ethics of precarity 111
universality 109, 114
   and singularity 109
   of apartheid 119
University of the Western Cape's Robben
      Island Mayibuye Archives 222 (n 5)
Ursprung des deutschen Trauerspiels 167
   (n 10)
US/USA *see* United States
'utopia of language' 151

V

Vale, Peter 2–3, 30–34 (n 2, 20, 22)
Van Bever Donker, Maurits 1, 28–29, 225,
   278
Van Coke, Francois 172–173, 181–182,
   185
Van Coke Kartel (VCK) 26, 172–186, 188
   (n 18, 21), 191 (n 32)
Van der Meulen, Lindy 183
Van Niekerk, Robert 271 (n 4)
Van Robbroeck, Lize 57, 62 (n 6)
Van Staden, Hanneli 187 (n 13)

VCK *see* Van Coke Kartel
Vertov, Dziga 252–254, 259, 262
Verwey, Cornel 180–181, 188 (n 23)
Vietnam 96, 97
Violent Femmes 190 (n 29)
Virgil 85
Virilio, Paul 253, 261, 263
vita activa 130
Vlakplaas 65
Voëlvry movement 188–189 (n 21, 28)
Von Goethe, Johann Wolfgang 149
'Vor dem Gesetz' 269

W

wa Azania, Malaika 44
Walder, Dennis 61 (n 3)
Walter Benjamin 166–167 (n 2, 9)
Waterwitch, Robert 269, 270 (fig), 271
   (n 2)
Way of the Dragon 258, 264
'We Refugees' 128
Weaver, Tony 266–267
Weber, Samuel 167 (n 9)
Weigel, Sigrid 167 (n 9)
Welcome to Our Hillbrow 28, 226, 232,
   236–237, 244–247 (n 13)
White Noise 182, 184
'White Power' 183
whiteness 182–184
   after 1994 184
   after apartheid 180–181, 183
   articulation 26, 182, 184
   as an 'erotogenic object' 11
   blackmail of 1–5
   decolonisation 11
   definition 12
   in post-1994 South Africa 173
   invisibility of 4
   mask 14
   mechanism of blackness/whiteness 5
   metaphysics of 4
   myths 13
Wie's bang 177, 185–186, 191 (n 32)
Williams, Coline 269, 270 (fig), 271 (n 2)
'Winter Garden' 152
'Winter in Tembisa' 199 (fig)

INDEX

The Wolf Man's Magic Word 127
Woodstock 190 (n 29)
Words of Light 167 (n 9)
World Bank 119
The Wretched of the Earth 11, 13–14, 105

X
xenophobia 238
xenophobic attacks 61 (n 3)

Y
Youth League 48

Z
Zapiro 57
Zinn, Howard 43–44
Žižek, Slavoj 58, 114, 118–119, 128, 222 (n 4)
Zuma, Jacob 57–59, 61 (n 3)

www.ingramcontent.com/pod-product-compliance
Lightning Source LLC
Chambersburg PA
CBHW020246030426
42336CB00010B/641